Of Rocks and Water

Towards an Archaeology of Place

edited by

Ömür Harmanşah

D1354241

Oxbow Books
Oxford and Philadelphia

Joukowsky Institute Publication 5

General series editor: Prof. John F. Cherry
Joukowsky Institute for Archaeology and the Ancient World
Brown University, Box 1837/60 George Street, Providence, RI 02912, USA

Published in the United Kingdom in 2014 by
OXBOW BOOKS
10 Hythe Bridge Street, Oxford OX1 2EW

and in the United States by
OXBOW BOOKS
908 Darby Road, Havertown, PA 19083

Published by Oxbow Books on behalf of the Joukowsky Institute

© Brown University, Oxbow Books and the individual contributors 2014

Paperback Edition: ISBN 978-1-78297-671-4
Digital Edition: ISBN 978-1-78297-672-1

A CIP record for this book is available from the British Library

Library of Congress Cataloging-in-Publication Data

Of rocks and water : towards an archaeology of place / edited by Ömür Harmansah.
   pages cm. -- (Joukowsky Institute publication ; 5)
Includes bibliographical references and index.
ISBN 978-1-78297-671-4
1. Landscape archaeology. 2. Landscape archaeology--Philosophy. 3. Place (Philosophy)
4. Rocks--Social aspects--History. 5. Water--Social aspects--History. 6. Human ecology--
History. 7. Social archaeology. I. Harmansah, Ömür
   CC77.L35O34 2014
   930.1--dc23
                              2014018518

Printed in the United Kingdom by Hobbs the Printers Ltd, Totton, Hampshire

For a complete list of Oxbow titles, please contact:

UNITED KINGDOM   UNITED STATES OF AMERICA
Oxbow Books   Oxbow Books
Telephone (01865) 241249   Telephone (800) 791-9354
Fax (01865) 794449   Fax (610) 853-9146
Email: oxbow@oxbowbooks.com   Email: queries@casemateacademic.com
www.oxbowbooks.com   www.casemateacademic.com/oxbow

Oxbow Books is part of the Casemate Group

*Front cover: Façade drawing of Eflatun Pınarı Spring Monument, near Beyşehir, Turkey.
Reproduced with permission from: Martin Bachmann and Sırrı Özenir, Das Quellheiligtum
Eflatun Pınar. Archaeologische Anzeiger 2004(I): 85–102, Abb. 32.
Back cover: Rock relief of the 12 gods of the underworld (Yazılıkaya near Boğazköy, Turkey,
Chamber B), Photograph by Ömür Harmanşah.*

Contents

List of Figures

Notes on Contributors

Wendy Ashmore is Professor of Anthropology at the University of California, Riverside. Her research centers on the social use and understanding of space, expressed in the archaeology of households, the analysis of civic planning in cities and towns, the study of ancient landscapes, and most recently, how gender affects and is affected by architecture and other kinds of spatial order. Publications include her monograph *Settlement Archaeology at Quiriguá, Guatemala*, and edited volumes *Voices in American Archaeology* (with D.T. Lippert and B.J. Mills), *Archaeologies of Landscape: Contemporary Perspectives* (with A.B. Knapp), and *Household and Community in the Mesoamerican Past* (with R.R. Wilk).

Matthew Canepa is Associate Professor of Art History and Classical and Near Eastern Studies at the University of Minnesota-Twin Cities. His research focuses on the intersection of art, ritual and power in the Eastern Mediterranean, Persia and the wider Iranian world. His first book, *The Two Eyes of the Earth*, was awarded the 2010 James Henry Breasted Prize from the American Historical Association for the best book in any field of history prior to the year A.D. 1000. Recent publications include articles on Iranian sacred spaces and the manipulation of Persian and Iranian identity through the natural and built environments. He is currently finishing a book exploring the transformation of Iranian identity, landscapes, architecture, and urbanism between Alexander and Islam.

John F. Cherry is Joukowsky Family Professor of Archaeology, Professor of Classics, and (by courtesy) Professor of Anthropology at Brown University. His fieldwork has focused on landscape archaeology and survey in Greece, but he has also worked in Great Britain, the United States, Yugoslav Macedonia, Italy, Armenia, and (currently) Montserrat. He is co-author or co-editor of 12 books and is at present writing a book entitled *Cretan Transformations*, on sociopolitical change on Crete at the turn of the third millennium B.C. He has been co-editor of the *Journal of Mediterranean Archaeology* for almost 25 years and is the General Series Editor for *Joukowsky Institute Publications*.

Thomas G. Garrison is a Lecturer in Anthropology and Archaeology at the University of Southern California. His research focuses on landscape archaeology in the Maya lowlands and the application of digital technologies to archaeological problems. He is the director of the Proyecto Arqueológico El Zotz in Guatemala, and is currently co-editing a volume on the first phase of research at the site.

Claudia Glatz is Lecturer in Mediterranean Archaeology at the University of Glasgow. Her research interests include the development of early social complexity, archaeological approaches to empire, the relationship of craft production and political power, as well as settlement and landscape studies, especially in border and transitional regions. Recent publications address practices of landscape monument construction and political competition in Bronze Age Anatolia and the western Zagros, and a range of approaches to the role and significance of plain pottery in Hittite Anatolia and its imperial relationships. She co-directs the Cide Archaeological Project, a survey on the west-central Turkish Black Sea coast, and the Sirwan Regional Project in the Kurdish Region of Iraq.

Ömür Harmanşah is Assistant Professor of Archaeology and Ancient Western Asian Studies at Brown University. He works and teaches in the fields of archaeology, architectural history and material culture of the ancient Near East, particularly Turkey, Iraq, and Syria. His academic interests revolve around questions of place and landscape, bodily performance, local knowledge, collective memory, and political ecology. He is the author of *Cities and the Shaping of Memory in the Ancient Near East* (Cambridge University Press, 2013), and is currently working on a cultural biography of rock reliefs and spring monuments in Anatolia and a critical archaeology of place. Since 2010, he has been directing the Yalburt Yaylası Archaeological Landscape Research Project, a diachronic regional survey in west-central Turkey.

Janet D. Jones is Professor of Classics and Ancient Mediterranean Studies at Bucknell University. Trained as a classical archaeologist at UNC-Chapel Hill, her research interests focus on the history of technology (particularly glass production) and the environmental impacts of preindustrial technologies. Recent publications include studies of Roman and Byzantine glass corpora from excavations in southern Jordan and scientific analyses of Iron Age glass finds from ancient Gordion (Turkey). She is currently examining the role of exploration and trade on the spread of technology along the Silk Road.

Andrew Kinkella is a full-time faculty member at Moorpark College in southern California, where he directs the Moorpark College Archaeological Program (MCAP). His current research focuses on how Maya cenotes (water-filled sinkholes) were used by the ancient Maya, specifically in terms of settlement location and water ritual. His dissertation, entitled *Draw of the Sacred Water: An Archaeological Survey of the Ancient Maya Settlement at the Cara Blanca Pools, Belize* (2009), is an analysis of the relationship between the Cara Blanca Pools (a string of 25 Maya cenotes) and local Maya centers in terms of settlement and ritual. This research includes an underwater component, where select pools are explored and mapped using diving equipment.

Gavin Lucas is Professor of Archaeology at the University of Iceland. His main research interests lie in archaeological method and theory, and the archaeology of the modern world. His most recent book was *Understanding the Archaeological Record* (Cambridge University Press, 2012) and he is co-editing a new series of volumes called *Archaeological Orientations* for Routledge. Recent fieldwork in Iceland includes excavations at a postmedieval episcopal manor, as well as an abandoned industrial fishing village, the latter as part of a larger collaborative project investigating modern ruins.

Lisa J. Lucero (Ph.D., UCLA 1994) is a AAAS Fellow and a Professor in the Anthropology Department at the University of Illinois at Urbana-Champaign. Her interests focus on the emergence and demise of political power, ritual, water management, the impact of climate change on society, and the Classic Maya. She has been conducting archaeology projects in Belize for over 20 years; her most recent project involves heading diving expeditions into cenotes looking for ancient Maya offerings and evidence for climate and landscape histories. Publications include her book *Water and Ritual: The Rise and Fall of Classic Maya Rulers* (University of Texas Press, 2006). She is an active member of the Maya arm of the Integrated History and Future of People on Earth (IHOPE), an organization seeking to address current problems by understanding our human past. She serves on the American Anthropological Association Task Force on Climate Change (2011–2014). Lucero has been working since 2008 with Roland Fletcher (Director, Greater Angkor Project; University of Sydney) on a comparative project on low-density urbanism, water management, and sustainability in the Tropics.

Ben Marsh is Professor of Geography and Environmental Studies at Bucknell University. Trained at Penn State University as a geographer within the cultural landscape tradition, his archaeological research focuses on ancient environmental change and archaeological site taphonomy. He has researched early land use and landscape evolution at the Iron Age site of Gordion in central Turkey for many years, most recently in the city's hinterland with the Gordion Regional Survey. He studies earth resources, environmental disruption, and human adaptation at a number of other Anatolian sites. His interest in landscapes of decline extends to long-term scholarship on nineteenth-century industrial landscapes and their economically challenged communities in the Susquehanna Valley in Pennsylvania.

Ali Mousavi is a visiting professor at the University of California, Los Angeles. His interests range from the archaeology of the second millennium B.C. in Iran to the archaeology of Iranian empires, notably the Achaemenid empire. He contributed to the nomination of the site of Pasargadae for inscription on the World Heritage List of UNESCO, and undertook a brief excavation at the site in 2006. He has published a book entitled *Persepolis: Discovery and Afterlife of a World Wonder* (De Gruyter, 2012), and a number of articles in scholarly journals.

Betsey Robinson is Associate Professor of History of Art and Classical Studies at Vanderbilt University. Her interests include Greek and Roman architecture and art, and ancient cities, sanctuaries, and landscapes. Since 1997 she has conducted research as part of the Corinth excavations of the American School of Classical Studies at Athens, focusing on water supply, architecture, and works of art in context. Her book *Histories of Peirene: A Corinthian Fountain in Three Millennia* (American School of Classical Studies at Athens, 2011) won the 2011 PROSE Prize for Archaeology and Anthropology. Her current research is on Hellenistic and Roman perceptions of landscapes and architecture.

Ian Straughn is the Joukowsky Family Librarian for Middle East Studies and Visiting Assistant Professor of Anthropology at Brown University. His research and teaching focus on the emerging field of Islamic-period archaeology where he has a special interest in the production of landscapes of the greater Levant. His fieldwork has ranged from Armenia to Egypt, with a professional career that has incorporated growing expertise in the transformation of cultural production and heritage politics across the Middle East. As an editor for the journal *Archaeological Dialogues* he has remained committed to pushing the boundaries of archaeological theory, particularly the relationship of text and object.

Lee Z. Ullmann is the Director of EducationUSA Chile. Before moving to Chile, Ullmann was a full-time lecturer in the Department of Art History and Archaeology at Columbia University. His research interests are concerned with the creation of, and movement within, the landscapes of Anatolia and the Near East. He is currently co-editing the *Brill Handbook of Hittite Landscape and Geography*.

Christopher Witmore is Associate Professor of Archaeology and Classics at Texas Tech University. His main research interests include Mediterranean Archaeology, especially Southern Greece; things and the new materialisms; land and chorography; the history of archaeology; science and technology studies; and media. He is the co-author of *Archaeology: The Discipline of Things* (University of California Press, 2012) and co-editor of *Archaeology in the Making: Conversations Through a Discipline* (Routledge, 2013). He is also co-editor, with Gavin Lucas, of the new Routledge series *Archaeological Orientations*.

Contributor Addresses

Wendy Ashmore
University of California, Riverside
Department of Anthropology
900 University Avenue
Riverside, CA 92521
wendy.ashmore@ucr.edu

Matthew P. Canepa
University of Minnesota
Department of Art History
271 19th Ave. South
Minneapolis, MN 55455
mpcanepa@umn.edu

John F. Cherry
Brown University
Joukowsky Institute for Archaeology
    and the Ancient World
Box 1837, 60 George Street
Providence RI 02912
John_Cherry@brown.edu

Thomas G. Garrison
University of Southern California
Department of Anthropology
Grace Ford Salvatori Hall
3601 Watt Way, Ste. 120
University Park Campus
Los Angeles, CA 90089
thomas.garrison@usc.edu

Claudia Glatz
University of Glasgow
Archaeology, School of Humanities
The Gregory Building
Lilybank Gardens
Glasgow G12 8QQ, UK
claudia.glatz@glasgow.ac.uk

Janet D. Jones
Bucknell University
Classics Department
1 Dent Drive
Lewisburg, PA 17837
jjones@bucknell.edu

Ömür Harmanşah
Brown University
Joukowsky Institute for Archaeology
    and the Ancient World
Box 1837, 60 George Street
Providence RI 02912
Omur_Harmansah@brown.edu

Andrew Kinkella
Moorpark College
Anthropology Program
7075 Campus Road
Moorpark, CA 93021
akinkella@vcccd.edu

Gavin Lucas
University of Iceland
Department of Archaeology
Saemundargata 2
101 Reykjavik, Iceland
gavin@hi.is

Lisa J. Lucero
University of Illinois at Urbana-
    Champaign
Department of Anthropology
607 S. Mathews Ave., MC-148
Urbana, IL 61801
Ljlucero@illinois.edu

Ben Marsh
Bucknell University
Department of Geography and Program
    in Environmental Studies
Lewisburg, PA 17837
marsh@bucknell.edu

Ali Mousavi
University of California, Los Angeles
Department of Near Eastern
    Languages and Culture
Humanities Building 378
Los Angeles, CA 90095–1511
amousavi@humnet.ucla.edu

Betsey A. Robinson
Vanderbilt University
Department of History of Art
Box 0274 GPC
230 Appleton Place
Nashville, TN 37203
betsey.a.robinson@vanderbilt.edu

Ian B Straughn
Brown University
Brown University Libraries and
    Department of Anthropology
Box A, Providence RI 02912
ian_straughn@brown.edu

Lee Z. Ullmann
Isabel Montt 3330 Dept. 4172
Vitacura, Santiago
Chile
lee.ullmann@gmail.com

Christopher Witmore
Texas Tech University
Department of Classical and Modern
    Languages and Literatures
2910 18th Street
Lubbock, TX 79409–2071
christopher.witmore@ttu.edu

Introduction:
Towards an Archaeology of Place

Ömür Harmanşah

Places are small, culturally significant locales that exist within a landscape.
They are meaningful to specific cultural groups through everyday experience
and shared stories associated with them. Places therefore gather a vast range
of things in their microcosm: both animate and inanimate entities, residues,
materials, knowledges, and stories. The material residues and cultural
associations that cluster around places run deep in their temporality. In
a remote spring site named İvriz in south central Turkey, at the northern
foothills of the Taurus Mountains, an impressive relief and an inscription
were carved on a living rock surface during the Middle Iron Age (eighth
century B.C.). The site was clearly sacred to the local Weather God of the
region (namely, Tarhunzas), and was incorporated into the state politics of
the local king Warpalawaš who sponsored the monument with Hieroglyphic
Luwian inscriptions and a monumental depiction of his encounter with
the deity (Figure 1.1). The site later continued to be populated with small
rock-cut altars, stele monuments, and the carving of other rock reliefs.
We hear from the seventeenth-century Ottoman traveller and geographer
Katip Çelebi, who gave a description of the still-standing rock relief in his
Cihannüma, and spoke about the site as "the spring of the prophet" – a site
of healing and pilgrimage (Harmanşah 2014). This continued sanctification
of the site in the early modern period clearly derives from its power as a place
of long-term cultural practice, its miraculous local geology of water gushing
out of the bedrock, and the layered material and visual corpus at the site.

Places are then generated and maintained by a spectrum of locally specific
practices, from the situated activities of daily users of space, on the one hand,
to the grandiose interventions of the political elite on the other. Combined,
these social practices continually produce hybrid material forms and spatial
configurations over time, and anchor communities to particular locales with

Figure 1.1. Rock relief of Warpalawaš at Ivriz, Turkey (author's photograph).

a sense of cultural belonging. They become assemblages of shared memories, always pregnant for improvised events, despite the common essentialist notion of local places as static or conservative. Places thus serve as meaningful nexuses of human interaction, and as sites of immediate everyday experience. Thomas J. Csordas (2002: 2) provides a concrete and very useful definition of experience as "the meaningfulness of meaning, immediate both in the sense of its concreteness, its subjective openness, its breakthrough to the sensory, emotional, inter-subjective reality of the present moment; and in the sense in which it is the unmediated, unpremeditated, spontaneous and unrehearsed upwelling of raw existence". The unmediated experience of place then allows an immersed, embodied interaction between persons and places, between human bodies and local geologies. This book explores precisely this relationship in a variety of landscapes and historical contexts across the ancient world(s).

On the grounds of new advances in landscape archaeology, spatial theory, analytical map-making technologies, and environmental research, archaeological field practices have recently leaped forward in their increasingly rigorous methodologies of addressing the temporal, spatial and material complexity of places, and have been adopting site-specific, locally nuanced surveying techniques. For example, more and more attention is paid to extra-urban sites such as rock-cut monuments, sacred springs, cairns, mountain-top sanctuaries, caves, quarries, mining sites, rural shrines, and water mills, which are often missed or understudied in standard surface survey projects that prioritize identifying settlement sites (Bradley 2000; Brady 2005; Zedeño and Bowser 2009). Such unusual locales challenge the traditional understanding of an archaeological site and therefore are often construed as marginal or epiphenomenal to the main structures of settlement in the landscape. Marginal places are studied or seen through the lens of imperial or multi-regional networks, while they are often literally imagined as border monuments or territorial markers. Another methodological problem with the study of such extra-urban or "landscape" monuments (rock reliefs, rock-cut tombs, spring monuments, etc.) is the long-held scholarly focus on the representational and epigraphic content of such monuments. Pictorial or iconographic analysis of rock reliefs have traditionally received attention for art-historical purposes, while the epigraphic content of their inscriptions are treasured for their contributions to the historical geography of various regions, because of the valuable site-specific information they provide. Rarely are these monuments considered as *archaeological places* in and of themselves, as locales of cultural practice and social memory, as repositories of material residues (Zedeño and Bowser 2009). Studying such places from archaeological, rather than historical or art historical, methodologies and interpretative perspectives opens up fresh ground for the production of new forms of knowledge. In fact, Laurent Olivier's groundbreaking, manifesto-like work *The Dark Abyss of Time* (2011) has pointed out that archaeology's strength comes from its being a discipline of memory rather than history, and therefore it is most suited to address the complex temporality of places of human experience, and places here are considered to be live presences in the contemporary world and not belonging to a fossilized, objectified past of canonical history.

Dissatisfied with past methodological limitations, archaeologists are beginning to address questions of long-term practice whereby the significance of place in the collective imagination and social memory continuously shifts. The political appropriation of particular local practices by the ruling elite introduces monumentality and state spectacles to these always already significant sites of cultural practice, while they are used, reused, and reconfigured by different cultural groups. Meaningful places are also often discussed in relation to bodily performance and movement through the landscape, perhaps best exemplified by ritual processions, state spectacles, and commemorations, as well as pilgrimages that constitute active routes linking places to broader networks of settlement and ecologies of dwelling (Inomata and Coben 2006).

This edited volume is the outcome of a workshop/colloquium that took place at Brown University's Joukowsky Institute for Archaeology and the Ancient World in March 2008, with the title *Drawing on Rocks, Gathering by the Water: Archaeological Fieldwork at Rock Reliefs, Sacred Springs and Other Places*. That event was intended to bring together academics who worked on similar questions concerning archaeological landscapes across the globe and specifically to focus on the making and unmaking of places of human interaction such as rock reliefs, sacred springs and lakes, cairns, ruins, and other meaningful places. The colloquium also provided a platform to discuss the experiences, the challenges, and the theoretical implications of working in the field and specifically at such unusual sites and landscapes. The intention was to bring to the table new archaeological perspectives on working at geologically and culturally distinctive locales where the particular geologies are encountered and uniquely reworked by local practices. It has been a long time since that gathering took place at Brown University's MacMillan Hall of the Geological Sciences, where a fairly small group of speakers and their discussants came together and were accompanied by a select and very alert audience. The format of the gathering was relatively unusual: six main speakers were invited to deliver substantial papers that were pre-circulated a few weeks ahead of the gathering to the group and the discussants. Each paper met its first challenge with a response from its discussant that immediately followed the delivery of the paper. The open forum discussions that followed each of these twin papers were intellectually provocative and constructive. In this edited volume, we have attempted to reflect, if not strengthen, this format by incorporating not only those six original papers, but also several short creative responses to those papers, some of which emerge from the responses delivered at the colloquium, while additional commentators were solicited in its aftermath. This is partly the reason why the publication of the volume has taken such an unusually long time. The book attempts to replicate the intellectual enthusiasm as well as the collegial and collaborative energy of the 2008 *Drawing on Rocks* colloquium.

Several of the contributions to the volume call into question the Cartesian bifurcation of the world into natural and cultural landscapes, while demonstrating through various case studies how such reductive splitting simply does not work when one deals with what Richard Bradley (2000) has famously called "the archaeology of natural places". In their contribution, Lisa Lucero and Andrew Kinkella introduce the idea of a highly animated sacred landscape where the nature-culture dichotomies collapse. Karstic features such as caves, springs, cenotes, and bodies of water function as portals into the underworld among the classical Maya, similar to beliefs within the rest of the Mesoamerican world (Garrison, this volume) and the Anatolian cultural imagination during the Late Bronze Age (Harmanşah, this volume). At Cara

Blanca in central Belize, a fascinating landscape of 23 water bodies (cenotes and lakes) where one finds much fertile agricultural potential and an abundance of water sources, the apparent absence of dense settlement is explained by what Lucero and Kinkella calls "the absence of the profane" – a certain decorum or ethics of dwelling that limited the exploitation of sacred landscapes among the classical Maya. Mayan architecture's mimetic embodiment of the karstic features of the sacred landscape even further supports the argument about the ambiguity between what is man-made and what is natural or supernatural. These karstic features and their architectural counterparts served as sites of ritual action where offerings were made to various divinities in the form of specially decorated ceramic vessels and other ritual objects. Lucero and Kinkella's field project at Cara Blanca presents us with an extraordinary example where an archaeological sensitivity to meaningful places and symbolically charged landscapes allows an alternative, nuanced understanding of a landscape that is otherwise classified as an anomaly according to strictly systematic, place-blind survey methods. Ashmore's brief review of places and place-making in ancient contexts situates Lucero and Kinkella's work into the broader context of the archaeology of places. Her critical perspective brings questions of memory, politics of place, movement (especially processions and pilgrimage) and experience into the picture. Thomas Garrison in his contribution elaborates on how caves, specifically, occupied the geographical imagination of mythical places of cultural origins, conceptualized as earth monsters, or served as canvases for pictorial representation among various Mesoamerican communities, for whom natural, modified, and man-made caves go beyond serving as sites of ritual activity.

Rock reliefs are images and inscriptions carved on living rock surfaces at symbolically charged, culturally significant, and/or geographically strategic locations in the landscape, and they constitute the main subject of research in several of the articles in this volume (Canepa, Ullmann, Harmanşah, Glatz, Robinson, Mousavi, and Straughn). From Bronze and Iron Age local communities of the Zagros mountains and the Akkadian kings of southern Mesopotamia, to Egyptian, Elamite, Hittite, Assyrian, and Persian rulers of antiquity, the practice had long-term application in the landscapes of the Middle East and the Eastern Mediterranean world. Likewise, for the Sasanian elites of Iran, carving ideologically charged and visually powerful images and inscriptions on rock surfaces at prominent extra-urban locations has been a technology of place-making and landscape politics in Western Asia. Canepa (2009: 57–78, 2010, this volume) understands rock reliefs as a powerful tool in constructing what he calls "topographies of power" and discusses the visual, spatial and ritual significance of rock reliefs as site-specific royal monuments. Remarkable in their claim to permanence in the landscape and their ambitious attempt to speak to future generations through what is carved onto the living rock, temporal longevity of rock reliefs oddly allows the authors of such durable monuments to establish particular relationships with the past and construct heritage landscapes of their own. As man-made features carved into the geology of place, rock reliefs appropriate the power of the place and the temporality of geological processes, entering a mimetic engagement with "nature". However, rock reliefs are rarely studied in relation to their local geological or micro-regional contexts, therefore their temporal and material complexity as *archaeological places* is usually ignored. It is precisely this methodological and theoretical bias that the papers in this volume choose to challenge.

Canepa's contribution reviews the long tradition of rock reliefs in Iranian history from the Lullubi of the Zagros to the Achaemenid Persian dynasts. Instead of blindly focusing on the iconographic or historical aspects of the monuments, Canepa presents insights into the local and regional landscapes and architectural ensembles into which the rock reliefs were placed. What is striking about these sites is how new Hellenistic and Sasanian reliefs were carved at deeply historical sites of the Achaemenid heritage and how such new carving events constitute performative engagements with the local manifestations of the Persian past. Rock reliefs are then simultaneously futuristic utopias that project themselves into an anticipated future while engaging deeply with the historical topographies of power. According to Canepa, rock reliefs introduce a certain form of performativity to particular sites of religious significance, state power, and ritual practice in the context of Iranian landscapes over a long period of time. As for the state performance, rock reliefs offered an excellent medium to present to its publics the "eternal and natural order of things" and to take over new territories with the perfect colonial metaphor and material practice of inscribing conquered landscapes (Canepa, this volume). Ian Straughn, as a profound storyteller, articulates the relationship between monuments built for eternity and their medieval afterlife – in particular, the architectural heritage politics of ruined monuments in early Islam. Straughn points to the methodological insufficiency and theoretical laziness of announcing a place as a site of memory, and leaving issues at that, but invites us to do the hard work, the retelling of the stories of ruined monuments highlighting their nuanced past, and political contestation across time of the ideological signatures of monuments in the landscape. Ali Mousavi reminds us of the deep history of rock-carving practice on the Iranian highlands, and the diachronic history of these monuments as sites of heritage, especially the transhistorical conversations between Elamite, Achaemenid, and Sasanian monuments.

Lee Ullmann's careful discussion of Hittite rock reliefs provides a similarly interrogative understanding of rock monuments, this time in the context of Anatolian landscapes. Ullmann's contribution presents a complex understanding of reliefs not simply as political propaganda, but as sites where Hittites used geological landscapes to construct places of ritual practice which then established a network of connections between settlements and regions. He excavates ancient texts and mobilizes GIS-based spatial analysis to understand the topographic features and geographical peculiarities of the Hittite rock reliefs in an interlinked and comparative way. Ullmann sees rock reliefs as a technology of constructing places of ritual and cult practice, but also as a way of conceptualizing the landscape as one moves through it. Claudia Glatz's commentary puts Ullmann's paper in perspective by contextualizing Ullmann's work in relation to the recent surge in scholarly interest on Anatolian landscape monuments, to which she herself has contributed significantly (Glatz 2009; Glatz and Plourde 2011). Glatz highlights the striking dichotomy within the study of Anatolian rock monuments between their role in the macro-scale imperial geographies and the particularistic aspects of each monument, and points out that successful interpretations will reside in the balanced intersection of the two perspectives that highlights locality versus globality, between the local cultural significance of places and their role in the networked territories of empires. The historical context of the making of the rock monuments testifies to this double perspective. Robinson's commentary presents us with a close and careful reading of Ullmann's contribution, while highlighting the Hittite engagements with natural topographies and local geographies both in the Boğazköy texts that are highlighted by Ullmann himself, and in the placement of rock reliefs in the landscape. Robinson pays close attention to the various possible functions that rock reliefs may have served in the Hittite context and welcomes Ullmann's proposal that the rock relief sites may have served as convenient way-stations for Anatolian armies, as already ritually significant locales. Having worked on the significance of water and spring monuments in classical antiquity, Robinson draws our attention to the remarkable Hittite interest in bodies of water and their everyday and cultic significance. This is a matter I take up in my own contribution.

In "Event, place, performance," I attempt to tackle the status of "place" in humanities and social sciences in the midst of discourses on globalization, transnationalism, and migration of the late twentieth and early twenty-first century. Place appears in contemporary anthropological, political, scientific and cultural studies discourses as a politically charged paradigm associated with questions of heritage, regional identity, ecological activism, and the defense of place against the pressures of neoliberal development projects. In this article, I propose that archaeology as a discipline can offer powerful tools to engage with places on the ground and through fieldwork, in order to understand their complexity, deep historicity, and cultural contingency. I suggest that this is only possible through a careful rethinking of our field methodologies, deliberate collaborations with other disciplinary fields such as anthropology and geology, and finally with a sincere, and politically engaged approach to its everyday realities and contemporary resident communities. Moving from the stories around the almond trees of Ayanis village in Eastern Turkey, to the caved source of the Loue river at Ornans in France and the famous realist painter Gustave Courbet's representations of it in his landscape paintings, and finally discussing the image-making practices of Assyrian rulers at the source of the Tigris river in southeastern Turkey, I define the deep historicity of places in relation to the events and performances of historical actors.

Ben Marsh and Janet Jones's contribution "Ruins within Ruins" provides an environmental and geomorphological overview for a historically and geographically nuanced understanding of places and landscapes. They do this ingeniously by exploring the powerful metaphor of the ruin, evoking not only the intensely emotional resonance of lived places with deep histories, but also alluding to the more physical aspects of archaeological landscapes that are always undergoing a material process of ruination. They brilliantly remind us that the geomorphological processes of change in micro-landscapes inform us about how the users of those landscapes relate to the past through the complex set of landscape features, such as ruins and deteriorated landscapes. Geomorphologically informed landscape biographies shift the focus of the study away from anthropocentric or site-based histories of a region, but draw on an ecological broad base of evidence that speaks to diachronic landscape processes that are at once cultural and natural. Contemporary landscapes therefore are always in the forefront of discussion, and archaeological landscapes are ruins through which one narrates the human interactions with and interventions into the environment. Important is the fact that these encounters are never purely authentic encounters with natural environments, but they are always mediated through an animated world that is always already at a state of ruination, teeming with memories, deep histories, stories, monuments, and traces of past human activities. According to Marsh and Jones, studying ruins and processes of ruination is a way to reflect on "entropic processes" such as "oxidation, abrasion, fracture, collapse, and weathering," therefore a delicate engagement with questions of temporality in the landscape. In the context of the lived environment, this also corresponds to processes such as alluviation, erosion, deforestation, alterations of vegetation, irrigation, and micro-climatic fluctuations. These correspond to cultural processes that have to do with the semantics of the environment, the shifts in the cultural significance of places, geographical shifts in the social imaginary, and new horizons in the meaning of particular landscapes. Ruins are therefore good to think with. The social life of contemporary ruins and an archaeology of the "heterogenous mass of our present" has recently been taken up by many theorists of archaeological thought, as a new and important avenue not just for archaeology, but also for humanities and the social sciences more broadly (Olivier 2011:62; see also Dawdy 2010; Shanks 2012). To exemplify their novel landscape biography approach, Marsh and Jones present the case of the environment around the site of Yassıhöyük (identified with the Iron Age capital city of Gordion), and demonstrate the complexity of long-term geomorphological processes around the site.

In his engaging commentary in dialogue with Marsh and Jones's contribution, John F. Cherry highlights the long-term processes of world landscapes becoming ruin after the onset of the Holocene, with all the dark associations of the concepts of ruin and ruination. According to him, the implications of such intricate natural/cultural processes are crucial, especially when one considers how the material record at particular places is strikingly well preserved, while others are being virtually erased. This unevenness of the material record in archaeological landscapes and the great history of erasure is perhaps one of the most significant contributions of geomorphology to archaeological field practice, as one realizes when reading Cherry's commentary. How successful are the archaeologists in this sense in "attending to ordinary places" when they are continuously attracted to the very special sites with high levels of preservation? Cherry further articulates an extremely stimulating aspect of landscape survey projects armed with geomorphologists today: the realization that severe alteration of landscapes was not just a feature of industrial modernity or Soviet-era agricultural practices, but pretty much part of the story all throughout the past at various scales.

The final contribution to the volume is Christopher Witmore's "(Dis)continuous Domains" where he presents the case for one of the most influential paradigms in anthropology and archaeology: the multi-sited approach. This is based on the very powerful idea that all places (Witmore's *topoi*) are relational (although perhaps some more than others). The things, the monuments, the artifacts, the bodies that we excavate at a particular place have far-reaching connections both spatially and temporally. Articulating in depth "an arbitration dispute between two Greek poleis, Hermion and Epidauros, in the second century B.C.," Witmore literally opens a new frontier of thinking for us on borders, border monuments, and their material relationships. As Elliott Colla ingeniously put it in his response to Witmore's paper, "pre-modern boundaries and frontiers – as opposed to modern border fences – are often rough-hewn both materially and conceptually," referring to the artfully crafted, gradually formed, politically contested and materially shaped nature of borders. Witmore's engaging and refreshing multi-sited intervention allows us to conceptualize meaningful continuities across the topographically discontinuous landscapes with an effective call for a "meticulous detailing of heterogeneous locales and linkages," fracturing "the flatlands of Euclidean space". Like a medieval relic of a saint's body-part circulated from shrine to shrine, things continuously link bodies to other times and other places in a myriad of ways, artfully. Stories, material practices, visualities, technologies, and knowledges are *folded into things*," to borrow further Witmore's mind-opening concepts. *Boleoi lithoi*, perhaps to be associated with the cairns in the Southern Argolid marking the borderlands between Hermion and Epidauros, are curiously informative, since they both constitute places themselves and define broader territories which are contested and always dynamic. *Boleoi lithoi* are witnesses to the very materialization of political disputes as real spaces in the landscape and sites of contention, while they embody far-reaching connections to urban centers, public monuments, and political powers. Witmore on the one hand meticulously weaves a dense fabric and a heterogeneous network of linkages, associations, and cultural practices around the *boleoi lithoi* and the cairns, moving from place to place, across a wide span of time and through the writings of travelers and topographers, both ancient and modern. On the other hand, he demonstrates strikingly that archaeology as a discipline and field practice has always been multi-sited by its very nature. Yet his dramatic intervention in the contemporary archaeology of places and landscapes invites us to pay closer attention to the dynamism of places over the long term, and in a way shows why it is incorrect to imagine places as self-contained and bounded, rather than distributed and connected.

It is only relevant to conclude the volume with Gavin Lucas's thoughtful response to Witmore's paper, entitled "Moving on". Here, Lucas poses challenging questions to relational ontologies via a critical reading of Graham Harman's work, while he takes us back to the strengths of "multi-sited archaeology." Among the avenues of research that multi-sited archaeology invites us to are the very specific relations between different places, and the myriad of forms of mobility between those places, the mobility of things, bodies, knowledges, and stories. These tangible mobilities are constitutive of places, and the study of movement and mobility may indeed answer why certain places are more connected to each other than others.

If we return to our notion of place, we see that the 15 contributions in this collection negotiate alternative readings of roughly hewn or delicately inscribed rocky places and venerated watery landscapes in different ways. A striking thread among many of the contributions is connectivity of places through the mobility of bodies, things, stories, and knowledges, and the need to understand places as part of a broader meshwork of relationships and associations. The special geologies of rocky and watery places, where nature performs its miracles, are at the forefront of human experience, while such sites are often associated with marginality and borderlands. At Hittite DINGIR. KAŠKAL.KUR monuments, at Sasanian rock reliefs, Classical Maya's cenotes, and at the Argolid's *boleoi lithoi,* the rocks constitute sites of arbitration, negotiation and political intervention towards the configuration of territory. The weathering surfaces of rock reliefs and their stubborn imagery witness the writing of new stories and open up new meanings in different historical contexts, while the landscape around them moves into new episodes of ruination. All contributions, however, point to the need for approaching archaeological landscapes as belonging to the present in their own way, and call for special field methodologies to get a grasp of their complexity.

What we sincerely and collectively hoped during the 2008 colloquium was to share ways of working at unusual places of geological and cultural significance and to contribute to the ever-increasing academic brainstorming about the notion of place and locality. However, more concretely we aimed at developing shared guidelines for the field, to address questions of site-specificity in archaeological field practice, and the necessary intellectual tools to understand past practices of drawing on rocks and gathering by the water. We hope that the conversations will continue.

References

Boivin, Nicole, and Mary Ann Owoc (eds.)
2004 *Soils, Stones, and Symbols: Cultural Perceptions of the Mineral World.* UCL Press, London.

Bradley, Richard
2000 *The Archaeology of Natural Places.* Routledge, London.

Brady, James Edward (ed.)
2005 *In the Maw of the Earth Monster: Mesoamerican Ritual Cave Use.* University of Texas Press, Austin.

Canepa, Matthew P.
2009 *The Two Eyes of the Earth: Art and Ritual of Kingship Between Rome and Sasanian Iran.* University of California Press, Berkeley and Los Angeles.
2010 Technologies of Memory in Early Sasanian Iran: Achaemenid Sites and Sasanian Identity. *American Journal of Archaeology* 114: 563–596.

Csordas, Thomas J.
2002 *Body/Meaning/Healing.* Palgrave Macmillan, New York.

Dawdy, Shannon
2010 Clockpunk Anthropology and the Ruins of Modernity. *Current Anthropology* 51: 761–793.

Glatz, Claudia

2009   Empire as Network: Spheres of Material Interaction in Late Bronze Age Anatolia. *Journal of Anthropological Archaeology* 28: 127–141.

Glatz, Claudia, and Aimée M. Plourde

2011   Landscape Monuments and Political Competition in Late Bronze Age Anatolia: An Investigation of Costly Signaling Theory. *Bulletin of the American Schools of Oriental Research* 361: 33–66.

Harmanşah, Ömür

2014   Stone Worlds: Technologies of Rock-carving and Place-making in Anatolian Landscapes. In *The Cambridge Handbook of the Bronze Age – Iron Age Mediterranean World*, edited by A. Bernard Knapp and Peter van Dommelen. Cambridge University Press, Cambridge, in press.

Inomata, Takeshi, and Lawrence S. Coben (eds.)

2006   *Archaeology of Performance: Theaters of Power, Community, and Politics.* Rowman Altamira Press, Lanham, MD.

Olivier, Laurent

2011   *The Dark Abyss of Time: Archaeology and Memory.* Translated by Arthur Greenspan. Rowman Altamira Press, Lanham, MD.

Shanks, Michael

2012   *The Archaeological Imagination.* Left Coast Press, Walnut Creek, CA.

Zedeño, María Nieves, and Brenda J. Bowser

2009   The Archaeology of Meaningful Places. In *The Archaeology of Meaningful Places*, edited by Brenda J. Bowser and María Nieves Zedeño, pp. 1–14. University of Utah Press, Salt Lake City.

A Place for Pilgrimage: The Ancient Maya Sacred Landscape of Cara Blanca, Belize

Lisa J. Lucero and Andrew Kinkella

In our everyday lives, we distinguish natural and cultural features of the landscape, where mountains belong to the natural world and buildings to the cultural one. Many groups in the past, however, did not envision their world in this dichotomous manner, but viewed it as a single entity. If people of the past did not dichotomize their world, neither should we. This is where landscape archaeology comes in, because it assesses the social relationships between people and the world in which they lived (Anschuetz et al. 2001), and stresses the multivocal aspects of landscapes through space and time (Bender 2002). This method is not about determining what people did to the landscape, but rather what they did with the landscape. In this sense, "Culture is the agent, the natural area is the medium, the cultural landscape is the result" (Carl Sauer, quoted in Anschuetz et al. 2001: 164). These relationships are dynamic and may not appear in the archaeological record as what one traditionally defines as a site. In other words, our imposition of archaeological terms does not necessarily reflect the "place" as it was in the past. We therefore must redirect our focus to place rather than site (cf. Bradley 2000: 147). After all, "the landscape is full of history, legend, knowledge, and power" (Anschuetz et al. 2001: 178).

The ancient landscape is imbued with sacred qualities. In some instances, people did not augment sacred places, but instead revered them in their natural state. For the Maya, the concept of sacred landscape is even reflected in their speech. For example, the Maya use the same term for mountain and temple – *witz* (Stuart 1987; Stuart and Houston 1994: 82). While they did not distinguish between culture and nature, they did distinguish between the upperworld, earth, and the underworld. The earth provided the contact point between the other realms (e.g., Bradley 2000: 13, 29), each reached by openings in the earth. For mountains, portals to the underworld or *Xibalba* consist of caves and standing bodies of water; for temples, they consist of doorways often decorated with cave imagery (Bassie-Sweet 1996).

The Classic Maya (A.D. 250–950) of southeastern Mexico, Belize, Guatemala, and the western parts of El Salvador and Honduras, lived in a tropical world that shaped their entire existence. Water was crucial in this rainfall-dependent society, given that the annual six-month dry season includes a four-month period when it did not rain at all (Scarborough 2003). At well-known Classic Maya centers such as Tikal, Calakmul, Caracol, and others, the Maya relied on massive artificial reservoirs to see them through the annual drought (Scarborough 2003). Water was plentiful during the six-month rainy season when farmers worked in their fields and where daily rain showers replenished water supplies and nourished growing plants. This setting, where agricultural land and water were critical for survival, makes areas with these resources in abundance particularly attractive to settle and farm, and archaeologists find noticeable settlement in such areas (Ford 1986, 1991). Areas that defy this common trend beg the question of what human necessities were more important than water and farming.

Cara Blanca in central Belize (Figure 2.1) is such a place, where agricultural land and abundant water sources are paired with only a moderate amount of settlement (Kinkella 2000, 2004, 2009). Rationally, especially given the annual drought, we should find evidence for dense settlement; but we do not. Did its sacred or supernatural qualities trump farming and water needs enough to prevent habitation and human interference? In this paper, we approach Cara Blanca as the Maya may have done, in order to explain how its 25 freshwater pools (cenotes) and lakes and steep escarpments intertwine with their worldview.

Unlike the typical situation at major centers, the Maya at Cara Blanca did not have to build artificial mountains (temples) or portals (reservoirs, temple entrances). The few structures and features found near pools, which appear to be ceremonial, suggest its sacred role. As a matter of fact, the limited construction may have increased its symbolic significance (cf. Bradley 2000: 107). Presented below are the results of several seasons of survey and test excavations that we explain through a sacred lens. We attempt to show that the Maya journeyed to Cara Blanca as a place of pilgrimage.

The Animated Landscape in Classic Maya Society

Any undertaking in understanding the ancient Maya must take into account what they faced living in the subtropics, a region with variously sized pockets of dispersed agricultural land and noticeable seasonal differences – namely, a six-month dry season and six-month rainy season. Average rainfall, depending

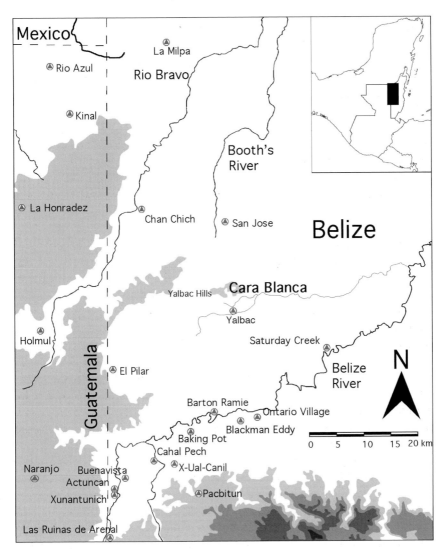

Figure 2.1. Location of Cara Blanca, Belize.

on the area, can range from 1350 to 3700 mm. To provide a sense of how important water is, one only has to take into account the fact that people can lose up to 10 liters per day through sweating, and as a consequence need to drink more water than their counterparts in temperate zones (Bacus and Lucero 1999). In addition to drinking water, the Maya depended on rainfall to grow maize, beans, squash, cacao, chili peppers, tobacco, pineapple, and so on. They lived in farmsteads dotted throughout the landscape near and in between centers, and basically were self-sufficient at the community level – in the rainy and agricultural season, anyway. Maya farmers relied on scattered and small-scale subsistence systems because of the dispersed nature of agricultural land and variable rainfall (Lucero 2006c). Thus, the highest settlement density and most powerful Maya centers are found in areas with the largest plots of prime agricultural land. Interestingly, these centers, including Tikal, Calakmul, Caracol, and Naranjo, emerged in areas that lacked permanent water sources such as lakes and rivers, which actually provided the means for rulers to acquire power (Lucero in press).

There are hundreds of civic-ceremonial centers with royal courts that had varying degrees of power. The most powerful Classic Maya kings in the southern lowlands emerged in areas with plentiful fertile land and pronounced seasonal variability (Lucero 1999b, 2002, 2003, 2006c). Rulers attracted and integrated farmers through sponsoring large-scale ceremonies, feasts, and ballgames (Ford 1996; Scarborough 1998). They drew people to centers by providing access to reservoirs during the dry season (the agricultural downtime) when many Maya had few options but to acquiesce to tribute demands for access to drinking water. The common farmer looked to kings to supplicate the gods to supply rain at the right time, since when the rains began and how much rain there was were critical factors in the agricultural regimen (Gunn et al. 2002; Lucero 2007; Marcus 2006). Centers located near rivers with smaller pockets of fertile land (i.e., fewer subjects or farmers) were not as powerful, because rulers did not have the means (reservoirs) to beholden others like those found at powerful centers.

Seasonal rainfall vagaries required continual supplications to the gods. The iconographic, hieroglyphic, and archaeological records leave little doubt of this fact. People prayed to ancestors, rain and maize gods, and other important deities at agricultural fields, near water sources and in public plazas, caves, and the home, as found among contemporary Maya groups (e.g., Vogt 1970, 1998). However, it was in the home where the material remains of their vibrant ritual life are most apparent. Domestic rites revolved around life, death, and renewal. Everything was cyclical, from the daily emergence and disappearance of the sun to their own cycle of life and death. Death was not the end of life so much as providing the stage for the beginning of life. Some contemporary Maya peoples even identify children or grandchildren as *kexol*, or "replacements" (Schele and Miller 1986: 266), signifying a connection between the living and the dead.

At present, we know the Maya conduct funerary rites in the creation of ancestors, which involve keeping a family member's remains close, by burying the deceased and grave goods under house floors (e.g., Vogt 1970). They perform dedication ceremonies to animate new houses and other objects; for the former, practices include the caching of objects under floors (e.g., Vogt 1993). Part of the renewal ceremony consists of terminating the old, for the New Year, for example, or after the death of a family member when life must begin anew. When a particular family member dies, they bury the deceased in the house floor, break and burn household items, raze the house, and build anew on top of the old. The new house then requires dedication rites to animate it – that is, for its transformation from a house to a home. Since all objects are animated, Maya perform termination rites to de-activate or de-animate them (e.g., Tozzer 1941: 151), thus releasing their soul; the Maya break or "kill" objects, partially destroy houses, and burn items and incense (Mock 1998). These same practices are indicated in the archaeological record based on the plethora of domestic dedication, funerary, and termination deposits (Lucero 2008). In fact, the depositional histories of Maya structures, small and large, reflect the continuous flow of ceremonial behaviors that in the end comprise much of the structure itself.

While dense with meaning, house rites only reveal one aspect of the Maya worldview. Outside the home is just as imbued with symbolic significance. Things in nature (such as springs, caves, water holes, mountains, etc.) that we define in our own view as non-living to the Maya were animated and played vital roles in their daily lives. Here we focus on openings in the earth and what they tell us about Classic Maya concepts of animated or sacred landscapes.

Portals to the Underworld

The karstic topography of the Maya lowlands consists of a limestone shelf pitted with caves and other openings. And because they open into the earth, they were and are considered by the Maya as portals to the underworld or *Xibalba* (Bassie-Sweet 1996), in which they left offerings (Andrews and Corletta 1995; Schele and Miller 1986: 42). Furthermore, these openings exude the very stuff of life – water. It is to be expected that sacredness embodies such places and that portals personify the source of water.

The earliest monumental Maya architecture is intimately linked to sacred natural features, particularly bodies of water, caves, and mountains (Stone 1992). At Copán, Fash and Davis-Salazar (2006: 134) suggest that "pyramids were mountains that provided an axis of communication with the gods and spirits; the courtyards surrounding them were the valleys and depressions that collected runoff, thereby creating shallow, watery ponds." Palenque, in contrast, had plentiful springs and streams, and thus only had to build artificial mountains (French et al. 2006). Water and cave iconography such as the Witz Monster (Schele and Mathews 1998: 43, 417) is found on temple doorways and signifies cave entrances (Puleston 1977; Rands 1953). Natural counterparts or "topographic shrines" were "closely allied with the notion of reciprocity ... reverence for the earth will yield harmony in the natural world and prosperity for humankind" (Stone 1992: 112). Their distance or isolation from centers and densely settled areas further added to their sacred qualities and served as ideal settings for communing with supernatural forces regarding hunting, rain, ancestors, agriculture, health, wealth, and so on.

Caves

Since many caves in the Maya area are wet environments with streams, springs, rivers, pools, small lakes, and waterfalls, it is not surprising that the Maya considered them as sources of water (Bassie-Sweet 1996: 10). Contemporary Maya collect *suhuy ha* or virgin water from caves for special ceremonies. Caves are places of abundance and material wealth. Gods dwell within them and their power is manifested in their control over lightning, rain, clouds, wind, the land, wild animals, health, crops, and wealth (Stone 1995: 40). "The interior of the mountain is ... where the owner [Earth God/Lord] keeps all types of wild animals" and is "filled with maize, water, or treasure" (Brady 1997: 603). In Yalcoba, Yucatán, "caves function ... as entry and exit points at the eastern and western horizons for celestial bodies, winds, and even human souls" (Stone 1995: 36). It is believed that the sun sets, or disappears, and rises, or emerges, through caves.

Caves are also places of creation from where humans emerged, as did maize (Bassie-Sweet 1996: 11; Stone 1997). Traditional Maya view certain mountains as lineage-mountains where ancestors reside (Bassie-Sweet 1996: 16, 24, 60). Such features in the landscape ritually define borders and manifest community identity. The Maya make pilgrimages to caves, sometimes from great distances, where they propitiate ancestors, the Earth Owner, rain deities, and so on (Stone 1997).

In some parts of the Maya area, caves are perceived as symbolic "steambaths" (e.g., Chamula, Chiapas, México) (Houston 1996: 138). A sweatbath not only cleanses the body, but also "restores heat" and eliminates fevers, which, along with other illnesses, can be "sweated out" (1996: 139). As such, they are also used during childbirth.

While caves are considered sacred, they also have dangerous aspects. The ambiguity of caves is a common belief among the Maya because of what can take place in caves, such as witchcraft or the extraction of souls. For example, in some parts of the Yucatán, the Maya believe that caves house disease-producing forces (Redfield 1941: 239). Caves are viewed as conduits for supernatural forces and in which the plagues of life were disposed. The

Maya deposit animated objects imbued with sacred and dangerous qualities. For instance, the Lacandon Maya dispose of god pots or *incensarios* in caves, because they still have dangerous animated attributes (McGee 1998). Evil spirits can inhabit caves; they are often associated with isolated and unprotected – that is, dark – areas where the dead reside (Moyes 2006: 26–31). In Amatenango, Chiapas, "dangerous spirits" are believed to live in caves and hills (Nash 1970: 23). Food is placed in front of them as offerings to the spirits so that they can carry illness into the cave and subsequently into the underworld. Cave-dwelling animals were thought to be the embodiment of demons, where they cast evil spells and perform sorcery. Maya caves, thus, provide the ideal place to conduct ritual violence (e.g., Brown 2004; Lucero and Gibbs 2007).

In pre-Columbian times, the Maya left offerings in caves. As a matter of fact, caves have some of the earliest evidence for ritual activities (e.g., Brady 1995). People from all over visited caves. For example, Naj Tunich, a cave in eastern Petén, Guatemala, has painted emblem glyphs on its walls indicating that visitors came from several areas (Brady 1989: 414). While the most common association of human remains in caves likely was ancestor veneration, the Maya also killed and/or placed sacrificial victims, or perhaps even witches, in caves. Stalagmites and stalactites have been found outside caves in several contexts, because they contain "spiritual power" (Brady et al. 1997a). In certain contexts, such as ballcourts found in every Maya center, the presence of items from caves likely signifies a connection to the Hero Twins defeating the Death Lords on the ballcourt in Xibalba, as depicted in Popol Vuh, the Maya origin story (Baron 2006; Christensen 2007).

Water Bodies

Bodies of water are also sacred features in Maya cosmology, and the Maya treated caves and water bodies much the same. As a matter of fact, the "Maya Underworld is characterized as water, which also is a physical attribute of limestone caves" (Stone 1992: 127). This similarity is expressed in the fact that both are openings in the earth in which supernatural entities resided, and in which the Maya left offerings.

Cenotes and lakes have different characteristics; surface rivers feed into lakes. Cenotes, found largely in the northern Maya lowlands, are "karstic solution features" (Brown 2006: 174) or sinkholes fed by the relatively high water table, and are sometimes the only source of water outside of rain (e.g., Redfield 1941: 119). In the southern Maya lowlands, especially inland, the water table is too low in most parts to percolate to the surface in cenotes. This fact makes Cara Blanca even more unique, since it is one of the few areas with cenotes in the southern lowlands.

More recently in the Yucatán, the Maya believe that cenotes are the source of wind (Redfield 1941: 118): "As the water makes its cycle, carried by the rain-gods from the cenotes up into the sky to fall as fertilizing rain upon the milpa, so the winds have their sources in the sea and pass up through the cenotes" (Redfield 1941: 118). While cenotes in town have both utilitarian and sacred features, those located in the "bush" or away from habitation have sacred qualities, and must be approached carefully (Redfield 1941: 119).

Water bodies often mark the center of communities and serve as an *axis mundi* (e.g., Brown 2006). At the Early Postclassic (c. A.D. 950–1150) site of Chichén Itzá in Yucatán, Mexico, one of the most famous cenotes, the Sacred Cenote, was connected to the center via a 400 m long causeway; the "utilitarian" cenote, however, was located in the center core (Brown 2006). At the Late Classic (c. A.D. 600–750) center of Dos Pilas, Guatemala, the Maya built the major temples and palace over caves and springs, a practice that occurred at other sites, to show a ruler's "control over water, and presumably over rain-making and fertility" (Brady and Ashmore 1999: 130). The Classic Maya placed the four largest reservoirs at Tikal approximately along the cardinal directions from the site core, a further indication of the symbolic significance of water bodies. And based on her analysis of water symbolism and artificial sunken pools and plazas, Fash (2005) argues that Copán's Late Classic residents built sacred pools in the site core.

At the Sacred Cenote of Chichén Itzá, the Maya built a ceremonial building so close to its edge that part of it has collapsed into the water, a pattern found at a few other sites including Chinkultic, Mexico and Cara Blanca. Edward H. Thompson first dredged the Sacred Cenote in 1904 and recovered figurines, masks, bells, cups, jade, ritually "killed" objects, representations of the Maya rain god Chak, gold and copper items, and human skeletal remains (Coggins 1992). Osteological studies indicate that the "inhabitants of the well" included 23 males, 12 females, and 43 subadults. Furthermore, skeletons show evidence for perimortem violence – that is, sacrifice or ritual violence (Anda 2007). In the early Colonial period in the sixteenth century, Bishop de Landa recorded that the Maya would sacrifice adults and children to Chak in times of drought (Tozzer 1941: 180, n. 948).

The ancient Maya also left offerings in lakes. For example, divers at Lake Amatitlán, Guatemala, recovered over 400 ceramic vessels depicting spider monkeys, various fruits, flowers, snakes, lizards, and human heads. Chak and Tlaloc, the latter the central Mexican storm deity, were also represented, as well as fertility and death gods (Borhegyi 1961). The stylistic diversity of the materials from Teotihuacan in central Mexico, the central Mexican highlands, the Maya area and other regions, indicates that the lake was a place of pilgrimage for different ethnic groups. Moreover, the waters at Lake

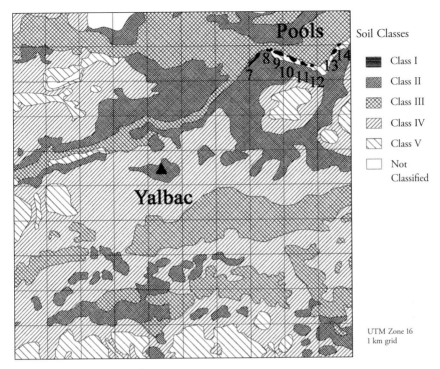

Figure 2.2. Agricultural soil types in the Yalbac and Cara Blanca Pools vicinity
(adapted from Kinkella 2009: fig. 4.4).

Amatitlán are quite warm, and people may have used the lake for curative
purposes; structures along the shore could have served as shrines (Borhegyi
1961). While archaeologists have investigated cenotes in the northern Maya
lowlands, southern Maya lowlands cenotes remain unexplored.

The Sacred Landscape of Cara Blanca, Belize

The Valley of Peace Archaeology (VOPA) project area in central Belize had
never been extensively explored prior to the beginning of our project in
1997. To get to know the area, we devised a survey strategy using a predictive
settlement model developed by Scott Fedick based on agricultural potential.
He evaluated agricultural potential using several factors including soil type,
root zone, susceptibility to erosion, workability, drainage, and inherent fertility
(Fedick 1988, 1995, 1996). Each cluster was assigned a Capability Class
(I–V), with Class I having the fewest and Class V having the greatest
limitations (Figure 2.2). Survey results correlated quite well with soil class

Soil Class	Structure/residential unit per km²
I	97/84
II alluvial	48/48
II non-alluvial	189/157
III	0
IV	0
V	19/11

Table 2.1.   Structure density in the VOPA area (from Lucero et al. 2004).

– except Cara Blanca (Lucero et al. 2004). Basically, outside of Cara Blanca, we found the highest settlement densities in Class I (alluvium) and Class II (well-drained upland) areas (Table 2.1).

Cara Blanca (literally "white face") consists of 25 water bodies extending east-west along the base of a limestone ridge c. 80–100 m high in the northern section of the VOPA area (Figure 2.3). It is in an uninhabited expanse of primary forest currently owned by a logging company, Yalbac Ranch. The central pools are defined as cenotes because of their steep-sided walls and clear water filtered through the limestone below, while the far eastern and western water bodies are more similar to lakes (i.e., with shallow shores and gradual change in water depth). Recently, geochemist and freshwater expert Patricia Beddows, who visited Cara Blanca in May 2008, confirmed that its central pools are deep pit cenotes (pers. comm., June 2008), which are formed from below (vs. collapsed dolines). The water level may fluctuate, but they are deep enough that there is more than enough water, even in the dry season. Most of the water is drainage from the Petén, Guatemala. A map compiled by Bryson Geological Services for Anschutz Corporation in 1974 shows an east-west fault with the north side uplifted (Robert Johnston, Castle Belize Ltd., pers. comm., 1998). The two rock types at the fault are defined as Kbc (Barton Creek Formation limestone and dolomite of the Cretaceous age, 70–65 million years) and Trb (Redbank Formation clay, sands and gypsum of Miocene-Pleistocene ages, 25–2 million years). Water bodies are ringed by Class V soils (black, poorly drained clayey soils) that flood during the rainy season. Immediately beyond these clayey soils are fertile Class II soils.

In the past several seasons we surveyed the area beginning at the secondary center of Yalbac (Graebner 2002) and paralleling the pools (Kinkella 2005, 2006, 2008, 2009). We started with a Brunton and tripod to establish a transect that ran 41.5° from traverse point YL at Yalbac to the closest pool, Pool 7, some 4 km distant (Kinkella 2006: figs. 3.1–3.2). In accordance with other survey projects in the Belize Valley area (see Ashmore 1996), we used a 400 m-wide transect; it is not possible to do complete coverage due

Figure 2.3. Aerial photo of one of the eastern pools at Cara Blanca.

to heavy jungle growth and the amount of time it would take. Twenty-five meters was the maximum line-of-sight distance possible; the survey team walked the transect back and forth at 50 m increments until a width of 400 m was attained. A Garmin Venture GPS was used in tandem with 1:50,000 government maps to record mounds, mound groups, pools, features, and elevations. Sketch maps were made of all solitary mounds and small mound groups using pace and compass. Larger mound groups were mapped using a total station.

Most of the survey was completed in summer 2007 (Kinkella 2008). Results have revealed the following locations of notable settlement clusters, each defined by a different set of characteristics (Figure 2.4):

1. The Yalbac site core
2. A large patch of Class II soil between Yalbac and Pool 7
3. The minor center of M104, two km northeast of Yalbac
4. A concentrated "lookout" area or pilgrimage destination on top of a high ridge above Pool 15
5. The area in the vicinity of Pool 1
6. The minor center of M124 immediately northwest of Pool 6

In most cases, mounds are typically located on slightly higher ground, likely to avoid flooding during the rainy season. The mounds range in size from less

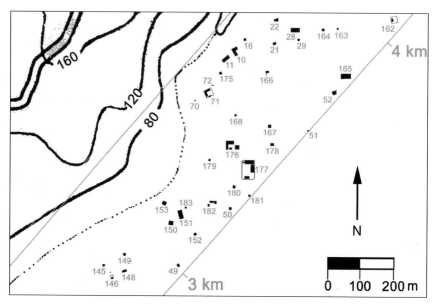

Figure 2.4. Settlement between Yalbac and the Cara Blanca Pools (from Kinkella 2009: 242).

than one meter to approximately 5 m in height (Kinkella 2006). The majority of surface ceramics, as well as those found in controlled excavations, date to the Late Classic period, or c. A.D. 700–900 (Kinkella 2000, 2009).

Large caves have not been found in the Cara Blanca area, likely due to the soft marl limestone present in the area – which would also explain the "white face" (i.e., so soft that pieces broke off, or "incompetent" limestone) (Beddows, pers. comm., June 2008). This being said, several smaller caves have been noted (c. 8 m deep from drip line with c. 4 m high ceiling) which may have been adequate for ritual purposes (see Kinkella 2009). The lack of large caves might also further increase the significance of the water bodies as the only major portals in the area (Patricia Beddows, pers. comm., June 2008).

We have visited the westernmost 16 of the 25 pools (nos. 1–16), four of which have associated structures near pool edges: Pools 1, 7, 8, and 9 (Figures 2.5–2.6). The survey we conducted in the surrounding cliffs to the north and *bajos* (seasonal swamps) to the south has thus far revealed little additional settlement. Soils are generally of poorer quality (Class III, IV, or V soils) with relatively severe restrictions for agriculture (Lucero et al. 2004). Pool 1 measures approximately 100 × 60 m and is surrounded by seven mounds (Figure 2.7). Looter's trenches show that the largest structure (Str. 1, 22 × 15 m, 4 m tall) is a vaulted range building consisting of six rooms,

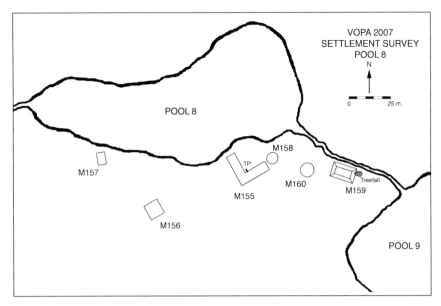

Figure 2.5. Settlement at Pool 8 (from Kinkella 2009: fig. 5.13).

three to a side, radiating out from a central spine wall with a series of four pillar-like walls that run the poolside length of the structure. It is similar in form to one of the range structures at the nearby center of San Jose (Str. C5) (Thompson 1939: 59–60). The structure sits so close to the pool's edge that it is eroding into the water. Test excavations at Str. 1 yielded predominantly (63%) Late Classic jars (c. A.D. 700–900) (Kinkella 2000, 2004) – not the typical domestic assemblage consisting of a more consistent distribution of jars, plates, bowls, and vases (Lucero 2001).

In 1998 two divers explored Pool 1 to c. 20 m below its surface without reaching bottom (c. 50+ m) and recovered two sherds from the steep sidewall at a depth of c. 10 m (Kinkella 2000; Osterholtz 1999). Since both sherds were found immediately below a Str. 1 looter's trench, we at first surmised that they comprised looter's debris (Kinkella 2000); however, recent research conducted by Kinkella indicates that the Maya may have purposely placed the sherds in natural or artificial niches along the cenote sidewalls.

A larger group of mounds is found approximately 400 m to the west of Pool 1, equidistant between Pools 1 and 2. Pool 2 is located about 1 km west-southwest of Pool 1, and Cara Blanca got its name from the steep white cliffs directly above it. The settlement includes a substantial number of mounds (c. 15), including several range structures and a sweatbath (M186) (Kinkella

Figure 2.6. Pool 9 (adapted from Kinkella 2009: fig. 5.15).

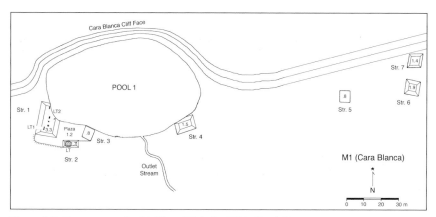

Figure 2.7. Structures at Pool 1 (from Kinkella 2009: fig. 4.7).

2008). We excavated a 1 × 1 m unit on one of the smaller structures (M170) in order to obtain ceramic sherds for dating purposes, but immediately came upon a burial (the only one so far encountered in the pool area). We left the remains in situ, but collected the remnants of two burial vessels from above the skull. Both dated to the Late Classic, and their styles suggest that its

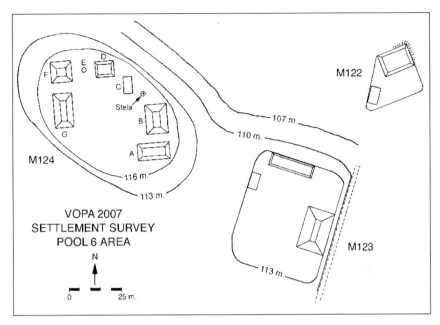

Figure 2.8. Settlement near Pool 6 including plain stela and altar (from Kinkella 2009: fig. 5.35).

inhabitants may have interacted more with people to the north at sites such as La Milpa, Chan Chich and others, rather than with Maya of the Belize Valley proper to the south.

Pool 7 (c. 130 × 30 m) is the westernmost pool, and settlement on its eastern side consists of eight low range structures forming a double plazuela group. In 2005, we placed a 1 × 1 m test pit in the middle of Plaza 2 to collect chronological information. As was the case elsewhere, virtually all ceramics date to the Late Classic (c. A.D. 700–900) and consist mostly of jars (Kinkella 2006). Pools 8 and 9 appear to comprise one settlement group and is the smallest of those yet observed around pools. Pool 8 (c. 70 × 30 m) has six small mounds along its southern edge, and Pool 9 (c. 300 × 60 m) has three low mounds on a single platform (M9) on the south side and is bordered on the northwest by a sheer cliff. One test pit was placed in a mound at each pool, but neither yielded much information, barring a few Late Classic ceramic sherds (Kinkella 2008).

Although it is not directly on the edge of the water, there is also settlement near one of the lakes, Pool 6, which appears to be the largest water body in the vicinity according to the government map. It is located on the eastern edge of the ridge system (Lucero 1999a). In the foothills above Pool 6, we found a mound group with a plain stela and altar (M124) (Figure 2.8). It sits on top of a small knoll, and has six structures built around a central plaza. Test excavations at the base of the stela yielded several Late Classic sherds, as did the test excavation at the corner of one of the structures (Kinkella 2008).

Cara Blanca pools are often covered with water lilies, which played an important role in Maya cosmology. We have briefly mentioned the artificial reservoirs at centers on which the Maya relied during annual drought, which water managers had to keep clean, a challenging feat. However, they clearly recognized the significance of the wetland biosphere and applied its principles by maintaining a balance of hydrophytic and macrophytic plants and other organisms to maintain clean water (Lucero in press). The presence of water lilies (*Nymphaea ampla*) is a visible indicator of clean water, since they are sensitive hydrophytic plants that can only flourish in shallow (1–3 m), clean, and still water (Conrad 1905: 116; Lundell 1937: 18, 26). The water lily is also associated with purity and is a symbol of abundance (Schele and Miller 1986: 46). Maya rulers appropriated water lilies to symbolize their abilities to bring forth prosperity (Lucero 1999b), and their representation is common in royal iconography, from painted ceramic vessels to carved monumental buildings and monuments (e.g., stelae and altars), bone, obsidian, shell, jade, and chipped stone. This cosmologically significant water flower is yet another sacred element found naturally in abundance at Cara Blanca.

We also noted crevices, rock shelters and undulating topography in several areas, including the immediate vicinity of the satellite center (M104), the largely uninhabited area near Pools 10 through 14, and especially in the drainage above Pool 15. While such an area is poor for farming, rock shelters may have been used for rituals, indicated by the sherds found at several of them. Further, one of the small mound groups mapped between Yalbac and Pool 7 (M6) includes a 3-m tall mound that is perched at the summit of a sheer cliff with a 6-m drop (Kinkella 2006: fig, 3.7). The cliff has a vertical fissure about 1.5 m wide and 5–6 m deep in the center, which travels directly underneath the front of the structure and is easily large enough for a person to fit into. This natural fissure into the earth may have had ritual significance, as well as its associated building.

Finally, even though "experiential" surveying (see Bender 2002) was not part of our plan, we could not help but notice the sometimes difficult terrain or the cool breeze that forewarned us of nearby portals. The view from the top of the ridge looking south is amazing, and likely was quite similar for the Classic Maya, though we will never know what they felt or thought about it. It is possible to see Cara Blanca from several kilometers to the south. Though we do not know if it was visible in the past due to tall trees, if it were, it would have served as an obvious beacon to signal the location of the sacred.

Discussion

The Maya constructed centers to function as artificial water mountains, where the site itself acted as a water collection device, directing water into the central reservoir system, which provided the means for centralizing power through water control. Such building was unnecessary at Cara Blanca. The bodies of water are relatively isolated from settlement and functioned as "shrines removed from daily life" (Freidel 1981: 380) where the Maya engaged in "scheduled periodic circulation of large numbers of people over broad sacred networks" (Freidel 1981: 378). Furthermore, during the Late Classic period there were "area-wide water cults, which included pilgrimages to 'sacred' water localities, and ritual offerings of elite goods and human victims to water and other deities" (Andrews and Corletta 1995: 112). This need became even greater at the end of the Late Classic when droughts struck (Lucero 2002, in press).

Sweatbaths, such as the one found between Pools 1 and 2, are also found elsewhere in the Maya area, even within temples and other types of monumental architecture (e.g., at Palenque and Piedras Negras, among others; Houston 1996). Some apparently were only "symbolic" ones since there is no evidence for fire or heating apparatus. Houston (1996: 135) suggests that, at the Palenque Cross Group, the sweatbath demonstrated the "connection between the Cross Group and mythological births" of Palenque's patron deities, and provided a place "linked to divine birth and purification" (1996: 147). While Houston focused on symbolic sweatbaths, recent excavations have revealed functional ones at large centers, small settlements, and even caves. Ethnographically, they are used for healing, purification, and transformation rites. "In indigenous communities today, sweatbaths are symbolically viewed as caves or entrances to the underworld…" (Child 2007: 242). The Maya at Cara Blanca did not need to build temples to house its sweatbath (M186), since hills are plentiful.

The concentration of so many pools in one area and the relatively small-scale and somewhat unique settlement indicate that Cara Blanca served as a sacred place to the ancient Maya, likely as a pilgrimage center (Kinkella 2009). Spanish documents detail the importance of pilgrimage at Cozumel, "centered on the Maya deity Ix Chel, the goddess of fertility, childbirth, divination, and medicine" (Patel 2005: 91). Pilgrimage sites could have acted as hubs that maintained group cohesion for a dispersed populace. Throughout Mesoamerica, people made pilgrimages for the sake of water deities, patron gods, and divine entities (Kubler 1985). Similarities to pilgrimage sites elsewhere (e.g., Cenote of Sacrifice at Chichén Itzá) and other types of evidence, such as the predominance of jars, indicate that

Cara Blanca served as a place of pilgrimage. Jars are used in the utilitarian movement of water, but they also can symbolize water creation and were used in water rites (Taube 2001). In fact, the Maya may have collected sacred or virgin water in jars for special ceremonies that took place either at the Cara Blanca pools or in nearby centers, similar to the Zinacantecos of highland Chiapas, Mexico, where shamans' assistants collect water from the seven sacred waterholes for curing ceremonies (Vogt 1993: 63–65). A comparison of Cara Blanca jars and artifacts with collections from the centers of Yalbac (c. 7 km distant), San Jose (c. 11 km distant), Saturday Creek (c. 11 km distant) and others, can reveal if people from different areas deposited offerings in pools and collected sacred water, something we plan to do in future once we dive several of the pools.

Other future plans include exploring the surrounding caves, in which we expect to find offerings. In 2008, Kinkella found several caves in the vicinity of Pool 15, one of which contained two hearth-like features. One of the features had a large jar rim laying on the surface. Interestingly, Moyes (2006: 567–569), in her analysis of Late Classic ceramics from several caves in Belize (e.g., Chechem Ha), found that jars were the most common vessel type recovered. Based on their placement and location, she goes on to suggest that associated rituals represent "a distinct Late Classic cave cult likely to have been associated with dry or drought conditions. Given the deep antiquity of Maya beliefs that associate caves with gods that control water, in a time of environmental crisis caves would have been the logical ritual venue to propitiate these deities" (2006: 568–569). The same could be argued for Cara Blanca. Interestingly, we have yet to see water levels drop in the pools, even at the height of the dry season.

Cara Blanca provides clues about the importance of the natural feature within the ancient Maya worldview, especially based on what is absent from such a water-rich area – the built, or in one sense, the profane. It is an excellent example of a "topography of ancient belief," to use a phrase from Bradley (2000: 20). The Maya journeyed to Cara Blanca because they valued "water mountains." This case illustrates how the Maya viewed their world; they were part of it, and did not separate it in what Western society defines as natural and cultural aspects. Just because people did not build "natural" places does not mean that supernatural forces did not build them (see Bradley 2000: 35). As such, the Maya did not interfere with such a place, even at the expense of their more basic needs – water and land.

In conclusion, the ancient Maya expended much effort at centers to build artificial mountains, caves, and pools. This effort was unnecessary at Cara Blanca, where natural places embodied the sacred. By the very absence of the constructed, the Maya left us with another view of the landscape, one we need to assess through a sacred lens. It is we, after all, who distinguish natural places from cultural ones. Many pre-modern societies, however, were "in harmony with nature" (Rykwert 1981: 75), while our methods typically are not. Cara Blanca has provided us the opportunity to "see" places just as central to the Maya, if not more so, than what they themselves added or built on the landscape. As a matter of fact, the Maya purposefully avoided building at Cara Blanca, so as not to interfere with this sacred place; there was no reason to change it from its natural state.

References

Anda, Guillermo de
  2007 Sacrifice and Ritual Body Mutilation in Postclassical Maya Society: Taphonomy of the Human Remains from Chichén Itzá's Cenote Sagrado. In *New Perspectives on Human Sacrifice and Ritual Body Treatments in Ancient Maya Society*, edited by Vera Tiesler and Andrea Cucina, pp. 190–208. Springer, New York.

Andrews, Anthony P., and Robert Corletta
  1995 A Brief History of Underwater Archaeology in the Maya Area. *Ancient Mesoamerica* 6: 101–117.

Anschuetz, Kurt F., Richard H. Wilshusen, and Cherie L. Scheick
  2001 An Archaeology of Landscapes: Perspectives and Directions. *Journal of Archaeological Research* 9: 157–211.

Ashmore, Wendy
  1996 Settlement Archaeology at Xunantunich, 1996. In *Xunantunich Archaeological Project: 1996 Field Season*, edited by Richard Leventhal, pp. 17–27. Submitted to the Department of Archaeology, Belize, Belmopan and Los Angeles.

Bacus, Elisabeth A., and Lisa J. Lucero
  1999 Introduction: Issues in the Archaeology of Tropical Polities. In *Complex Polities in the Ancient Tropical World*, edited by Elisabeth A. Bacus and Lisa J. Lucero, pp. 1–11. Archeological Papers of the American Anthropological Association 9. American Anthropological Association, Arlington, VA.

Baron, Joanne P.
  2006 The Origins and Placement of the Ballcourt at Yalbac. *Research Reports in Belizean Archaeology* 3: 235–246.

Bassie-Sweet, Karen
  1996 *At the Edge of the World: Caves and Late Classic Maya World View.* University of Oklahoma Press, Norman.

Bender, Barbara
  2002 Time and Landscape. *Current Anthropology,* Supplement 43: 103–112.

Borhegyi, Suzanne de
  1961 Gifts to the Rain God. *Lore* 11(4): 122–128. Milwaukee Public Museum, Milwaukee.

Bradley, Richard

2000   *An Archaeology of Natural Places.* Routledge, London.

Brady, James E.

1989   *An Investigation of Maya Ritual Cave Use with Special Reference to Naj Tunich, Peten, Guatemala.* Ph.D. Dissertation, University of California, Los Angeles. University Microfilms, Ann Arbor.

1995   A Reassessment of the Chronology and Function of Gordon's Cave 3, Copan, Honduras. *Ancient Mesoamerica* 6: 29–38.

1997   Settlement Configuration and Cosmology: The Role of Caves at Dos Pilas. *American Anthropologist* 99: 602–618.

Brady, James E., and Wendy Ashmore

1999   Mountains, Caves, Water: Ideational Landscapes of the Ancient Maya. In *Archaeologies of Landscape: Contemporary Perspectives,* edited by Wendy Ashmore and A. Bernard Knapp, pp. 124–145. Blackwell, Oxford.

Brady, James E., Ann Scott, Hector Neff, and Michael D. Glascock

1997a   Speleothem Breakage, Movement, Removal, and Caching: An Aspect of Ancient Maya Cave Modification. *Geoarchaeology* 12: 725–750.

Brady, James E., Ann Scott, Allan Cobb, Irma Rodas, John Fogarty, and Monica Urquizú Sánchez

1997b   Glimpses of the Dark Side of the Petexbatún Project: The Petexbatún Regional Cave Survey. *Ancient Mesoamerica* 8: 353–364.

Brown, Clifford T.

2006   Water Sources at Mayapán, Yucatán, Mexico. In *Precolumbian Water Management: Ideology, Ritual, and Politics,* edited by Lisa J. Lucero and Barbara Fash, pp. 171–185. University of Arizona Press, Tucson.

Brown, Linda A.

2004   Dangerous Places and Wild Spaces: Creating Meaning with Materials and Spaces at Contemporary Maya Shrines on El Duende Mountain. *Journal of Archaeological Method and Theory* 11: 31–58.

Child, Mark B.

2007   Ritual Purification and the Ancient Maya Sweatbath at Palenque. In *Palenque: Recent Investigations at the Classic Maya Center,* edited by Damien B. Marken, pp. 233–262. Altamira Press, Lanham, MD.

Christenson, Allen J.

2007   *Popol Vuh: The Sacred Book of the Maya.* Originally published 2003. University of Oklahoma Press, Norman.

Coggins, Clemency C. (ed.)

1992   *Artifacts from the Cenote of Sacrifice.* Memoirs of the Peabody Museum of Archaeology and Ethnology Vol. 10, No. 3. Harvard University, Cambridge.

Conrad, Henry S.

1905   *The Waterlilies: A Monograph of the Genus* Nymphaea. Carnegie Institute of Washington Publication No. 4. The Carnegie Institute of Washington, Washington, D.C.

de Montmollin, Olivier
   1995   *Settlement and Politics in Three Classic Maya Polities.* Prehistory Press, Madison, WI.

Eber, Christine
   1995   *Women and Alcohol in a Highland Maya Town: Water of Hope, Water of Sorrow.* University of Texas Press, Austin.

Fash, Barbara W.
   2005   Iconographic Evidence for Water Management and Social Organization at Copán. In *Copán: The History of an Ancient Maya Kingdom*, edited by E. Wyllys Andrews and William L. Fash, pp. 103–138. School of American Research, Santa Fe.

Fash, Barbara W., and Karla L. Davis-Salazar
   2006   Copan Water Ritual and Management: Imagery and Sacred Place. In *Precolumbian Water Management: Ideology, Ritual, and Politics*, edited by Lisa J. Lucero and Barbara W. Fash, pp. 129–143. University of Arizona Press, Tucson.

Fedick, Scott L.
   1988   *Prehistoric Maya Settlement and Land Use Patterns in the Upper Belize River Area, Belize, Central America.* Unpublished Ph.D. Dissertation, Arizona State University, Tempe. University Microfilms, Ann Arbor.
   1995   Land Evaluation and Ancient Maya Land Use in the Upper Belize River Area, Belize, Central America. *Latin American Antiquity* 6: 16–34.
   1996   An Interpretive Kaleidoscope: Alternative Perspectives on Ancient Agricultural Landscapes of the Maya Lowlands. In *The Managed Mosaic: Ancient Maya Agriculture and Resource Use*, edited by Scott L. Fedick, pp. 107–131. University of Utah Press, Salt Lake City.

Fedick, Scott L., and Anabel Ford
   1990   The Prehistoric Agricultural Landscape of the Central Maya Lowlands: An Examination of Local Variability in a Regional Context. *World Archaeology* 22: 18–33.

Ford, Anabel
   1986   *Population Growth and Social Complexity: An Examination of Settlement and Environment in the Central Maya Lowlands.* Arizona State University Anthropological Papers No. 35. Arizona State University, Tempe.
   1991   Economic Variation of Ancient Maya Residential Settlement in the Upper Belize River Area. *Ancient Mesoamerica* 2: 35–46.
   1996   Critical Resource Control and the Rise of the Classic Period Maya. In *The Managed Mosaic: Ancient Maya Agriculture and Resource Use*, edited by Scott L. Fedick, pp. 297–303. University of Utah Press, Salt Lake City.

Freidel, David A.
   1981   The Political Economy of Residential Dispersion Among the Lowland Maya. In *Lowland Maya Settlement Patterns*, edited by Wendy Ashmore, pp. 371–382. University of New Mexico Press, Albuquerque.

Freidel, David A., and Jeremy A. Sabloff
   1984   *Cozumel Late Maya Settlement Patterns.* Academic Press, Orlando.

French, Kirk D., David S. Stuart, and Alfonso Morales
    2006 Archaeological and Epigraphic Evidence for Water Management and Ritual at Palenque. In *Precolumbian Water Management: Ideology, Ritual, and Politics*, edited by Lisa J. Lucero and Barbara W. Fash, pp. 144–152. University of Arizona Press, Tucson.

Gunn, Joel, Ray T. Matheny, and William J. Folan
    2002 Climate-Change Studies in the Maya Area. *Ancient Mesoamerica* 13: 79–84.

Haviland, John B.
    1977 *Gossip, Reputation, and Knowledge in Zinacantan.* University of Chicago Press, Chicago.

Hellmuth, Nicholas N.
    1987 *The Surface of the Underworld: Iconography of the Gods of Early Classic Maya Art in Peten, Guatemala.* 2 vols. Foundation for Latin American Anthropological Research, Culver City.

Helmke, Christophe G.B.
    2006 A Report of the 2005 Season of Archaeological Investigations at Pook's Hill, Cayo District, Belize. In *The Belize Valley Archaeological Reconnaissance Project: A Report of the 2005 Field Season*, edited by Christophe G.B. Helmke and Jaime J. Awe, pp. 39–92. Institute of Archaeology, National Institute of Culture and History, Belmopan.

Helmke, Christophe G.B., and Jaime J. Awe
    2005 The Ancient Maya Sweathbath at Pook's Hill. *Belize Today* 5(1): 24–26.

Hooten, E.A.
    1940 Skeletons from the Cenote of Sacrifice at Chichen Itza. In *The Maya and their Neighbors: Essays on Middle American Anthropology and Archaeology*, edited by Clarence L. Hay, Ralph Linton, Samuel K. Lothrop, Harry L. Shapiro, and George C. Vaillant, pp. 272–280. Appleton Century, New York.

Houston, Stephen D.
    1996 Symbolic Sweatbaths of the Maya: Architectural Meaning in the Cross Group at Palenque, Mexico. *Latin American Antiquity* 7: 132–151.

Ishihara, Reiko
    2007 Bridging the Chasm between Religion and Politics: Archaeological Investigations of the Grietas at the Late Classic Maya Site of Aguateca, Peten, Guatemala. Unpublished Ph.D. dissertation, University of California, Riverside.
    2008 Rising Clouds, Blowing Winds: Late Classic Maya Rain Rituals in the Main Chasm, Aguateca, Guatemala. *World Archaeology* 40: 169–189.

Kinkella, Andrew
    2000 Settlement at the Sacred Pools: Preliminary Archaeological Investigations at the Late Classic Maya Site of Cara Blanca, Belize. Unpublished M.A. Thesis, California State University, Northridge.
    2004 The Pools at Cara Blanca: Archaeology in the Valley of Peace Above and Below the Water. *Research Reports in Belizean Archaeology* 1: 93–102.
    2005 Forty-Two Degrees, and Straight on 'Till Morning: 2004 Settlement Survey in the Yalbac Area. In *Results of the 2004 Valley of Peace Archaeology Project: The Temples*

and Ballcourt of Yalbac, edited by Lisa J. Lucero, pp. 50–56. Report submitted to the Institute of Archaeology, National Institute of Culture and History, Belize.

2006   Two Transects Are Better Than One: 2005 Settlement Survey in the Yalbac Area. In *Results of the 2005 Valley of Peace Archaeology Project: Yalbac Architecture and Settlement*, edited by Lisa J. Lucero, pp. 39–45. Report submitted to the Institute of Archaeology, National Institute of Culture and History, Belize.

2008   Over the Bajo and Through the Pools: The 2007 Settlement Survey Transect from Yalbac to the Cara Blanca Pools. In *Results of the 2007 Valley of Peace Archaeology Project: Yalbac's Settlement*, edited by Lisa J. Lucero, pp. 19–114. Report submitted to the Institute of Archaeology, National Institute of Culture and History, Belize.

2009   Draw of the Sacred Water: An Archaeological Survey of the Ancient Maya Settlement at the Cara Blanca Pools, Belize. Unpublished Ph.D. dissertation. University of California, Riverside.

Kubler, George

1985   Pre-Columbian Pilgrimages in Mesoamerica. In *Fourth Palenque Round Table, 1980*, edited by Elizabth P. Benson, pp. 313–316. The Palenque Round Table Series Vol. VI. The Pre-Columbian Art Research Institute, San Francisco.

Lucero, Lisa J.

1999a Politics and Ritual in the Valley of Peace Area, Belize: Results of the 1998 Season. In *The Second (1998) Field Season of the Valley of Peace Archaeological (VOPA) Project*, edited by Lisa J. Lucero, pp. 1–12. Report submitted to the Department of Archaeology, Ministry of Tourism, Belize.

1999b Water Control and Maya Politics in the Southern Maya Lowlands. In *Complex Polities in the Ancient Tropical World*, edited by Elisabth A. Bacus and Lisa J. Lucero, pp. 34–49. Archeological Papers of the American Anthropological Association No. 9. American Anthropological Association, Arlington, VA.

2001   *Social Integration in the Ancient Maya Hinterlands: Ceramic Variability in the Belize River Area*. Anthropological Research Paper No. 53. Arizona State University, Tempe.

2002   The Collapse of the Classic Maya: A Case for the Role of Water Control. *American Anthropologist* 104: 814–826.

2003   The Politics of Ritual: The Emergence of Classic Maya Rulers. *Current Anthropology* 44: 523–558.

2006a Agricultural Intensification, Water, and Political Power in the Southern Maya Lowlands. In *Agricultural Strategies*, edited by Joyce Marcus and Charles Stanish, pp. 281–305. Cotsen Advanced Seminars No. 2. The Cotsen Institute of Archaeology, UCLA, Los Angeles.

2006b The Political and Sacred Power of Water in Ancient Maya Society. In *Precolumbian Water Management: Ideology, Ritual, and Politics*, edited by Lisa J. Lucero and Barbara Fash, pp. 116–128. University of Arizona Press, Tucson.

2006c *Water and Ritual: The Rise and Fall of Classic Maya Rulers*. University of Texas Press, Austin.

2007   Classic Maya Temples, Politics, and the Voice of the People. *Latin American Antiquity* 18: 407–427.

2008   Memorializing Place among Classic Maya Commoners. In *Memory Work: Archaeologies of Material Practices*, edited by Barbara J. Mills and William H. Walker, pp. 187–204. School for Advanced Research Press, Santa Fe.

In press Water Management in Lowland Mesoamerica. In *Water and Humanity: Historical Overview*, edited by Vernon L. Scarborough and Yoshinori Yasuda. History of Water and Civilization Vol. VII, general editor, Fekri Hassan. UNESCO International Hydrological Programme (IHP).

Lucero, Lisa J., Scott L. Fedick, Andrew Kinkella, and Sean M. Graebner
2004 Ancient Maya Settlement in the Valley of Peace Area, Belize. In *Archaeology of the Upper Belize River Valley: Half a Century of Maya Research*, edited by James F. Garber, pp. 86–102. University Press of Florida, Gainesville.

Lucero, Lisa J., and Sherry A. Gibbs
2007 The Creation and Sacrifice of Witches in Classic Maya Society. In *New Perspectives on Human Sacrifice and Ritual Body Treatments in Ancient Maya Society*, edited by Vera Tiesler and Andrea Cucina, pp. 45–73. Springer, New York.

Lundell, Cyrus
1937 *The Vegetation of Petén*. Carnegie Institute of Washington Publication No. 478. The Carnegie Institute of Washington, Washington D.C.

Marcus, Joyce
2006 The Roles of Ritual and Technology in Mesoamerican Water Management. In *Agricultural Strategies*, edited by Joyce Marcus and Charles Stanish, pp. 221–254. Cotsen Advanced Seminars No. 2. The Cotsen Institute of Archaeology, UCLA, Los Angeles.

Marx, Robert F.
1975 *The Underwater Dig: An Introduction to Marine Archaeology*. Henry Z. Walck, New York.

McGee, Ron J.
1998 The Lacandon Incense Burner Renewal Ceremony: Termination and Dedication Ritual among the Contemporary Maya. In *The Sowing and the Dawning: Termination, Dedication, and Transformation in the Archaeological and Ethnographic Record of Mesoamerica*, edited by Shirley B. Mock, pp. 41–46. University of New Mexico Press, Albuquerque.

Mock, Shirley B.
1998 Prelude. In *The Sowing and the Dawning: Termination, Dedication, and Transformation in the Archaeological and Ethnographic Record of Mesoamerica*, edited by Shirley B. Mock, pp. 3–18. University of New Mexico Press, Albuquerque.

Moyes, Holley
2005 The Sweatbath in the Cave: A Modified Passage in Chechem Ha Cave, Belize. In *Stone Houses and Earth Lords: Maya Religion in the Cave Context*, edited by Keith M. Prufer and James E. Brady, pp. 187–211. University Press of Colorado, Boulder.

2006 The Sacred Landscape as a Political Resource: A Case Study of Ancient Maya Cave Use at Chechem Ha Cave, Belize, Central America. Unpublished Ph.D. dissertation, SUNY Buffalo.

Nash, June
1970 *In the Eyes of Ancestors: Belief and Behavior in a Mayan Community*. Waveland Press, Prospect Heights, IL.

Neiman, Fraser D.
   1997   Conspicuous Consumption as Wasteful Advertising: A Darwinian Perspective
          on Spatial Patterns in Classic Maya Terminal Monument Dates. In *Rediscovering
          Darwin: Evolutionary Theory and Archeological Explanation*, edited by C. Michael
          Barton and Geoffrey A. Clark, pp. 267–290. Archeological Papers of the American
          Anthropological Association No. 7. American Anthropological Association,
          Arlington, VA.

Osterholtz, Anna
   1999   Underwater Archaeology of the Maya Area: A History and Study of the
          Methodological Approaches for the Recovery and Treatment of Cultural Materials
          Recovered from a Freshwater Environment. Honors Thesis, New Mexico State
          University, Las Cruces.

Patel, Shankari
   2005   Pilgrimage and Caves on Cozumel. In *Stone Houses and Earth Lords: Maya Religion
          in the Cave Context*, edited by Keith M. Prufer and James E. Brady, pp. 91–112.
          University Press of Colorado, Boulder.

Prufer, Keith M.
   2005   Shamans, Caves, and the Roles of Ritual Specialists in Maya Society. In *In the Maw
          of the Earth Monster: Mesoamerican Ritual Cave Use*, edited by James E. Brady and
          Keith M. Prufer, pp. 186–222. University of Texas Press, Austin.

Prufer, Keith M., Phil Wanyerka, and Monica Shah
   2003   Wooden Figurines, Scepters, and Religious Specialists in Pre-Columbian Maya
          Society. *Ancient Mesoamerica* 14: 219–236.

Puleston, Dennis E.
   1977   Art and Archaeology of Hydraulic Agriculture in the Maya Lowlands. In *Social
          Process in Maya Prehistory: Studies in the Memory of Sir Eric Thompson*, edited by
          Norman Hammond, pp. 449–467. Academic Press, London.
   1983   *Settlement Survey of Tikal*. Tikal Report No. 13; University Museum Monograph
          50. The University Museum, University of Pennsylvania, Philadelphia

Rands, Robert L.
   1953   The Water Lily in Maya Art: A Complex of Alleged Asiatic Origins. *Bureau
          of American Ethnology Bulletin* No. 151, pp. 75–153. Smithsonian Institution,
          Washington, D.C.

Redfield, Robert
   1941   *The Folk Culture of Yucatan*. University of Chicago Press, Chicago.

Rykwert, Joseph
   1981   *On Adam's House in Paradise: The Idea of the Primitive Hut in Architectural History*.
          2nd edn. MIT Press, Cambridge, MA.

Sanders, William T.
   1977   Environmental Heterogeneity and the Evolution of Lowland Maya Civilization. In
          The Origins of Maya Civilization, edited by Richard E. W. Adams, pp. 287–297.
          University of New Mexico Press, Albuquerque.

Saul, Frank P., and Julie M. Saul

    1989   Osteobiography: A Maya Example. In *Reconstruction of Life from the Skeleton*, edited by M. Yasar Iscan and Kenneth A.R. Kennedy, pp. 287–302. Willey Liss, New York.

Scarborough, Vernon L.

    1993   Water Management in the Southern Maya Lowlands: An Accretive Model for the Engineered Landscape. *Research in Economic Anthropology* 7: 17–69.

    1996   Reservoirs and Watersheds in the Central Maya Lowlands. In *The Managed Mosaic: Ancient Maya Agriculture and Resource Use,* edited by Scott L. Fedick, pp. 304–314. University of Utah Press, Salt Lake City.

    1998   Ecology and Ritual: Water Management and the Maya. *Latin American Antiquity* 9: 135–159.

    2003   *The Flow of Power: Ancient Water Systems and Landscapes.* School of American Research Press, Santa Fe.

Scarborough, Vernon L., Fred Valdez, and Nicholas Dunning (eds.)

    2003   *Heterarchy, Political Economy, and the Ancient Maya.* University of Arizona Press, Tucson.

Scarborough, Vernon L., and Gary C. Gallopin

    1991   A Water Storage Adaptation in the Maya Lowlands. *Science* 251: 658–662.

Schele, Linda, and David Freidel

    1990   *A Forest of Kings: The Untold Story of the Ancient Maya.* William Morrow, New York.

Schele, Linda, and Peter Mathews

    1998   *The Code of Kings: The Language of Seven Sacred Maya Temples and Tombs.* Touchstone Books, New York.

Schele, Linda, and Mary Ellen Miller

    1986   *The Blood of Kings: Dynasty and Ritual in Maya Art.* George Braziller, New York.

Sharer, Robert J.

    1994   *The Ancient Maya.* 5th edn. Stanford University Press, Stanford.

Stone, Andrea

    1992   From Ritual in the Landscape to Capture in the Urban Center: The Recreation of Ritual Environments in Mesoamerica. *Journal of Ritual Studies* 6: 109–132.

    1995   *Images from the Underworld: Naj Tunich and the Tradition of Maya Cave Painting.* University of Texas Press, Austin.

    1997   Precolumbian Cave Utilization in the Maya Area. In *Human Uses of Caves*, edited by Clive Bonsall and Christopher Tolan-Smith, pp. 201–206. BAR International Series 667. Archaeopress, Oxford.

Stuart, David

    1987   *Ten Phonetic Syllables.* Research Reports on Ancient Maya Writing No. 14. Center for Maya Research, Washington, D.C.

Stuart, David, and Stephen Houston

    1994   *Classic Maya Place Names.* Dumbarton Oaks, Washington, D.C.

Taçon, Paul S.C.
　　1999　Identifying Ancient Sacred Landscapes in Australia: From Physical to Social. In *Archaeologies of Landscape: Contemporary Perspectives*, edited by Wendy Ashmore and A. Bernard Knapp, pp. 33–57. Blackwell, Oxford.

Taube, Karl A.
　　2001　The Breath of Life: Symbolism of Wind in Mesoamerica and the American Southwest. In *The Road to Aztlan: Art from a Mythic Homeland*, edited by Virginia Fields and Victor Zamudio-Taylor, pp. 102–123. Los Angeles County Museum of Art, Los Angeles.

Thompson, J. Eric S.
　　1939　*Excavations at San Jose, British Honduras*. Carnegie Institution of Washington Publication No. 506. Carnegie Institution, Washington D.C.
　　1970　*Maya History and Religion*. University of Oklahoma Press, Norman.

Tozzer, Alfred M.
　　1941　*Landa's Relación de Los Cosas de Yucatán*. Papers of the Peabody Museum of American Archaeology and Ethnology No. 28. Harvard University, Cambridge.

Vogt, Evon Z.
　　1970　*The Zinacantecos of Mexico: A Modern Maya Way of Life*. Holt, Rinehart and Winston, New York.
　　1993　*Tortillas for the Gods: A Symbolic Analysis of Zinacanteco Rituals*. 2nd edn. University of Oklahoma Press, Norman.
　　1998　Zinacanteco Dedication and Termination Rituals. In *The Sowing and the Dawning: Termination, Dedication, and Transformation in the Archaeological and Ethnographic Record of Mesoamerica*, edited by Shirley B. Mock, pp. 21–30. University of New Mexico Press, Albuquerque.
　　2004　Daily Life in a Highland Community: Zinacantan in Mid-Twentieth Century. In *Ancient Maya Commoners*, edited by Jon C. Lohse and Fred Valdez, Jr., pp. 23–47. University of Texas Press, Austin.

Vogt, Evon A., and David Stuart
　　2005　Some Notes on Ritual Caves among the Ancient and Modern Maya. In *In the Maw of the Earth Monster: Mesoamerican Ritual Cave Use,* edited by James E. Brady and Keith M. Prufer, pp. 155–185. University of Texas Press, Austin.

Walker, William H., and Lisa J. Lucero
　　2000　The Depositional History of Ritual and Power. In *Agency in Archaeology*, edited by Marcia-Anne Dobres and John Robb, pp. 130–147. Routledge, London.

— 3 —

On Ancient Placemaking

Wendy Ashmore

Meaningful places are the product of enduring locations where people's practices accumulate, along with stories and memories shared about individual and collective experience there (Basso 1996; Zedeño and Bowser 2009). Landscape has become a central frame for identifying practices and memory archaeologically, as Lucero and Kinkella's chapter demonstrates (this volume). Indeed, Lucero has led in fomenting such work (Walker and Lucero 2000; Lucero 2008, 2010).

Several intersecting lines of thinking advance work in these areas, expressed in and beyond study of the ancient Maya. Phenomenological archaeologists, mainly in Britain, have long espoused the insights to be gained from this kind of approach; others caution the risks in what they see as estimating experiences of past times in ancient settings today, and in attributing meaning to everything encountered (Tilley 1994, 2008; see Binford 1981; Barrett and Ko 2009). *Can* observers today glean meanings held in times long past? Among phenomenology advocates, scientific positivists, and skeptics of both, studying materiality of ancient practices rises to the fore of means to infer what places would have meant to long-ago generations, in historically and culturally contingent contexts (Bender 2006; Mills and Walker 2008).

From all theoretical perspectives, five often convergent themes emerge as critical factors for identifying and understanding meanings of meaningful places, in the past and today: the multivocality of memory-making; the crucial role of people's movements; multi-sensory perception in shaping meaning; importance of the diverse elemental aspects – water, air, fire, earth – of the landscape experienced; and expanded domains in which meaningful places are recognized to occur. Some of these directions, especially the last three named, elicit new methods for their investigation. Implicit in all of these themes is, as well, the importance of contingent history and the biographies of meaningful places.

First, memory-making is far from homogenous or continuous at any place
deemed meaningful (Rodman 1992; Barrett 1999; Bradley 2003; Mills and
Walker 2008). Identifiably diverse standpoints of those who make use of a
given locality imply that meanings attached there will be correspondingly
diverse and multivocal. Archaeological examples include inferences from
the temple districts of medieval south Indian Vijayanagara (Fritz 1988;
Mack 2004), from two public plazas at eighth-century Maya Quiriguá
(Ashmore 2009), and from the marked class differences among the people
who experienced these places. Tensions as well as cohesion between rulers,
ruled, and the factions among them, play out in public arenas such as these,
in archaeologically discernible ways.

Second, experience and memory-making within a meaningful place, as
well as transit among multiple such locales, implies the central role of people's
movements across the landscape. "A place is not a free-floating entity; it
is connected to other places in a web of associations and practices" (Kok
2008: 69). Increasing attention to processions and pilgrimage highlights
ritual aspects of movement between locations, complement longstanding
interest in more purely economic moves (Thomas 1993; Patel 2005; Parker
Pearson et al. 2006; Ashmore and Blackmore 2008; Snead et al. 2009).
Documenting displacement of groups and individuals due to conflict has
a long and growing history of archaeological interest for understanding the
impact of and *on* meaningful places in displaced people's lives (Bender 2001,
2006; Ferguson and Preucel 2005).

Third, underlying the multivocal and movement-filled experience of
meaningful places, landscapes comprise rich and varied elements – earth, air,
water, sky – perceived through multiple senses. Growing attention attaches
to sensory and sensual dimensions of imbuing and understanding meaning
in place (Kus 1992; Howes 2006; Frieman and Gillings 2007). Privilege
traditionally accorded sight for orientation and place recall finds increasing
challenge, as archaeologists and others recognize the impacts of sound, smell,
touch, and even taste. From the festal cacophony of sound at large public
gatherings in the Andes, to "waterfalls of song" among the Kaluli of Papua
New Guinea, to controlled aural input of music, chant, and other sounds in
the amphitheatre of Chaco Canyon, inferred and even measurable sensory
attributes of particular places demonstrably shape and enhance significantly
the social meanings instilled through these events (Feld 1996; Moore 2005;
Stein et al. 2007). Some have inferred that sounds of a practice rival the
product in importance (Rainbird 2002).

Fourth, all human senses engage input from varied elemental landscapes
of earth, water, air, and sky. For example, evidence from the deep open
chasm at Maya Aguateca points to dramatic, choreographed articulation of

temperature and breeze regularities, sound-play, and the mix of the visible with the unseen, all toward royally-commissioned rituals for calling rain to an increasingly parched political capital and its farms (Ishihara 2008). Stillness or moving air, mists, and changing ambient temperature are as critical to the performances as are the ritual objects and practices invoked, adjacent to the royal palace, to seek rain for the young maize. More solidly, varied soils and minerals of the earth likewise inspire expanded attention, augmenting economic with social and symbolic importance that, though creation and use, makes places meaningful (Richards 1996a; Kus and Raharijaona 1998; Boivin and Owoc 2004; Brown 2004; Houston et al. 2006; see also Bradley 2000). Carefully selected and assembled construction materials often recreate cosmic structure in the built environment, imbuing the place with deep meaning (Charles et al. 2004; Bell 2007).

Fifth, challenge to primacy of the visual sense for engaging meaningful places is matched by growing appreciation for the true breadth of physical domains in which such places occur. Maya landscape studies now fruitfully embrace terrestrial, underground, and celestial locations, appropriate to the three vertical layers of the Maya cosmos (Ashmore 2004). The explosive growth in Maya cave archaeology attests to the importance of such places for understanding the conceptual, social, and ritual world (Brady and Prufer 2005; Prufer and Brady 2005). At the same time, and as Lucero and Kinkella highlight in their chapter, concerted efforts pursue meanings attached to aquatic settings and to the meaningful articulation of aquatic, terrestrial, and other worlds (Richards 1996b, 2008). Long-standing interest in near-shore places and wetlands inspires renewed attention (Coles 1985; Purdy 1988; McKillop 2005); one productive recent focus is the virtually unanticipated array of wetland ritual locales from Netherlands antiquity of 2500 B.C.–A.D. 450 (Kok 2008).

In all the foregoing, place biographies of memory-making and the cumulative remembering and forgetting of their meanings infuse placemaking. Whether temporally continuous or disjunctive, human association with a place endows it with meaning. The challenges for archaeologists are to identify the attachment of meanings to a place, and then to interpret their significance.

References

Ashmore, Wendy
> 2004   Ancient Maya Landscapes. In *Continuities and Changes in Maya Archaeology: Perspectives at the Millennium*, edited by Charles W. Golden and Greg Borgstede, pp. 95–109. Routledge, London.
> 2009   Biographies of Place at Quirigua. In *The Archaeology of Meaningful Places*, edited by Brenda J. Bowser and María Nieves Zedeño, pp. 15–31. University of Utah Press, Salt Lake City.

Ashmore, Wendy, and Chelsea Blackmore
> 2008   Landscape Archaeology. In *Encyclopedia of Archaeology*, edited by Deborah Pearsall, pp. 1569–1578. Elsevier, Oxford.

Barrett, John C.
> 1999   The Mythical Landscapes of the British Iron Age. In *Archaeologies of Landscape: Contemporary Perspectives*, edited by Wendy Ashmore and A. Bernard Knapp, pp. 253–265. Blackwell, Oxford.

Barrett, John C., and Ilhong Ko
> 2009   A Phenomenology of Landscape: A Crisis in British Landscape Archaeology? *Journal of Social Archaeology* 9(3): 275–294.

Basso, Keith H.
> 1996   *Wisdom Sits in Places: Landscape and Language Among the Western Apache.* University of New Mexico Press, Albuquerque.

Bell, Ellen E.
> 2007   Early Classic Ritual Deposits within the Copan Acropolis: The Material Foundations of Political Power at a Classic Period Maya Center. Ph.D. dissertation, University of Pennsylvania, Philadelphia.

Bender, Barbara
> 2001   Landscapes On-the-Move. *Journal of Social Archaeology* 1(1): 75–89.
> 2006   Place and Landscape. In *Handbook of Material Culture,* edited by Chris Tilley, Webb Keane, Susanne Küchler, Mike Rowlands, and Patricia Spyer, pp. 303–314. Sage, London.

Binford, Lewis R.
> 1981   *Bones: Ancient Men and Modern Myths.* Academic Press, New York.

Boivin, Nicole, and Mary Ann Owoc (eds.)
> 2004   *Soils, Stones, and Symbols: Cultural Perceptions of the Mineral World.* UCL Press, London.

Bradley, Richard
> 2000   *The Archaeology of Natural Places.* Routledge, London.
> 2003   The Translation of Time. In *Archaeologies of Memory*, edited by Ruth M. Van Dyke and Susan E. Alcock, pp. 221–227. Blackwell, Malden MA.

Brady, James E., and Keith M. Prufer (eds.)
> 2005   *In the Maw of the Earth Monster: Mesoamerican Ritual Cave Use.* University of Texas Press, Austin.

Brown, Linda A.

2004 Dangerous Places and Wild Spaces: Creating Meaning with Materials and Space at Contemporary Maya Shrines on El Duende Mountain. *Journal of Archaeological Method and Theory* 11(1): 31–58.

Charles, Douglas K., Julieann Van Nest, and Jane Buikstra

2004 From the Earth: Minerals and Meanings in the Hopewellian World. In *Soils, Stones, and Symbols: Cultural Perceptions of the Mineral World*, edited by Nicole Boivin and Mary Ann Owoc, pp. 43–70. UCL Press, London.

Coles, John M.

1985 *Archaeology of Wetlands*. Edinburgh University Press, Edinburgh.

Feld, Steven

1996 Waterfalls of Song: An Acoustemology of Place Resounding in Bosavi, Papua New Guinea. In *Senses of Place*, edited by Steven Feld and Keith H. Basso, pp. 91–135. SAR Press, Santa Fe, NM.

Ferguson, T.J., and Robert W. Preucel

2005 Signs of the Ancestors: An Archaeology of Mesa Villages of the Pueblo Revolt. In *Structure and Meaning in Human Settlements*, edited by Tony Atkin and Joseph Rykwert, pp. 185–207. University of Pennsylvania Museum, Philadelphia.

Frieman, Catherine, and Mark Gillings

2007 Seeing is Perceiving? *World Archaeology* 39(1): 4–16.

Fritz, John M.

1986 Vijayanagara: Authority and Meaning of a South Indian Imperial Capital. *American Anthropologist* 88(1): 44–55.

Houston, Stephen, David Stuart, and Karl Taube

2006 *The Memory of Bones: Body, Being, and Experience among the Classic Maya*. University of Texas Press, Austin.

Howes, David

2006 Scent, Sound and Synaesthesia. In *Handbook of Material Culture,* edited by Chris Tilley, Webb Keane, Susanne Küchler, Mike Rowlands, and Patricia Spyer, pp. 161–172. Sage Publications, London.

Ishihara, Reiko

2008 Rising Clouds, Blowing Winds: Late Classic Maya Rain Rituals in the Main Chasm, Aguateca, Guatemala. *World Archaeology* 40(2): 169–189.

Kok, Marjolijn S.M.

2008 The Homecoming of Religious Practice: An Analysis of Offering Sites in the West Low-lying Parts of the Landscape in the Oer-IJ Area (2500 B.C.–A.D. 450). Ph.D. dissertation, University of Amsterdam, Rotterdam.

Kus, Susan

1992 Toward an Archaeology of Body and Soul. In *Representations in Archaeology*, edited by Jean-Claude Gardin and Christopher S. Peebles, pp. 168–177. Indiana University Press, Bloomington.

Kus, Susan, and Victor Raharijaona

1998 Between Earth and Sky There are Only a Few Large Boulders: Sovereignty and

Monumentality in Central Madagascar. *Journal of Anthropological Archaeology* 17(1): 53–79.

Lucero, Lisa J.

2008   Memorializing Place among Classic Maya Commoners. In *Memory Work: The Archaeologies of Material Practice*, edited by Barbara J. Mills and William H. Walker, pp. 187–205. School for Advanced Research Press, Santa Fe NM.

2010   Materialized Cosmology among Ancient Maya Commoners. *Journal of Social Archaeology* 10(1): 138–167.

Mack, Alexandra

2004   One Landscape, Many Experiences: Differing Perspectives of the Temple Districts of Vijayanagara. *Journal of Archaeological Method and Theory* 11(1): 59–81.

McKillop, Heather

2005   Finds in Belize Document Late Classic Maya Salt Making and Canoe Transport. *Proceedings of the National Academy of Sciences* 102(15): 5630–5634.

Mills, Barbara J., and William Walker (eds.)

2008   *Memory Work: Archaeologies of Material Practices*. School for Advanced Research Press, Santa Fe.

Moore, Jerry

2005   *Cultural Landscapes in the Ancient Andes*. University Press of Florida, Gainesville.

Parker Pearson, Mike, Josh Pollard, Colin Richards, Julian Thomas, Christopher Tilley, Kate Welham, and Umberto Albarella

2006   Materializing Stonehenge: The Stonehenge Riverside Project and New Discoveries. *Journal of Material Culture* 11(1/2): 227–261.

Patel, Shankari

2005   Pilgrimage and Caves on Cozumel. In *Stone Houses and Earth Lords: Maya Religion in the Cave Context*, edited by Keith M. Prufer and James E. Brady, pp. 91–115. University Press of Colorado, Boulder.

Prufer, Keith M., and James E. Brady (eds.)

2005   *Stone Houses and Earth Lords: Maya Religion in the Cave Context*. University Press of Colorado, Boulder.

Purdy, Barbara A.

1988   *Wet Site Archaeology*. Telford Press, Caldwell, N.J.

Rainbird, Paul

2002   Making Sense of Petroglyphs: The Sound of Rock Art. In *Inscribed Landscapes: Marking and Making Place*, edited by Bruno David and Meredith Wilson, pp. 93–103. University of Hawai'i Press, Honolulu.

Richards, Colin

1996a   Henges and Water: Towards an Elemental Understanding of Monumentality and Landscape in Late Neolithic Britain. *Journal of Social Archaeology* 1(3): 313–336.

1996b   Monuments as Landscape: Creating the Centre of the World in Late Neolithic Orkney. *World Archaeology* 28(2): 190–208.

2008   The Substance of Polynesian Voyaging. *World Archaeology* 40(2): 206–223.

Rodman, Margaret C.

    1992   Empowering Place: Multilocality and Multivocality. *American Anthropologist* 94(3): 640–656.

Snead, James E., Clark L. Erickson, and J. Andrew Darling (eds.)

    2009   *Landscapes of Movement: Trails, Paths, and Roads in Anthropological Perspective.* University of Pennsylvania Press, Philadelphia.

Stein, John, Rich Friedman, and Taft Blackhorse

    2007   Revisiting Downtown Chaco. In *Architecture of Chaco Canyon*, edited by Stephen H. Lekson, pp. 199–223. University of Utah Press, Salt Lake City.

Thomas, Julian

    1993   The Politics of Vision and the Archaeologies of Landscape. In *Landscape: Politics and Perspective,* edited by Barbara Bender, pp. 19–48. Berg, Oxford.

Tilley, Christopher

    1994   *A Phenomenology of Landscape.* Berg, Oxford.

    2008   *Body and Image: Explorations in Landscape Phenomenology 2.* Left Coast Press, Walnut Creek, CA.

Walker, William H., and Lisa J. Lucero

    2000   The Depositional History of Ritual and Power. In *Agency in Archaeology,* edited by Marcia-Anne Dobres and John Robb, pp. 130–147. Routledge, London.

Zedeño, María Nieves, and Brenda J. Bowser

    2009   The Archaeology of Meaningful Places. In *The Archaeology of Meaningful Places,* edited by Brenda J. Bowser and María Nieves Zedeño, pp. 1–14. University of Utah Press, Salt Lake City.

Origins and Fertility:
Mesoamerican Caves in Deep Time

Thomas G. Garrison

Caves are one of the most pervasive symbols in Mesoamerican iconography, from northern Mexico down through Costa Rica. Lucero and Kinkella (this volume) have provided a succinct summary of the diverse meanings of caves in the ancient and modern Maya worldviews. These meanings and others are prevalent throughout Mesoamerican civilizations. In this brief marginalia I review some of the evidence for cave iconography and beliefs in Mesoamerica outside of the Maya area. I argue that the major themes of origins and fertility conveyed by cave iconography and mythology are due to their role as residences in early agricultural communities prior to the emergence of the Olmec as the first major Mesoamerican civilization in c. 1400 B.C., and that the civilizational ideas surrounding caves were born out of a Mesoamerican deep-time during which caves represented more than just sacred spaces. Here I will discuss some of the major ideas surrounding caves for the Aztec, Teotihuacan, and the Olmec. These civilizations represent a spatio-temporal cross-section of Mesoamerican culture history, although this is in no way meant to be an exhaustive survey.

Aztec Caves

The Aztec (or Mexica) were a Nahua group that arrived in Central Mexico no later than the early fourteenth century A.D. (Coe and Koontz 2008). Like other Nahua peoples, the Aztec claimed descent from the great Toltec civilization of the Early Postclassic (A.D. 900–1150). They also claimed descent from the Chichimec, a stereotypically wild and savage group from the north, who dressed in animal hides and hunted with bows and arrows. According to some versions of the Aztec origin myth, the earliest Aztecs emerged from a place called Chicomoztoc, or "Seven Caves." This mythological place of origin is depicted in numerous Colonial-Period documents from the town of Cuauhtinchan, including the *Historia Tolteca-Chichimeca* (Kirchhoff et al. 1976) and the *Mapa de Cuauhtinchan #2* (Carrasco and Sessions 2007). Other Aztec myths cite caves or the interiors of mountains (an analog for caves or caverns) as the origin place for the moon, the sky, corn, and humans themselves (Heyden 1981; Taube 1993).

Teotihuacan Caves

Northeast of modern Mexico City lie the ruins of the ancient metropolis of Teotihuacan. Often considered the greatest city of Pre-Columbian Mesoamerica, this site was a dominant center of power from c. A.D. 1 to around A.D. 650 (Sugiyama 2005: 1). The major architectural features of Teotihuacan were built in relation to the natural landscape surrounding the valley, with the large Cerro Gordo being of particular importance (Manzanilla 1997: 122; Sugiyama 2005: 46–47). Manzanilla and her colleagues (1994) carried out a geophysical survey of the Teotihuacan Valley and concluded that the caves throughout the landscape may have made this valley a symbolic Tlalocan for the people living there, Tlalocan being a Nahuatl term for a mythical place of great wealth that was home to the rain deity, Tlaloc. While this concept is more directly affiliated with the Aztec civilization, it is believed to have originated earlier in Mesoamerican culture history.

In 1971, a modified natural cave was found to run underneath the Pyramid of the Sun, the largest structure at the site and one of the most massive structures in the New World (Heyden 1975, 1981). The cave was partitioned by a series of walls and there was once a spring flowing through it (Heyden 1981: 3). The Pyramid of the Sun is believed to be associated with the Teotihuacan Storm God (later *Tlaloc* for the Aztecs), the Mesoamerican concept of a Mountain of Sustenance (*tonacatepetl* in Nahuatl), and forming one half of a replicated mountain-cave complex. While Manzanilla and colleagues (1994) have used remote-sensing data to suggest that the Pyramid of the Sun cave extends further to the east and west as part of a more integrated system of tunnels and caverns, it seems likely that the tunnel was deliberately shaped by the Teotihuacanos in the form studied by Heyden (1975, 1981). Heyden (1975) argues that the cave underneath the Pyramid of the Sun was a place of origin for Teotihuacan, analogous to the Aztec mythical concept of Chicomoztoc.

Olmec Caves

Moving back into the Mesoamerican Formative Period (c. 2000 B.C.–A.D. 300, but with variations depending on the region) there are a number of Olmec or Olmec-influenced sites that display strong connections to the cave concepts discussed here and by Lucero and Kinkella. First, there are actual caves in the Mexican state of Guerrero where Olmec-style paintings have been found. Deep within Juxtlahuaca Cave (Gay 1967; Grove 1972) there is a series of paintings which include a jaguar, a feathered serpent, and a probable Olmec ruler wearing a jaguar-skin costume. In this case, the depths of the caves are being associated with wild and mythical animals commonly associated with Mesoamerican rulership. Given the known connotations that caves have with origins, it appears that in this case the cave was a source for royal power. At nearby Oxtotitlan Cave (Grove 1970), there are numerous paintings depicting jaguars, a feathered serpent, and Olmec rulers. Painting I-d in this cave depicts a human and jaguar having sexual intercourse, which Grove (1972: 161) interprets as the symbolic birth of the "Jaguar-People" (i.e., the Olmec).

Caves are prevalent in the art and iconography of numerous Olmec and Olmec-influenced sites as well. There are a number of table-top altars from the sites of San Lorenzo and La Venta that depict putative rulers emerging from niches, which are interpreted as caves. The best example of this type of monument is La Venta Altar 4. This well-preserved monument depicts a figure emerging from a cave that doubles as the mouth of a sky monster. Vegetation at the corners shows that the main figure is being connected to the natural as well as the cosmological world. The ropes connecting the cave figure to another figure have been alternatively interpreted as being bindings or genealogical ties (Grove 1973; Taube 1995; Pool 2007: 116, 139). Perhaps the latter interpretation is more accurate given the strong connections with origins and fertility in other Mesoamerican cave iconography.

The site of Chalcatzingo in the Mexican state of Morelos is argued to have been either Olmec or Olmec-influenced, despite its distance from the Olmec heartland (Grove 1987). Monument I at the site is one of a series of bas-relief rock carvings found at the base of two volcanic mountains that overlook the site. This monument, nicknamed "El Rey," depicts a probable ruler sitting in a cave with speech scrolls or wind emerging from its entrance. Three rain clouds float above with a number of rain drops shown falling around the cave, emphasizing the connection between the cave and agricultural fertility. Monument IX at this site is a free-standing monument that seems to depict the same cave from Monument 1, except this time from a frontal perspective. The "cave" is a stylized earth-monster maw and it has been suggested that the monument may have functioned as a ritual passage for people or objects (Angulo Villaseñor 1987: 141). Heyden (1981: 20) has interpreted the Chalcatzingo cave as a representation of an oracle.

Archaic Antecedents

The first inhabitants of ancient Mesoamerica were Paleo-Indian hunter-gatherers who arrived sometime after 14,000 years ago. Around 8000–7500 B.C. the climate in Mesoamerica became noticeably drier as a result of the Holocene Climatic Optimum (sometimes called the Hypsithermal Period). This climate change coincided with the extinction of the last of the Pleistocene megafauna and a reduction in previously abundant wild food staples. The human adaptation to this climate change resulted in the so-called Desert Culture, first defined in the Great Basin of the United States (Jennings and Norbeck 1955). The Desert Culture defines the Archaic Period (8000–2000 B.C.) of ancient Mesoamerica. People of the Desert Culture became more sedentary and developed new ways of processing wild grains through the use of ground-stone tool technology.

Long-term research projects in the Tehuacán Valley, Puebla, and the Oaxaca Valley (both in Mexico), have established extended human occupation in caves and rock shelters throughout the Archaic Period. Richard MacNeish (1967) found preserved maize cobs in a number of dry caves in the Tehuacán Valley. These cobs show an increasing nutritional productivity through time as early Mesoamericans refined agricultural techniques (Smith 1999). In Oaxaca, Kent Flannery (1986) directed excavations at Guilá Naquitz, a cave site with the earliest evidence for domesticated squash (Smith 2000). In these cases we have evidence of early agriculturalists actually living in caves for thousands of years.

Discussion

Cave iconography created by the civilizations of ancient Mesoamerica has many themes. Origins and fertility (both human and agricultural) are common themes conveyed by art relating to caves. While it is nearly impossible to prove, I find it possible that the prominence of caves in later art is directly related to the fact that the ancestors of the Formative, Classic, and Postclassic civilizations physically lived in caves. Caves and rock shelters triggered cultural memories from a hazy Mesoamerican deep-time in which there was a shared origin story. Perhaps through time myths were created and altered depending on local circumstances and cultural idiosyncrasies, but there were still the root concepts of origins and fertility spanning over 3500 years of civilizational development in ancient Mesoamerica. The diversity of other cave associations elaborated by Lucero and Kinkella, and also discussed by Heyden (1975, 1981) and Stone (1995) make caves some of the most polyvalent symbols in Mesoamerica. I would argue that the longevity of the cave as a cultural fixture accounts for the diversity in its meaning. In a region filled with cultural diversity, the idea of the cave was something that bound all Mesoamerican people to a common origin and symbolized the fertility of their people and their land.

References

Angulo Villaseñor, Jorge
    1987   The Chalcatzingo reliefs: An Iconographic Analysis. In *Ancient Chalcatzingo*, edited by David C. Grove, pp. 132–158. University of Texas Press, Austin.

Carrasco, David, and Scott Sessions
    2007   *Cave, City, and Eagle's Nest: An Interpretive Journey through the Mapa de Cuauhtinchan No. 2.* University of New Mexico Press, Albuquerque.

Coe, Michael D., and Rex Koontz
    2008   *Mexico: From the Olmecs to the Aztecs.* Thames and Hudson, New York.

Flannery, Kent V.
    1986   *Guilá Naquitz.* Academic Press, New York.

Gay, Carlo T.E.
    1967   Oldest paintings of the New World. *Natural History* 76: 28–35.

Grove, David C.
    1970   *The Olmec Paintings of Oxtotitlan Cave, Guerrero, Mexico.* Studies in Pre-Columbian Art and Archaeology No. 6. Dumbarton Oaks, Washington, D.C.
    1972   Olmec Felines in Highland Central Mexico. In *The Cult of the Feline: A Conference in Pre-Columbian Iconography*, edited by Elisabeth P. Benson, pp. 153–164. Dumbarton Oaks, Washington, D.C.
    1973   Olmec Altars and Myths. *Archaeology* 26: 128–135.
    1987   *Ancient Chalcatzingo.* University of Texas Press, Austin.

Heyden, Doris
    1975   An Interpretation of the Cave Underneath the Pyramid of the Sun in Teotihuacan, Mexico. *American Antiquity* 40: 131–147.
    1981   Caves, Gods, and Myths: World-view and Planning in Teotihuacan. In *Mesoamerican Sites and World-views*, edited by Elisabeth P. Benson, pp. 1–39. Dumbarton Oaks, Washington, D.C.

Jennings, Jesse D., and Edward Norbeck
    1955   Great Basin Prehistory: A Review. *American Antiquity* 21: 1–11.

Kirchhoff, Paul, Lina Odena Güemes, and Luis Reyes García
    1976   *Historia Tolteca-Chichimeca.* Instituto Nacional de Antropología e Historia, Mexico.

MacNeish, Richard S.

1967   An Interdisciplinary Approach to an Archaeological Problem. In *Prehistory of the Tehuacan Valley, Vol. 1: Environment and Subsistence*, edited by Douglas S. Byers, pp. 14–24. University of Texas Press, Austin.

Manzanilla, Linda R.

1997   Teotihuacan: Urban Archetype, Cosmic Model. In *Emergence and Change in Early Urban Societies*, edited by Linda R. Manzanilla, pp. 109–121. Plenum, New York.

Manzanilla, Linda R., Luis Barba, René Chávez, Andrés Tejero, Gerardo Cifuentes, and Nayeli Peralta

1994   Caves and Geophysics: An Approximation to the Underworld of Teotihuacan, Mexico. *Archaeometry* 36: 141–157.

Pool, Christopher A.

2007   *Olmec Archaeology and Early Mesoamerica.* Cambridge University Press, Cambridge.

Smith, Bruce D.

1999   *The Emergence of Agriculture.* New ed. Scientific American Library, New York.

2000   Guilá Naquitz Revisited: Agricultural Origins in Oaxaca, Mexico. In *Cultural Evolution: Contemporary Viewpoints*, edited by Gary M. Feinman and Linda R. Manzanilla, pp. 15–60. Kluwer Academic/Plenum, New York.

Stone, Andrea J.

1995   *Images from the Underworld: Naj Tunich and the Tradition of Maya Cave Painting.* University of Texas Press, Austin.

Sugiyama, Saburo

2005   *Human Sacrifice, Militarism, and Rulership: Materialization of State Ideology at the Feathered Serpent Pyramid, Teotihuacan.* Cambridge University Press, Cambridge.

Taube, Karl A.

1993   *Aztec and Maya Myths.* University of Texas Press, Austin.

1995   The Rainmakers: The Olmec and their Contribution to Mesoamerican Belief and Ritual. In *The Olmec World: Ritual and Rulership*, edited by Jill Guthrie, pp. 83–103. The Art Museum, Princeton University, N.J.

Topographies of Power: Theorizing the Visual, Spatial and Ritual Contexts of Rock Reliefs in Ancient Iran[1]

Matthew P. Canepa

Introduction

The practice of creating monumental rock reliefs enjoyed a rich history in ancient Western Asia, spanning from the mid-third millennium B.C. until as recently as the nineteenth century A.D. While their techniques and approaches often differed, the Lullubi, Hittites, Egyptians, Assyrians and Elamites all shaped their kingdoms and empires with rock-cut sculpture or inscriptions, leaving richly marked and contested landscapes. When, in the seventh century B.C., Iranian-speaking peoples established themselves as imperial overlords in Western Asia, the vestiges of these ancient topographies of power challenged and stimulated their own engagement with this practice.[2] Indeed, Iranian kings and those influenced by Iranian culture became some of the most prolific patrons of rock-cut sculptures and inscriptions and adapted this ancient commemorative practice to serve Iranian religious and royal traditions. Monumental rock reliefs became one of the most privileged expressions of royal power for Persian kings of kings and later Middle Iranian dynasties, such as the Arsacids and Sasanians, who contended for the mantle of rightful Iranian sovereign. Local rulers, such as the Mithradatids of Pontos, the kings of Elymaïs, or the Orontids of Commagene, who all aspired to the forms and ideologies of Iranian kingship, adapted the larger imperial tradition of rock reliefs as well. By late antiquity the many rock reliefs that marked the rugged, rocky landscape of the Iranian plateau, northern Mesopotamia, Anatolia and the Hindu Kush served as a constant

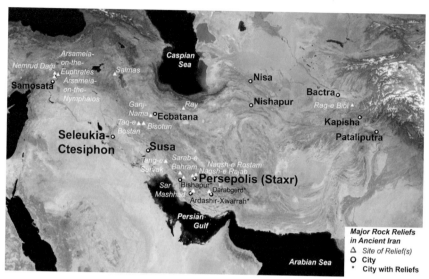

Figure 5.1 Map of the sites of major rock reliefs in the ancient Iranian world.

challenge and stimulation for succeeding and competing dynasties – Iranian or otherwise (Figure 5.1).

The Iranian rupestrian heritage began to receive the attention of European travelers, diplomats and missionaries in the fifteenth century (Vanden Berghe 1983: 13–16; Mousavi 2002; Errington and Curtis 2007; Canepa 2013). As well as initiating scholarly interest, in several cases, their sketches and descriptions preserve valuable information about reliefs damaged or destroyed in the intervening years.[3] The late nineteenth and early twentieth century brought the systematic documentation of the most prominent and accessible reliefs, often as corollaries to large-scale excavations conducted at nearby sites.[4] With greater access to Iran in the period between the Second World War and the 1979 revolution, archaeologists were able to publish many new rock reliefs in previously inaccessible regions. Efforts in the second half of the last century to catalogue and systematically document the reliefs have provided scholarship with important tools for studies of the reliefs and Iranian culture in general.[5] Except for one new relief discovered this past decade in Afghanistan, the corpus of Iranian reliefs established by the end of this period has remained largely unchanged.[6]

The focus of much scholarship on rock reliefs has centered on their internal content: dating, composition, iconographic elements, and the identification of figures.[7] As Iran's tumultuous history has left both a dearth of textual evidence and a fragmentary art and architectural heritage, rock reliefs serve as one of the few unquestionably authentic primary sources (Canepa 2009: xvii–xviii). By necessity scholars from many disciplines have mined these reliefs to provide data for studies of Iranian cultural, political and art history. A smaller cadre of art historians and archaeologists has studied the internal visual elements of rock reliefs, whose contents often stand in for lost panel or wall paintings, textiles and architectural ornament, whose subject matter they often shared. These studies have been quite productive for understanding the reliefs' subject matter and have advanced our knowledge of ancient Iranian culture. Their general approach, however, has often dissected the reliefs from their natural environment and wider cultural context in the process.

   In this study I widen the scope of inquiry to take into account the reliefs' relationship with their natural and man-made environments and examine how rock reliefs shaped Iranian cultural experience. My goal is to establish a foundation for a new approach to Iranian rock reliefs that focuses on the interactions among Iranian rock reliefs' sculptural or epigraphic contents and their environmental, urban, and ritual contexts. I explore how Iranian sovereigns marked their kingdoms with monumental features in rock, including figural sculpture and inscriptions, carved from the living rock and freestanding steles. As an important tool used to manipulate their kingdoms' experience of time, memory, and the sacred, rock reliefs' full impact emerged from their relationship with the wider landscape and nearby human activity.

Rock Reliefs as a Royal Practice in the Iranian World

The kings of kings of the Achaemenid Persian empire (c. 550–c. 330 B.C.) were the first Iranian-speaking sovereigns to carve monumental rock reliefs. They creatively adapted it, along with many other elements of kingship taken from their conquered lands. The first Persian king of kings to sponsor a monumental rock relief was Darius I (r. 522–486 B.C.). Like many aspects of Achaemenid kingship, Darius I established forms and precedents of Achaemenid rock reliefs that his dynastic successors followed. The dynasty's and Darius I's first foray into this ancient practice occurred on a grand scale at the sacred mountain of Bīsotūn, (OPers. *Bagastāna*, "place of the gods"). There he carved a massive figural sculpture three meters high and five and half meters long and a monumental trilingual inscription on and beneath the relief sculpture (Figure 5.2).[8] The relief portrays Darius in conversation with a symbol of the great god, Ahura Mazda, while trampling a defeated rival for the throne and lording over nine bound captives in different ethnic dress, each representing a defeated usurper and rebellious province (Garrison 2009). The basic composition of the relief evokes, and was likely inspired by, much earlier royal iconographic traditions, as represented in a variety of media (Wiesehöfer 1995: 13; Luschey

Figure 5.2 The monumental rock relief and inscriptions of Darius I at Bīsotūn, Iran, created in multiple phases from 522–518 B.C.

1990, 1974: 114–149; Feldman 2007: 268). While the reliefs of the Assyrian kings were carved much more recently, six reliefs created in the region around 1,500 years earlier provide the closest precedents in the sense of topography and composition (Postgate and Roaf 1997). A relief carved by the Lullubi king, Annubanini, was located only 100 km to the west. Although the identity of these kings were long forgotten, Darius engaged with this local monumental and environmental experience of triumphal iconography when he carved his much larger and more elaborate expression.

The content of the great Bīsotūn relief stemmed from Darius I's wider propaganda program aimed at presenting a coherent narrative explaining the turmoil surrounding the deaths of the sons of Cyrus and Darius I's own rise to power.[9] The relief's ultimate significance, however, derived from its permanent association with the sacred mountain. Archaeological evidence indicates that the site was occupied since prehistoric times and, in addition to hosting a sacred area, was the site of a pre-Achaemenid fortress (Luschey 1990). Some have even suggested that the fortress was the very place mentioned in the inscription where Darius I captured and killed his rival, Gaumata, portrayed begging for mercy above (Brown 2001). Writing after the age of Darius I, Ctesias describes the mountain as "sacred to Zeus," and the site of a paradise (OIr. *pairi.daiza*).[10] The sanctuary precinct walls are still visible in aerial imagery and ran approximately 180 m from one cliff spur to another (Kleiss 1996, 1970; Bernard 1990: 319). Within the precinct a sloping hillside leads up to a rubble field, which, in turn, abuts the cliffs. The hillside was divided into two artificial terraces, with an area with evidence of cult activity on the southern ledge of the upper terrace. The terrace below Darius I's relief, now covered with its debris, was likely a site of cult activity under the Medes and in the early Achaemenid era. A rock-cut stairway led from the rubble field to a third zone, which looked down upon Darius I's rock relief and preserves evidence of cult activity. Whatever occurred on these terraces, the relief appropriates the mountain's significance as both a sacred site and as a landmark on an important transcontinental artery. Given its close connection to the upper terrace, it is possible that Darius I's relief could have obliterated a pre-Achaemenid relief.

On a smaller scale, Darius I carved a monumental inscription at a major east-west pass through the Alvand range near a waterfall. Located about 12 km southwest from the royal residence, Ecbatana, the site is known today by the toponym Ganjnāma (Brown 2001). The relief consists of a 2 × 3 m recessed rectangle with Old Persian, Babylonian and Elamite versions of the same inscription. Holes in the rock indicated that some sort of covering protected it. Like Bīsotūn, this smaller-scale relief greets the great thoroughfare that linked together the Iranian plateau and Mesopotamian plain and, again like Bīsotūn, it appears that a sacred platform of some sort stood above the relief (Brown 2001). Although executed on a different scale, Bīsotūn and Ganjnāma both engaged with road networks and the potential flow of viewers that they implied. Later generations of Achaemenid kings created rock reliefs to associate themselves with their predecessors. Unlike Bīsotūn, which no other Achaemenid king of kings sought to rival, Xerxes I, son and successor of Darius I, replicated his smaller-scale relief at Ganjnāma, creating an inscription of similar size and content underneath. In an even more explicit example, Xerxes I carved a trilingual inscription on the face of the citadel rock of Van, ancient Tušpa (Summers 1993: 85). In the inscription Xerxes states that, "King Darius, who was my father, by the will of Ahura Mazda, created much that was good, and he gave orders to dig out this place, where he did not create a carved inscription. Thereafter, I gave orders to carve this inscription" (Xerxes I, Van Inscription 17–25).

As rock reliefs accumulated at certain sites, carving one became a tool by which a sovereign could associate himself with his predecessors, and even a necessary and expected physical and visual expression of his legitimacy within a long dynastic tradition. In this light, Darius I's other great rock-cut creation, his monumental tomb, established a precedent that all his successors followed, formally as well as topographically. Within 7 km from Persepolis, Darius began what evolved into the Achaemenid royal necropolis at the site known today as Naqš-e Rostam (Figure 5.3). While the Bīsotūn relief

Figure 5.3 The site of at Naqš-e Rostam, Iran with a view (right to left) of the
           Achaemenid tombs identified as those of Artaxerxes, Darius I, Xerxes I.
           Below, the Sasanian reliefs of Bahrâm II, Šāpūr II, Šāpūr I, Bahrâm I, Narseh,
           and an unfinished relief (perhaps initiated by Ḵosrow II) with an early modern
           inscription in its center.

remained unique in terms of Achaemenid rock art, Darius I's tomb had a
deeper influence on Persian royal practice. Previous Persian royal tombs were
freestanding masonry structures and Darius I's tomb presents a clear break
in tradition. Three succeeding Achaemenid kings of kings carved tombs
carefully replicating Darius I's original at Naqš-e Rostam, as did two created
on the Kūh-e Raḥmat, the mountain which flanked Persepolis.[11] In contrast
to Bīsotūn, Van and Ganjnāma, which flanked major roads, Naqš-e Rostam
was in the heart of the homeland of the Persians and closely associated with
the ceremonial palace of Persepolis. At the end of the dynasty, it appears
no Achaemenid king would consider *not* creating one. The Achaemenid
tombs were cruciform and the upper portion of the monument carried
relief sculpture portraying personifications of all provinces of the empire
supporting a throne. The throne, in turn, supported a scene of the king of
kings standing before a fire altar in communication with the divine symbol.
Below, a rock-cut entranceway evoked the façade of a Persian palace with
bull-protome columns. Only the tomb of Darius I carried an extensive royal
inscription, which, in this case, occupied the negative space of the upper
register. The interior contained the rock-cut sarcophaguses of the king of
kings and his family. In this way, the Achaemenids, beginning with Darius,
combined the genre of the royal rock relief with the Iranian religious practice

of using ossuaries to encase human remains in some durable material to prevent ritual pollution of the soil (Canepa 2010c; Hutter 2009).

After the fall of the Achaemenids, rock reliefs temporarily receded as a royal medium within Pārsa. Outside the province, however, a wide variety of royal patrons began to incorporate the practice into their artistic and ideological arsenal. Seleucid governors, Arsacid kings of kings and local provincial dynasts all engaged with this ancient royal practice according to their means to execute them (on the Arsacid reliefs, see Boehmer and von Gall 1973; Vanden Berghe and Schippmann 1985; Kawami 1987). As with many aspects of Persian culture, Alexander's invasions ruptured the Achaemenid tradition of rock reliefs. Achaemenid sculptural forms, iconographies, and inscriptional conventions largely fell out of favor. In general, rock art became much more diverse in form and function and incorporated new artistic developments from the wider world of Hellenistic Asia. Apart from royal reliefs, private individuals created a variety of smaller-scale rock-cut tombs as pious acts. These appear in regions as diverse as the Persian home province, Media, and Kharg Island (Haerinck 1975; Huff 2004; Potts 2004). In addition to these smaller ossuaries, local gentry in Persia and Media carved a few larger reliefs in a manner that, in some cases, vaguely evoked their cruciform shape, or, in other cases, the idea of a columned façade, though using Greek architectural forms rather than Persian bull columns. As provincial creations, they did not come close to matching the intricacy and refinement of the great royal reliefs. Rather than hosting rock-cut sarcophagi dedicated to individuals, these post-Achaemenid reliefs were *daxmas*: that is, places to expose dead bodies for air burial and collect the cleaned bones of a larger number of individuals (Huff 2004: 596–602).

A reclining Herakles created at Bīsotūn in honor of a Seleukid governor is the only rock sculpture surviving on the Iranian plateau from the Seleukid era (c. 312–c. 140/39 B.C.) (Kleiss 1970: 144–146; Luschey 1974: 114). It portrays in a naïve sculptural style a weary Herakles reclining on his lion skin after his labors, drinking from a cup. Behind him, his bow and club appear to lean against an inscribed relief stele. An inscription, carved in Greek and Aramaic, accompanied it and dates it to 148 B.C., indicating, quite ironically, that it was completed only months before the Arsacids swept away Seleukid control in this region (inscription reported as a side note in Robert 1963: 76). It is no coincidence that the only Seleukid-era rock relief was carved at Bīsotūn, as the sheer spectacle of Darius' relief still made a very deep impression on the Hellenistic world, although its original patron and meaning were forgotten (Ctesias [in Diodorus, 2.13.1–2.13.2]; Diodorus:17.110.5; Isidore of Charax:5; Luschey 1990: 292–293). The Herakles relief engages the topography of Bīsotūn's famous sanctuary as it evolved in the Hellenistic age. The Herakles relief marks the entrance to the ancient sanctuary, where the precinct walls met the rock face. Given this placement and its subject matter, the relief likely received cult offerings or simple veneration from visitors to the sanctuary. The only other example of a major rock-cut feature from the Seleukid era is located about 145 km southeast of Lake Urmia. The rock-cut caves of Karafto, which included an apotropaic inscription invoking Herakles, likely served as a Seleukid garrison (Von Gall 1978, 2009; Bernard 1980; Tubach 1995).

While not in Iran proper, a valley outside the Seleukid royal residence of Antioch-on-the-Orontes hosts a mysterious Seleukid-era rock relief. Lying to the east of the city, it consists of the 4.5-m high bust of a beardless male figure with a smaller, draped male figure standing on its shoulder holding some sort of staff or torch. The late Roman author, Malalas, preserves an urban legend on the origin of the relief, calling it an image of Charon, which he ascribes as a talisman against the plague (Malalas 205.8–205.13; Downey 1961: 103–104). Both figures appear to wear a Phrygian cap, indicating to early surveyors that it portrayed the god Mithras attended by Attis (Renan 1865). Religious subject matter and perhaps a cultic function parallel the Bīsotūn Herakles; however, without further comparanda, at this point we can only speculate if such a genre of rock-cut, monumental statuary existed in the Seleukid era inspired by Iranian rock reliefs, or if this was simply a coincidence.

The Arsacid dynasty (248 B.C.–c. 224 A.D.) carved the majority of the rock reliefs it sponsored at Bīsotūn and a substantial settlement grew up here (Alibaigi et al. 2012). Like the Seleukid Herakles, they were located near ground level and engaged the entranceway into the sanctuary. Mithradates II (c. 124 –88/87 B.C.) carved a relief on the ground level to the west of the high cliff supporting Darius I's relief and to the east of the Seleukid Herakles (Vanden Berghe 1983: 118–119). The composition of the relief, which portrays the king of kings receiving satraps, adapts the composition of Darius I's relief overhead and portrays a series of figures in profile standing one after the other before the king. An equestrian victory of Gotarzes II Geopothros (Gōdarz ī Gēw, r. 38–51 A.D.) crowned by a victory was later carved to east of this relief. Although very abraded, the relief portrays the king among armored cavalrymen, unhorsing their rivals, with a winged victory crowning the king. Given their orientation, running along the lower rock face, and their relationship with the Herakles relief at the sanctuary's entrance, both of these reliefs likely lined the road to the sanctuary. The field to the north of the sanctuary precinct contains a free standing boulder (the "Parthian stone") which carries a relief on two of its faces depicting scenes of a male figure offering incense at an altar. One of the sacrificing figures is identified as Vologases, possibly one of the five Arsacid kings of kings with this name (Luschey 1990: 293; von Gall 1996a: 60–71,

1996b: 85–88; Boyce 2000, 2003). The reliefs are both oriented towards the sanctuary, implying a spatial connection between the act of sacrifice portrayed and the sanctuary to the south.

While Arsacid courtly engagement with the genre was limited, several Arsacid client kings began to carve rock reliefs as the dynasty declined. Under Arsacid overlordship, the Middle Iranian kings of Elymaïs cultivated a certain independence (Hansman 1998). The kings of this region produced more reliefs than their Arsacid overlords (Vanden Berghe and Schippman 1985). While their formal qualities are often quite crude, the reliefs of Elymaïs reflect current Parthian visual culture and adapt its conventions of royal iconography, portrayals of religious activity, and conventions of figural representation.

Before the fall of the Achaemenids, rock-cut tombs flourished in many parts of Anatolia, especially in Lycia and Caria (Shahbazi 1975; Miller 2002). Proud of their Persian and Macedonian ancestry, the kings of Pontos created tomb monuments that evoked Persian royal practices while engaging with the Hellenistic *koiné* of the region.[12] Although they superficially bear Greek forms and join a long history of Anatolian rock-cut tombs, the associated inscriptions and evidence of ritual practice present some of the closest royal correspondences to Achaemenid funerary traditions from Hellenistic era (Canepa 2010c). Like Pontos, the Orontid kings of Commagene celebrated their dual Persian and Macedonian roots (Facella 2006; Mittag 2011). Antiochos I (69–34 B.C.), the main innovator in cult and artistic activity in the kingdom of Commagene (162 B.C.–A.D. 17), engaged with this very ancient royal practice within the larger formal context of his deliberately "hybrid" Hellenic and Iranian court.[13] He created *hierothēsia,* sanctuaries dedicated to royal and divine cult, at several sites throughout his kingdom. Every major *hierothēsion* makes extensive use of stone relief steles, which mark the surrounding landscape. Most employed earthworks, such as rock tumuli or artificial caves, to shape the natural landscape.

Once the Sasanian dynasty (c. 224–651 A.D.) consolidated power, monumental rock reliefs enjoyed an incredible resurgence in Persia. Under the Sasanians monumental relief carving served as a cornerstone of royal legitimation to the point that it came to be a self-consciously royal practice and the preserve of the Sasanian dynasty within their empire. Indeed, the number of rock reliefs that Sasanians sponsored in their empire rivaled and surpassed the volume of all other royal dynasties, Iranian or otherwise, with their kings and courtiers sponsoring almost 40 reliefs (Canepa 2013).[14] The Sasanians set out with a vengeance to focus the accumulated landscape of power that confronted them discretely around their dynasty. Their reliefs often impose a filter through which many earlier dynasties' creations must be viewed.

Ardašīr I (r. 224–239/40), the founder of the Sasanian empire, drastically restricted the royal prerogatives enjoyed by his subject kings. Ardašīr I was brutally effective in this campaign, and a variety of sources reflect the anxiety that this program generated among those rulers who now found themselves under his control (Canepa 2009: 18). While we do not have the same level of textual corroboration, the empirical evidence of the rock reliefs indicate that they were also included among those practices Ardašīr I felt compelled to control: after he took power, no one but the king of kings, and in one exceptional case, the chief magus, carved a monumental rock relief. Not surprisingly, the central visual focus of all Sasanian rock reliefs was almost without exception the Sasanian king of kings. The sovereigns portrayed themselves engaged in a variety of activities with varying levels of compositional complexity, from multi-figured scenes of equestrian battles or hunting to elegantly simple scenes of the king receiving the royal diadem from a divinity or enthroned frontally receiving the homage of his court.[15] The majority of the Sasanian reliefs depicted scenes of divine investiture and triumph over internal or foreign enemies, often in combination with these other themes (De Waele 1989: 811).[16]

While some functions of the Sasanian rock reliefs paralleled those of their predecessors, taken as a whole, the way the Sasanians deployed them indicates a uniquely uniform approach. The Sasanian kings created reliefs at a number of different types of sites. Some were in close proximity to a city and roads leading to and from it. Another group clustered near important Achaemenid reliefs. Still others were located in more remote areas, drawn to natural features like spring-fed pools, rivers and mountains. Yet others claimed symbolic space at the borders of or within conquered territory. While they never created tombs for themselves in the manner of the Achaemenids, the Sasanian kings paid close attention to the traditions of Achaemenid relief sculpture and inscriptions. They periodically added their inscriptions or reliefs onto sites or structures favored by the earlier dynasty and based their own sculptural forms on Achaemenid precedents (Canepa 2010b).

Physical, Visual and Ritual Inscription of Space and Time

In order to understand their role in Iranian kingship and impact on Iranian culture, it is important to bring rock art and inscriptions into focus as royal technologies that could shape a culture's practical relationship and experience of space, time, memory and the sacred (Canepa 2010b). We must look beyond the bound of the reliefs themselves and be attuned to how their internal contents and very presence potentially shaped viewers' perceptions of their surroundings. While a cohesive debate does not yet exist, several contemporary theoretical discussions have the potential to shed light on the phenomenon among ancient Iranian cultures. Studies involving the social or political experience of space have grown up in several disciplines, most notably anthropology, sociology, and geography. The reciprocal and mutually constituting relationship between peoples and their environment is the focus of many studies (e.g., Howard et al. 2013; Rodning 2010). In this light, rock art and inscriptions were important tools used to transform open-ended "space" into symbolic "place," as explored in different ways by the other studies in this volume.

Rock reliefs, and the network of practices that engaged with them, inscribed meaning on the landscape and shaped individual's relationship to it. Speaking broadly, the fundamental power of the rock relief was its ability to merge a viewer's experience of its visual or epigraphic content with that of the site and any historical, religious, or political significance associated with the site. Rock reliefs thus "functioned" by compelling a relationship in the experience of the viewer between the images or, in the case of inscriptions, words that they carried, the natural or man-made features at a site, and the activities that took place there. This could be put to many purposes; however, as an elite technology and often an exclusively royal prerogative, Iranian rock reliefs played a special role in shaping a kingdom's experience of royal power by shaping the populace's experience of and relationship with important sites in their environment.[17]

The topographical setting of these reliefs reinforced and interacted with their content. The very physical presence of these durable images or inscriptions could claim local territory, mark holy spaces at sites such as springs, caves, or mountains, and appropriate sites that were important to the general populace or in the dynastic memory of previous regimes. Patrons were drawn to sites that people were drawn to. Thus rock reliefs often cluster at such religiously important natural features as mountains, caves, oases, and springs, or sites such as canyons, river fords, and mountain passes which controlled the passage of important military or trade routes. Water, as well as fire, air, and earth, was sacred in Iranian religions, and spring-fed pools and riverside canyons were especially popular sites for rock reliefs (Callieri 2006; Canepa 2013: table 45.1).[18] Mountains, plateaus, and other elevated areas often functioned as sacred spaces in Iranian culture and were often the sites of both grand architectural complexes and smaller-scale artistic and architectural embellishment. Like those created near water, the visual impact of rock reliefs on or at the base of hills or mountains shaped viewers' and worshippers' experience of the intrinsic holiness of the natural feature. A relief at a virgin site, and the royal attention implicit in it, could proclaim that that site was special and noteworthy, even if it was not connected with previous cultural activity. In this way, rock reliefs could transform sites that had a special significance in the personal history of a king into a site that had a wider cultural and social importance.

In addition to the powerful interaction between the contents and location of reliefs, patrons and viewers alike often forged close connections between rock reliefs and ritual practices performed at the site or elsewhere. At the most basic level, this ritual interaction could be as simple as portraying an important ritual activity taking place. The contents of rock reliefs portrayed ritual performances such as coronations, victory celebrations, and courtroom ritual. Such images could include scenes of sovereigns sacrificing at an altar, or courtiers and subject people performing ritual obeisance to a sovereign. They could engage the site before them or refer to practices and places at a distant remove. For example, the "Parthian Stone" at Bīsotūn presents reliefs of individuals offering incense and was oriented in the direction of the sanctuary. Many of Šāpūr I's reliefs portray defeated kings honoring the king of kings with ritual acts of obeisance. The enduring medium ensured the eternal performance of such honored rituals, and perpetuated the respect shown to a god or sovereign.

More difficult to access, yet no less intriguing, are the moments where the rock reliefs themselves were integrated into rituals performed at the site or when reliefs received direct cultic veneration, be they state-sanctioned or "vernacular" interpretations of the reliefs. Although static themselves, rock reliefs' perennial proximity to holy substances and sites such as water, fire, or mountains, implies that a variety of ritual activities were performed next to them and animated them. Underscoring the power of rock reliefs to claim and participate in the rituals of sacred spaces, recent excavations before the cluster of Elymaean reliefs at Ḵong-e Nowrūzi exposed a sacred terrace with bronze offerings, such as bells and arrowheads. This open-air sanctuary, dated by radiocarbon to within 150 B.C. and 75 A.D., superceded an Elamite sanctuary, indicating the antiquity of the cult site (Messina and Mehrkian 2011a, 2011b). These offerings parallel those at nearby Parthian-era sanctuaries, such as Bard-e Nešānda and Masjed-e Solaymān.

While other personages joined them, the main focus of almost every Iranian rock relief was a king, a god, or both. The image of a sovereign or god demanded behavioral changes from the viewing subject. Thus, the Seleukid Herakles at Bīsotūn could have received simple cultic devotion from any who passed into the sanctuary, while referring in a metaphorical sense to the satrap in whose honor it was created. The Achaemenid, Seleukid, Arsacid, Orontid, and Sasanian sovereigns all received ritual deference from their courtiers and subjects and, in certain cases, their images would demand the same treatment as the living king (Wiesehöfer 2007).

Once a part of the substance of site, the rock reliefs affected those who came into contact with them and what went on at the site. At the most important sites, rock reliefs developed reciprocally and interdependently with ritual practice. A ritual could lead to a new inscription commemorating it or imply a new meaning for a rock relief. New reliefs within a ritual environment could modify the performance and significance of a ritual. The kings of kings created their visual and spatial environments with the knowledge that they would provide a focus for ritual activities. These ritual activities, in turn, commented on and shaped further additions. Approaching Iranian rock reliefs, the spaces they inhabited and the activities that went on around them as an expressive whole enables one to coherently interpret the linkages between the rich variety of visual, sensual, spatial, and emotional constituents that an experience of such images marshaled, as well as the organizing effect they potentially had on the memories and imaginations of the viewer. Since artistic features and ritual practice could become so interwoven with the landscape, it is not surprising to observe that an alteration in the fabric of one had implications for that of the other.

Having introduced this interpretative approach, I turn to three important tasks that rock reliefs fulfilled in the Iranian world. I first explore the role of rock reliefs in maintaining memory and manipulating a culture's understanding and experience of the past. I then examine how rock art and inscriptions could articulate regional topographies of power, around either a city or a province. Finally I consider how inscriptions and rock art could negotiate the identity of a sovereign or empire. In this regard I look at how rock reliefs could project a politically sanctioned vision of the world into the peripheries of an empire, extending the visual presence of a sovereign, while simultaneously presenting to the center a vision of peoples and powers on the periphery as conquered, subservient and meek.

Rock Reliefs, Sites, and Rituals of Memory

Given their manifestly durable nature, it should come as no surprise that monumental rock reliefs played an especially important role in the way several Iranian powers understood the past and their methods to preserve their own memory for future generations. In terms of square footage and number, the majority of rock reliefs patronized by the Achaemenid dynasty in their home province of Pārsa were funerary. As such, a complex set of ritual practices devoted to the memory of the deceased king of kings enveloped and animated the Persian court's and populace's experience of the Achaemenid rock-cut tombs (Canepa 2010c). The site that Darius I selected for his tomb, called today by its New Persian nickname of Naqš-e Rostam, eventually developed into the principle royal necropolis for the Achaemenid kings of kings. It hosts the majority of Achaemenid funerary reliefs, though later in the dynasty rock-cut tombs were carved behind the Palace of Persepolis. Naqš-e Rostam marked the final spur of a mountain known today as the Ḥosayn Kūh, lying within processional distance of roughly 6.25 km to the north of the palace of Persepolis, and 25 km south of Cyrus I's capital, Pasargadae (Schmidt 1970: 7). The basic Achaemenid constituents of Naqš-e Rostam are four Achaemenian funerary reliefs, those of Darius I, Xerxes I, Artaxerxes I, and Darius II, and one tower of fine ashlar masonry known as the Ka'ba-ye Zardošt ("the Ka'ba of Zoroaster").

All Achaemenid tombs at Naqš-e Rostam, as well as those started later at Persepolis, conform to the design and size of Darius I's tomb: cruciform, with a tomb chamber entrance at the center reached through a relief façade that evoked the façade of a Persian *apadāna* (audience hall). The upper register portrays a scene of the king of kings in conversation with the great god, Ahura Mazda, and venerating a fire altar, while standing on a throne supported by representatives of his provinces. Only Darius I's tomb carries a monumental trilingual inscription. Although the tomb's inscription would have been completely illegible even to the few who were literate, given the height of the tomb from the original ground level, it still functioned as a generalized visual marker of power. The interior of the rock-cut tombs contained multiple rectangular burial chambers, just over human scale (Schmidt 1970: fig. 32). The grand visual spectacle of the tombs looming on the horizon powerfully maintained the memory of the Achaemenid kings of kings and marked the landscape as intrinsically important for them. Complementing the tomb monuments, funeral processions and rituals and, more importantly, commemorative rituals performed before the tombs for the benefit of the kings' souls linked the tombs into the wider world of Persian courtly ritual (Canepa 2010c). Elamite tablets from the Persepolis Fortification Archive mention the funerary monuments (šumar) of the Achaemenid kings and record the supplies reserved for the performance of rituals for the benefit of their soul carried out at the tombs (Henkelman 2003, 2008: 287–291, 429–432, 546; Canepa 2010c). Officials who served the king in life received the post of "keeper of the tomb" as a high honor. They and their servants offered sacrifices to the gods on behalf of the kings at the tombs and ensured the monuments themselves were kept in good repair (Canepa 2010c).

While the Achaemenid empire lasted, the court and populace would have experienced the rock-cut tombs, as well as the earlier freestanding tombs of Cyrus and his family, as inextricable from the ritual performance before them. After the dynasty fell to Alexander, the reliefs became decoupled from their original, specific significance; eventually, the tombs were separated from the specific memory of the Achaemenid dynasty altogether. Despite this loss in memory the rock reliefs and tombs themselves persisted, looming large on Iran's physical and ideological horizons for centuries thereafter. Subsequent rulers, from the Seleukids to the Qājārs, created rock reliefs at these sites as a means to gain control of these important monuments and claim the still impressive features as ideological bulwarks for their regime. It is no coincidence that the only extant rock reliefs on the Iranian plateau created by the Seleukid and Arsacid courts were carved at Bīsotūn, a site that was important due to its sanctuary, location on the trade routes, and Darius I's own prestigious relief. The Seleukid Herakles and the remains of Gotarzes II's equestrian combat scenes have little to do compositionally with Darius I' relief, but capitalized on the cultural prominence of the site. Mithradates II's relief (now known only through a traveler's sketch) suggests a subtle formal influence from the Achaemenid relief carved above, especially with regards to the repeated profiles of his courtiers paying homage (Vanden Berghe 1983: 118–119). The overall result was the beginning of a new 'cumulative aesthetic,' where the reliefs of previous dynasties inspired and challenged the activities of later regimes.

The Sasanian kings of kings developed an especially complex set of memory practices in which rock reliefs played an especially prominent role (Canepa 2010b). The Sasanians used rock-cut sculpture and inscriptions to appropriate sites and structures that were prominent under previous dynasties, even those from which they were separated by hundreds of years. The Sasanians were particularly drawn to the sites that were important to the Achaemenids and the material vestiges of this great Persian heritage served as the raw material for their own memorial and monumental practices (Canepa 2010b). Although the exact history of the Achaemenid dynasty was forgotten, the new dynasty understood the Achaemenids to be their ancestors and, eventually, their connection to the even more ancient and legendary Kayānid dynasty. Rock reliefs served as an important tool in the Sasanians' cadre of memory technologies and one of their most important tools to enliven what was originally a silent, inert past. Once they had achieved supreme power, the early Sasanian kings began to sponsor rock reliefs at sites throughout Persia and eventually their empire. The region around Persepolis and the site of Naqš-e Rostam in particular developed into a site that was incredibly important for the Sasanian dynasty's sense of its past and connection to their ancient ancestors, both semi-mythological and historical. At Naqš-e Rostam, the Sasanian kings completed eight bas-relief sculptures, more than at any other site, and the second king of the dynasty carved an extensive trilingual inscription into the site's Achaemenid tower.

At the most basic level, the close contiguity among Sasanian rock reliefs and Achaemenid tombs implied a relationship of identity and lineage between the two temporally distant dynasties. This link physically instantiated a claim that eventually formed one of the cornerstones of early Sasanian ideology. In addition to physical and visual proximity, the Sasanians re-enveloped the site with ritual practice. Šāpūr I dedicated two-fifths of his monumental inscription on the Ka'ba-ye Zardošt to establishing a cult celebrating the memory of his family, dynasty and court (ŠKZ: 33–50). Internal clues in the inscription as well as corroborating evidence elsewhere at Naqš-e Rostam suggest that the cult was based at the site. The form and content of the inscription, which records the foundation of major sacred fires (ādur) for the soul and memory (pad amā ruwān ud pannām) of Šāpūr himself, his queen of queens and three of his sons, parallels that of Achaemenid memorial ritual (Šāpūr, Ka'ba-ye Zardošt inscription [hereafter ŠKZ]: 33–34; Canepa 2010b: 583). This suggests that the Sasanians could have reinvigorated, or reinvented, Achaemenid rituals preserved in oral history or epics, if they were not still alive. Šāpūr I's inscription presents a valuable record of ritual activity that engaged and reanimated the site. It also provides a possible view into cultic activities performed alongside their rock reliefs that the later kings might have instituted at this or other sites. These activities, although grounded on rock reliefs, went far beyond simply associating themselves with the Achaemenid remains: the rupestral and ritual practice focused on the site created a coherent experience of a single genealogical, visual, and spatial whole.

Regional Topographies

Rock reliefs were instrumental in creating regional topographies of power. They shaped the landscape, conforming it to the identity of a king or dynasty, and imposed a royally sanctioned experience of the space and natural features of a sovereign's realm. The local kings of Elymaïs, semi-independent vassals of the Arsacid kings of kings, were some of the most prolific patrons of rock reliefs in the Middle Iranian era, though as a regional power they were far from the core of the empire (Vanden Berghe and Schippmann 1985).[19] In Elymaïs, rock reliefs clustered at a seven different sites, often on large boulders rather than mountain cliffs. Among these, the site of Tang-e Sarvak was the most important sanctuary of the kings of Elymaïs and hosted 13 reliefs and several inscriptions (Haerinck 2005). The themes of these reliefs include scenes of investiture of the local king by the Arsacid king of kings, courtiers paying homage to the local king, hunting and banqueting scenes, and kings offering sacrifice before a sacred stone (betyl). These reliefs accumulated over the years with succeeding local rulers compelled to add their images to these sites that increasingly became associated with both divine and royal power. The content and subject matter of the reliefs suggest that the majority were dedicated to negotiating the relationship between the local rulers and the sites and traditions of power in the region.

Among the many Parthian-era reliefs in Elymaïs, those of Ḵong-e Nowrūzi (also called Ḵong-e Azhdar) were carved at what was an ancient Elamite sanctuary. It features a large, freestanding boulder that preserves a rock relief of a king on horseback and page in profile with several nobles standing frontally to the right (Vanden Berghe and Schippmann 1985: 33–38; Potts 1999: 354–406). New archaeological work suggests that the horseman was an earlier feature and the figures on the right, as well as the two diadem-bearing eagles, were added later, possibly effacing a previous relief on that section of the rock face (Messina and Mehrkian 2011a). While the horseman resembles the Hellenized portraits of the Arsacid king of kings Mithradates I (171–139/8 B.C.), it also evokes the portraits of several of the early first century B.C. Elymaean kings named Kamnaskires, whose numismatic portraits drew from the image of the Arsacid king of kings (Messina and Mehrkian 2011b). The frontal composition and iconography of the standing figures differ markedly from those of the horseman. The iconographic features of the main standing figure evoke coin portraits of a later Kamnaskires, Kamnaskires-Orodes (c. early to mid-second century A.D.). The evidence suggests this later king added his relief to manipulate the significance of a popular and ancient sanctuary and associate himself with his predecessor portrayed in the preexisting relief.

The kingdom of Commagene, wedged between the Roman and Parthian empires, capitalized on its dual Persian and Macedonian heritage as the two great powers encroached on either side. Antiochos I of Commagene (r. 69–36 B.C.), whose reforms reshaped the public cult of his the kingdom, used monumental figural relief sculpture and inscriptions to reshape the symbolic topography of his kingdom and engage Iranian traditions of kingship. The symbolic center of Commagene, as well as its highest point visible from miles around, was Antiochos I's burial site and seat of cult rendered to him, his ancestors and the gods: the mountain-top *hierothēsion*, referred to by its modern toponym Nemrud Dağı. [20] While not carved out of the living rock, Antiochos set up two sets of colossal statue groups of himself enthroned among the gods on the east and west of his grave tumulus (Figure 5.4). Relief slabs portraying the king clasping hands with the gods appeared before or next to the colossal sculpture groups on both terraces. Lines of relief steles portraying the king's Seleukid, Achaemenid and Orontid ancestors flanked eastern and western terraces and were designed to line the northern processional way that connected the terraces.

Figure 5.4 The hierothēsion of Antiochos I of Commagene. View of the west terrace. Nemrud Dağı, Turkey, c. mid-first century B.C.

Rock reliefs, steles and earthworks made what had been a very tenuous claim and connection to Persian identity monumental and permanent. Antiochos I set up similar reliefs slabs portraying the king with the gods lining the processional way at Arsameia-on-the-Nymphaios, modern Eski Kahta, Adıyaman province (Figure 5.5). A deep cave served as the cultic focus of the site. A monumental inscription, the longest in Anatolia, marked the cave's entrance and outlined Antiochos I's newly instituted dynastic cult (on the cult, see Waldmann 1973; Koch 2002: 281–301). About 15 km to the southwest of Nemrud Dağı, on the plain below, a monumental tumulus with relief slabs on columns at the cardinal points marked the burial site of the royal Commagene woman. Antiochos I carved a monumental rock relief 25 km to the northeast of Nemrud Dağı, at the citadel of Arsameia-on-the-Euphrates, modern Gerger (Figure 5.6). Identified by its inscription as Antiochos's grandfather Samos I, the male figure wearing royal "Persian" robes offers a libation. Its placement on the cliff side orients the relief towards the peak of Nemrud, which was visible across the valley. The figure's sacrificial gesture, mirrored in Nemrud's ancestor steles, honors those who occupy the *hierothēsion* on the sacred mountain, "the abode of the gods." The mountain of Nemrud Dağı, with its artificially augmented peak, dominated the entire region. The *hierothēsioi* themselves provide important examples of ritual-

Figure 5.5   Stele with Antiochos I of Commagene clasping hands with Artagnes-Herakles-Ares and the cave sanctuary and inscription at the *hierothēsion* of Arsameia-on-the-Nymphaios. Eskı Kahta, Turkey.

Figure 5.6 Rock relief and inscription of of Samos I, sponsored by Antiochos I of
Commagene at the citadel of Arsameia-on-the-Euphrates. Gerger, Turkey,
c. mid-first century B.C.

visual interaction and memory practices; however, in this discussion, what
is more significant is the way the *hierothēsioi* and rock reliefs articulated the
wider symbolic topography of Commagene. A common "liturgy," the visual

dominance of Nemrud Dağı, and visual and topographic correspondences of the images' ritual actions bound all sites together into a meaningful whole.

While Antiochos I of Commagene worked within the bounds of a small kingdom, inscribing it with a uniquely centralized and unified vision, the Sasanian kings of kings used rock art to shape multiple regions across their home province, and, eventually, their empire. At their simplest, they could focus on natural features sacred to Iranian religion such as mountains or springs, and in the supreme expression, they were constellated around newly founded cities. This is most readily evident in the actions of the first two Sasanian kings of kings, but their immediate successors creatively adapted their precedents. We have seen the early importance of the Achaemenid necropolis of Naqš-e Rostam, but once they became kings of kings, the Sasanian sovereigns began to construct regional topographies of power in largely untouched areas. Concentrations of reliefs accumulated at several sites first throughout the province, then throughout the empire, indicating that the Sasanians developed the practice of cultivating ritually linked, monumental zones in their home province of Pārs. The founder of the dynasty, Ardašīr I (r. 224–239/240), introduced a number urban memorial practices that evolved under his successors into a tradition of Sasanian royal urbanism. The founders of these royal cities conceived of them as standing at the center of a "memorial zone" with features such as palaces and fire temples in the urban center complemented by rock reliefs. While the Achaemenid reliefs clustered around a few important sites, the Sasanian reliefs extended the experience of a symbolically rich territory to new previously untouched sites (Canepa 2010b: 572–573). The rock reliefs they created in the vicinity of cities such as Ardaxšīr-Xwarrah and Bīšāpūr marked and shaped the surrounding natural environment and could extend quite a distance into the countryside and along routes to and from the city.

In addition to articulating the regions around cities, Sasanian kings of kings created rock reliefs at relatively isolated sites, claiming important local features like springs or mountaintops with rock-cut sculpture. The subject matter of these reliefs varied: when a Sasanian king created a rock relief at a water source, he would carve it almost without exception as close to the water as possible (Callieri 2006). In addition to embellishing sites that the first two kings of the dynasty brought to prominence, Bahrām II, who was a particularly prolific patron, created reliefs at many regional sites throughout Pārs. The relief of Sarāb-e Bahrām, which portrays the king of kings enthroned and flanked by adoring courtiers, was carved into the cliff face before a natural spring. His reliefs at Sar Mašhad, Barm-e Delak, Guyūm and Sarāb-e Qandil were located near or a comfortable distance from the nearest large settlement and some were the likely sites of royal retreats

(Ghasemi 2009; Overlaet 2009b, 2010; Haerinck and Overlaet 2009). Their subject matter ranges from a dramatic hunting scene to simple compositions portraying the king with his queen or courtiers.

The grandest of such sites, Ṭāq-e Bostān, not only claimed a water source and marked the site of a royal retreat, but incorporated the architecture and rituals of the Sasanian palace into the rock and the site's stunning natural setting (Luschey 1996b). Ṭāq-e Bostān was located in northern Iran, along the route that led from the Iranian plateau down onto the Mesopotamian plain. The site of the last reliefs of the fourth century and the final resurgence of royal rock reliefs in the seventh century, Ṭāq-e Bostān was closer to Ctesiphon than Pārs and likely served as a high-elevation refuge from the heat of Mesopotamia. The site itself originally hosted a Sasanian paradise – that is, a royal hunting enclosure and pleasure garden – and the basic forms of two of the rock reliefs evoke the hidden courtly environment of the palace. Three reliefs were carved into the rocky spur of a mountain: two fourth-century reliefs sponsored by Ardašīr II, Šāpūr III, and one by Ḵosrow II, which dates to the seventh century.[21] In the Sasanian era, water from the spring flowed directly in front of the cliff and reliefs, from which square stone platforms or "landings" extended (Callieri 2006: 341). A rock-cut stairway leads up the rockface behind the reliefs, allowing access to an artificial platform on top of the relief of Ḵosrow II, before continuing further up the rockface to a natural terrace halfway up the mountain.

Both fourth-century reliefs, Ṭāq-e Bostān I and Ṭāq-e Bostān II, associate their patrons with Šāpūr II. Ṭāq-e Bostān I, is the most prominent commemoration of Šāpūr II's defeat of the invasion of Julian ("the Apostate") in A.D. 363, which its patron, Ardašīr II, participated in. Its reference to it, in the form of Julian's dead defeated body, is, however, subordinate to the relief's overarching assertion of Ardašīr II's legitimacy in the succession (Hollard 2010; Canepa 2013). The next relief carved at the site, that of Šāpūr III, presents a simple composition within an innovative architectural context: a rock-cut barrel vault, or *ayvān*. In its final state, the relief portrays the standing figures of two kings of kings, Šāpūr II and his son and the patron Šāpūr III (Vanden Berghe 1983: 92, 145; for a new view, see Overlaet 2011). Like the dome, the *ayvān* marked privileged spaces such as a royal audience hall or fire temple. Given the placement of the statues above eye level, it is very likely that the king of kings actually used the rock-cut *ayvān* as a temporary throne hall.

With the end of the fourth century, Sasanian royal patronage shifted decisively away from the monumental rock relief. After an abeyance of nearly three centuries, Ḵosrow II (A.D. 590–628) revived the genre, executing the final relief of the dynasty, again at Ṭāq-e Bostān (Figure 5.7). Known as the "Great Ayvān," the relief creates a deep barrel vault in the cliff. The rear of the

Figure 5.7 The Great Ayvān at Ṭāq-e Bostān, begun by Ḵosrow II (590–628), portraying, in the upper rear register, the king of kings crowned by goddess Anāhīd and god Ohrmazd.

ayvān is divided into an upper and lower portion; the upper scene portrays a scene of divine investiture, with the king of kings receiving diadems from the divinities Ohrmazd and Anāhīd. The lower level of the rear face contains a high-relief sculpture of the king of kings with a nimbus surrounding his head, mounted, fully armored and holding a lance and shield.[22]

By at least the time of Ḵosrow II, the site was incorporated into a large hunting paradise, and the side relief panels of Ḵosrow II's rock cut *ayvān* carry extensive sculptural representations of the king of kings at the hunt. On the right panel, mostly unfinished, the king of kings hunts deer in an enclosure with a bow. The left panel depicts the king of kings hunting boars from a boat in a marsh enclosed by netting with many elephants beating the brush to flush out the animals. In the center, a second figure of the king faces the viewer after a successful hunt prominently displaying a nimbus around his head, the visual representation of his *xwarrah*, which he just re-enlivened and displayed while at the hunt.

Parallels with descriptions of the Sasanian audience hall at Ctesiphon suggest that the relief functioned as a sort of microcosmic setting for the royal throne while the king entertained at the site (Canepa 2009: 139). While the right side-wall of the relief was never finished, it was likely that the *ayvān* entered into use. Grooves that accommodated door pivots mark the right and left sides of the *ayvān*'s entrance. Just like the royal throne room, the interior of the relief was a restricted site, indicating, along with its shape, that it could have served that purpose while the king of kings held court while relaxing at his hunting reserve. The proximity of the imperial presence and concomitant royal court and hunting rituals thus had the potential to interact closely with the reliefs. This was the last relief brought to any sort of completion by a Sasanian king; however, it is possible that Ḵosrow II was the patron of a large, unfinished relief near Bīsotūn. Known today as the Tarāš-e Farhād, the site consists of a terrace held up by a retaining wall 150 m long, which fronts a sheer rock face with a roughly chiseled face 200 m wide × 30 m high (Luschey 1990, 1996a). If completed, it would have been the largest royal rock relief in Iran. Ḵosrow II likely planned to carve a rock-cut *ayvān* similar to the one at Ṭāq-e Bostān, which would have similarly provided a dramatic setting for him to hold court when visiting the Bīsotūn's paradise, while permanently claiming and marking the famous sacred mountain.

Rock Reliefs and the Images and Topography of Empire

While regional powers like the kings of Elymaïs, Antiochos of Commagene, or the pre- and early imperial Sasanians could order their own regions, only true imperial powers and the mightiest of kings could attempt to do this supraregionally. Several sovereigns of the Achaemenid, Arsacid, and Sasanian dynasties used rock reliefs to inscribe an imperially formed experience of spaces on their empires. Through their location, subject matter, or simply sculptural forms, certain Iranian rock reliefs focused on defining their patron's ability to control a global empire. The patrons directed these statements both to the inhabitants of their own empire and to conquered regions. Three strategies were especially popular. Rock reliefs could mark and control key points on trade or military routes, often within the heartland of the realm, ensuring that all who traveled by them would view their message. Conversely, the strongest kings projected their presence and vision of the world into regions far from the imperial center, carving rock reliefs that marked and claimed sites in newly conquered territory. Finally, the content of certain rock reliefs, created both in imperial centers and at strategic transitory locations, sought to negotiate the sovereign's relationship to global systems of power.[23]

The Egyptians, and especially the Assyrians, deployed rock reliefs in their imperial holdings to mark and claim space, activities that likely challenged the first Achaemenid king also to do so (Harmanşah 2007; Shafer 2007). The Achaemenid rock reliefs at Bīsotūn, Ganjnāma, and Van claimed important sites on the main east-west routes from the Iranian plateau through the Mesopotamian plain and into Anatolia. The monumental inscriptions of Ganjnāma and Van, illegible to all but a few, functioned simply as an imperial "brand" on the rock face claiming it for the king, something the content of the Van inscription all but admits. Bīsotūn's pictorial content directly portrayed how Darius I crushed all resistance to his rule and brought the Persian empire firmly under his control. Long after the actual historical moment of rebellion and upheaval, the relief, which clothed each of the yoked and shackled leaders of the rebellious provinces in stereotyped ethnic dress, presented a constant statement of Achaemenid imperial control over these peoples and the empire's willingness to apply divinely sanctioned violence to keep them in that position (Lincoln 2007: 17–22). The king repeated this statement in Babylon, by erecting a glazed brick version of the Bīsotūn relief along the sacred way leading from the Ishtar Gate, near the palace (Seidl 1999, 1976). Although he executed it in a much less durable medium, the monument temporarily claimed Babylon's most sacred urban thoroughfare in a manner parallel to his use of rock reliefs.

With the arrival of the Arsacids, the strongest kings again used rock reliefs to project their presence into restive regions far from the imperial center. They also continued a long tradition of vassals paying homage to their imperial overlord. These include Bīsotūn I, where Mithradates II (123–88/87 B.C.) stands receiving the submission of his governors. Reflecting this, Tang-e Sarvāk II depicts a simple scene of homage with vassals literally lined up behind the local Elymite prince who is enthroned (Seidl 1976: 76–77).

The Sasanian empire presents several complex examples of the imperial role of rock reliefs. Šāpūr I's prodigious military successes and innovations in royal ideology made a deep impact on Persian identity and visual culture. Under Šāpūr I, Sasanian royal ideology underwent a rapid series of developments that reformed the bounds and claims of Iranian kingship, providing an ideological and visual bulwark to the military expansion started by his father. Sasanian kingship and its symbolism of power became self-consciously imperial, and the king of kings claimed to rule both Iranian and non-Iranian lands (Ērān ud Anērān) (Canepa 2009: 54–55). His rock reliefs reflected and buttressed this shift in Sasanian desire to portray themselves as kings of kings of peoples beyond the traditional borders of Iran, both in their subject matter and location. Šāpūr I sponsored a number of reliefs that unequivocally represent foreign sovereigns, specifically the Romans and Kušāns. Interestingly, all of these were executed at sites in the Sasanian homeland of Pārs in southwestern Iran, either at the emerging Sasanian *lieu de mémoire* of Naqš-e Rostam or his own newly created city of Bīšāpūr.

Spurred by his Roman and Kušān victories, Šāpūr I developed visual and spatial techniques to imagine control over Iran and non-Iran, and showcased them most spectacularly in six monumental reliefs.[24] Šāpūr I never commissioned a victory monument in the Roman empire, which is not surprising since the Persians did not hold the western territories they invaded. Although they were devastating, his military activities against Rome were really more of a series of raids, rather than the long-term incorporation of any sizable portion of its territory, as was the case with the Kušān empire. However, this did not stop Šāpūr from portraying his victories over the Romans as wars of conquest in reliefs created in the heart of Iran. Šāpūr I's Roman victories are the sole subject of his relief at Naqš-e Rostam, and this same theme remains the central focus of Bīšāpūr I, II, and III. They portray the king of kings mounted with the three Roman emperors he claims to have killed, or captured and made to pay tribute (Canepa 2008: 58). This scene of Roman victory later forms the central focus of Šāpūr I's multi-figure reliefs Bīšāpūr III and II, which extend his dominance over Kušān South Asia as well (Figure 5.8; Herrmann 1980: 9–30, 1983: 11–21). Although they differ in size and integrate a different number of figures and registers, they both portray the king of kings receiving the submission of conquered peoples, backed up by rows of the Sasanian nobles. These two reliefs deal with roughly the same subsidiary themes: a demonstration of the support of the Sasanian nobles for Šāpūr I and subjection or obeisance of select sovereigns and peoples from both Ērān ud Anērān. In these much more complex compositions, the reliefs incorporate Philip's act of submission with those of the other kings, linking the Roman scene to additional scenes portraying the subjection of other peoples. Within a wider exploration of the theme of sovereignty over Iran and non-Iran, the Roman emperors' acts of obeisance overlap with the other Kušāns who stand in supplication or submission before Šāpūr (Canepa 2009: 71–75). A few kings who succeeded Šāpūr I attempted to portray themselves as conquerors of foreign peoples. Though few could

Figure 5.8   Rock relief of Šāpūr I (Bīšāpūr II) portraying (left to right), the Persian
nobility, the king of kings with the Roman emperors Phillip the Arab,
Valerian and Gordian III and multiple subject peoples.

boast equal accomplishments to back up their claims beyond trade missions
or holding the line against subsequent Roman invasions, they were portrayed
in their rock reliefs in a similarly triumphal light (Overlaet 2009a).

Given their intense efforts to establish control over their empire, it should
come as no surprise that Šāpūr I created rock reliefs in conquered regions
outside the Iranian plateau and Mesopotamia, the two main poles of Sasanian
power. A relief sculpture at the site of Salmās near Lake Urmia, now in Iranian
Azerbaijan but once in the marchlands along the border of Armenia, depicts
Ardašīr I with Šāpūr I as co-regent investing two Armenian governors with
their insignia (Vanden Berghe 1983: 67). Since the Achaemenids, Armenia
had been included in the Iranian sphere of influence and the Sasanians
included it as a constituent of *Ērān*. However, this incorporation was uneasy,
and the fact that its royal family was a scion of the overthrown Arsacid
dynasty made it especially important for the Sasanians to assert control over
this region. The relief itself betrays a rough, provincial style, indicating that
the will and the image of the sovereign extended to the provinces, but not
court artisans. No matter the style, the relief visually demonstrated that the
Sasanians controlled the local hierarchy and bears testament to their control
over the region's topography.

To the east, the newly discovered Sasanian rock relief at Rag-e Bībī in present-day Afghanistan was carved deep within the conquered territory of what had been the heart of the northern portion of the Kušān empire (Grenet 2005; Grenet et al. 2007). Rag-e Bībī portrays Šāpūr I, who took the northern and western territories of the Kušān empire. Šāpūr I carved a relief on a cliff that flanked the main north-south route from Bactra (Balk) to Kāpiśa (Bagram), connecting Bactria with the Indian subcontinent, thus claiming the global space of the trade route, as well as marking the local topography of his new subjects (Grenet et al. 2007: 260). Although it is heavily damaged, the subject matter is recognizable, portraying the king of kings hunting rhinoceroses. The subject matter of the relief subtly alludes to Šāpūr I's victories over the Kušāns, integrating this South Asian quarry into a traditional portrayal of royal power: the royal hunter. Such reliefs marked formerly hostile topography, creating a tangible, permanent visual reminder that the land was now a satellite in a larger realm. While we can safely conclude that Šāpūr I, just as Darius I before him, intended such a relief to inspire fear, awe, and obedience in any beholder who would be traveling on the route that it marked, we do not know how successful he was in this aim. The reliefs endure, but – save vandalism – any lewd gestures or verbal abuse, to which viewers on the route likely subjected the relief, were ephemeral. Similarly we can only imagine the tactics that individuals living in conquered regions whose landscape had been marked by the imperial center undertook to integrate or subvert the rupestral violence that had been inflicted on their landscapes.

Conclusions

In this chapter, I have outlined an approach to the study ancient Iranian rock reliefs that focuses simultaneously on their visual contents, spatial contexts, and practical roles in shaping the environment and Iranian kingship. Royal rock reliefs presented a visual representation of the "world as it should be" in an awe-inspiring and permanent medium. They offered not just a view of the sovereign or survey of the terrestrial world, but often a glimpse of the supernatural world as well, shaping the viewer's imagination with a politically authorized representation of what is normally unseen. Images such as Darius I's Bīsotūn relief, and Ardašīr I's investiture scene at Naqš-e Rostam, provide tangible proof of divine sanction for the political order of things. In the case of Ardašīr I's relief, its starkly symmetrical composition presents vivid visual equations of the king of kings and the Great God, on the one hand, and the defeated Arsacid king and the Demon of Demons, Ahriman, on the other (Duchesne-Guillemin 1982; Canepa 2010b: 576). Whether you respected the regime or not, in beholding what would have been an awe-inspiring spectacle, such a relief would place you, the viewer, in your politically and metaphysically sanctioned place. If you were an aristocrat, it would place you within the hierarchy through the visual cues of prominently represented official symbols of rank and office. If you were a menial laborer, this rare glimpse into the courtly world, normally in over-life-sized images, was certainly intended to overawe you, and the visual presence of the king would demand the same deference as the actual king.

The extensive inscriptions Darius I carved presented ideologically correct narratives justifying the king's action, reinforcing his claims to act with divine agency or reinforce his dynastic claims. While their locations, high up on cliff faces, did not allow the passerby to read them casually, they persisted as grand and permanent visual reminders of the content, which the king circulated across the empire in other media. In the case of Bīsotūn or his tomb at Naqš-e Rostam, the inscription was reinforced and illuminated by the relief sculpture. Indeed, like figural sculpture, the impact of inscriptions primarily came from their visual impact, since most viewers would not have been able to read them due to illiteracy or simply because they were deliberately carved high above the viewer's standpoint. Oral recitations could have mediated their content and could have been an important element in intertwined ritual activities performed before them.

Beyond their subject matter, rock reliefs acted as permanent symbolic anchors in a potentially shifting sea of expressive events, ritual actors, and viewers that came before them. This power determined how patrons deployed them, and viewers experienced their impact through their understanding of the landscape. Other media, including wall painting, sculpture in the round, architectural relief sculpture, stucco, silver or gold plate, seals and gems, or textiles, often paralleled the visual programs of monumental rock reliefs. However, the durability of the medium had a special power to imply that whatever vision the reliefs represented, even if it was the claim of a newly minted regime, was as ancient and immutable as the living rock into which it was carved. This ability to transform the contingent and ephemeral into the eternal and natural order of things was the basis of rock relief's power to forge a permanent links between a dynasty and site, or a dynasty and an earlier regime that had previously marked a site.

In this regard, a rock relief could link the patron to earlier prestigious reliefs by incorporating aspects of their formal elements, or by simply being carved in close contiguity. The potential for a relief's internal contents to interact with a site's significance lay at the core of many sovereigns' choice of site and content. Most importantly, patrons often created rock reliefs at sites that hosted ritual activity and intended their creations to interact with that ritual activity either directly or indirectly. Bīsotūn, Tang-e Sarvak, and Naqš-e Rostam all served as sanctuaries, and kings added their reliefs in order to shape the significance of the activities performed there and associate themselves with them. Conversely, rock reliefs could sacralize sites with important natural features, such as springs, and render them an appropriate focus for ritual activity. They could inscribe a social and political meaning onto sites that a culture considered to be significant because of some preexistent natural importance, religious symbolism, or simply a pragmatic utility.

In addition to marking out individual natural features as culturally and politically significant, rock reliefs could define a wider symbolic topography, of a region or even of an empire. At certain sites, such as Naqš-e Rostam, Bīšāpūr, or Bīsotūn, rock reliefs proliferated around the reliefs of previous dynasties or members of the same dynasty (Iranian or otherwise). Those added to sites that were important to previous dynasties and bore their accumulated changes could graft the patron's own contributions and identity onto the preexisting reliefs. Conversely, rock reliefs could be used as colonizing tools to efface the existence and usurp the claims of defeated regimes. The accumulation of rock reliefs at certain sites, combined with activities performed there, provided the viewer participant a direct spatial and visual experience of their relationship to prestigious pasts. Rock reliefs were an especially important feature of newly founded cities in the Sasanian era, and served as a technique by which an ambitious sovereign could create a regional topography of power, focused specifically on his deeds (Canepa 2010b: 572–574). The contents of the rock relief could bring an image of the center to the periphery of the empire and vice versa. The experience of multiple rock reliefs strategically sited along a major trade route could, in a sense, inculcate in the mind of the viewer the notion that the sovereign not only controlled those specific sites, but the spaces through which the route ran. The combination of these various techniques made it possible for sovereigns to claim cross-continental space.

Rock reliefs presented a constant challenge and inspiration to those who controlled the Iranian plateau or competed to be a rightful Iranian king. Cataclysmic upheavals cyclically fractured Iranian culture and broke most technical and artistic continuities, but despite losses in memory and even efforts on the part of victors to efface the images of the vanquished, the practice of carving relief sculpture or inscriptions re-emerged century after century as a royal prerogative. As the landscapes of ancient Iran accumulated a rich complement of rock reliefs from forgotten or half-understood dynasties, the images that they contained provided a timeless store of raw material for later Iranian kings to creatively refashion. In addition, the landscapes that they inscribed preserved the partial experience of kingdom- or empire-wide topographies of power. Even if the empires that made them were defunct, the topographies of power of previous generations and previous ages still affected the present inhabitants' perception of the landscape and inspired their own activities. In a sense, the rock reliefs themselves ensured the genre's continued survival and reappearance, as the sheer grandeur of even half-understood rock features stimulated new kings to experiment and reinvent the genre. Long after the fall of the Sasanian empire, rock reliefs drew the attention of the succeeding Islamic regimes. Either effaced in an attempt to sever ties with the pre-Islamic past, or manipulated and aggrandized to manufacture new connections with the ancient kings, these ancient topographies of power affected, and arguably continue to affect, the experience of the landscape of Iran and Iranian identity.[25]

Notes

1. Research for this project was made possible by a Charles A. Ryskamp Fellowship from the American Council of Learned Societies. Thanks to my research assistant, Kevin Kallmes, for his meticulous work in helping me prepare the manuscript for publication. Transliterations of Iranian languages and related abbreviations conform to those established by *Encyclopaedia Iranica*; abbreviations otherwise follow those of the *American Journal of Archaeology*.

2. As opposed to the more geographically restricted nation-state or region, in ancient Iranian studies "Iranian" refers to several peoples who self-consciously considered themselves to be Iranian (Av. *airiia-*/MPers. *ēr*/ Bactrian *airia*) or spoke an Iranian language. These Iranian peoples further classified themselves according to the region they inhabited (Persian), or their dynasty (Achaemenid, Arsacid, Kušān, Sasanian etc.). In addition, several Hellenistic kingdoms, such Mithradatid Pontos or Orontid Commagene, adopted aspects of Iranian culture and kingship and played up their distant Iranian roots. Thus, this study encompasses the royal rock reliefs from Anatolia to South Asia. On nineteenth- and twentieth-century scholarly and political uses and abuses of Iranian studies, see Lincoln 1999; Arvidsson 2006.

3. For example, the full contents of the Arsacid relief of Mithradates II at Bīsotūn are only known from the 1673 sketch of J. Grélot (Vanden Berghe 1983: 119).

4. Persepolis: E.F. Schmidt 1940, 1953, 1957, 1970; Bīšāpūr: Ghirshman 1956–1971; Ardāxšīr-Xwarrah/Fīrūzābād: Huff 1971, 1972, 1976, 1999.

5. Iranian rock reliefs are identified by their New Persian place-name and, if there are multiple reliefs at a site, a number which corresponds to a topographical place, not the order in which they were carved Canepa (2013).

6. See Canepa 2013 for a survey of the sites and literature.

7. Foundational catalogs of rock reliefs in Iran: Vanden Berghe 1983; Vanden Berghe and Schippmann 1985 (with caution to some of the attributions). Outside the Iranian plateau, but created under Iranian cultural influence: Shahbazi 1975; von Gall 1988, 1971. To this must be added the relatively newly discovered relief of Šāpūr I in present-day Afghanistan: Grenet et al. 2007. See also Canepa 2009, 2010b, 2010c, 2013; Overlaet 2009a, 2009b, 2010, 2011; Soudavar 2009; Thompson 2008; Grenet et al. 2007; Movassat 2005; Levit-Tawil 1993; de Waele 1989; Kawami 1987; and the bibliography below.

8. The Lullubi reliefs at Sar-e Pol could have inspired Darius I's composition, although the way the subject matter is dealt with in it are entirely contemporary (Luschey 1990; 1974: 114–149; Wiesehöfer 1995: 13; Feldman 2007.

9. The text and image were replicated and circulated in other media (Seidl 1976: 125–130; Luschey 1990; Feldman 2007); on the propaganda campaign, see Lincoln 2007: 8–13.

10. In Diod. 2.13.1–2. Reflecting the Iranian name, Diodoros (17.110.5) calls the site *theoprepestatē* ("fitting for the gods") (Schmidt 1990); on the Achaemenid paradise, see Lincoln 2012: 1–104.

11. These later tombs lack inscriptions and are identified from their relative wear and style. The final tomb, begun at Persepolis presumably for Darius III, was never finished (Schmidt 1970: 77–107).

12. Strab.: 12.3.39; Fleischer 2009. Mithradates VI boasted of both his royal Persian and Macedonian descent, counting as his ancestors Cyrus, Darius, Alexander, and Seleukos I (Just. *Epit.* 38.7.1).

13. For the rock relief at Arsemeia-on-the-Euphrates (Gerger), see Tanabe 1998: 153–163 (images only, without commentary); for the inscription, see Dörner and Naumann 1939: 16–21; Waldmann 1973: 141.

14. As well as Vanden Berghe's catalogue overview, the main documentary publications of the Sasanian rock reliefs include: Schmidt 1970; Herrmann and Howell 1977; Herrmann 1980, 1981, 1983; Herrmann et al. 1989; Fukai and Horiuchi 1969–1972; Huff 1984; Vanden Berghe 1986a. Most other literature is collected in Vanden Berghe's *Bibliographie analytique* (1981–1995); for post-1995 material, see Canepa 2013.

15. The two reliefs at Naqš-e Rostam and Naqš-e Rajāb that portray the chief priest, Kirdīr, serve as the exceptions to this rule. Kirdīr's bust reliefs are subordinate to previously-executed royal reliefs and are dependent on them.

16. For a recent attempt to argue that divine figures in Sasanian rock reliefs were intended as priests/priestesses, despite the evidence of inscriptions (and the absence of evidence for "priestesses" in Sasanian Zoroastrianism), see Overlaet 2013.

17. "Symbolic – that is, *conventional* and *conditional* – stimulations, which act only on condition they encounter agents conditioned to perceive them, tend to impose themselves unconditionally and necessarily when inculcation of the arbitrary abolishes the arbitrariness of both the inculcation and the significations inculcated" (Bourdieu 1977: 76).

18. As an interesting point of comparison, the site of Nahr al-Kalb bears the rupestral marks of millennia of conquerors, from Egyptian and Assyrian kings down to modern European colonizers, and local authorities such as Byzantine provincial governors and 20th century Lebanese politicians (Volk 2008).

19. On the Parthian impact on Sasanian reliefs, see Vanden Berghe 1987.

20. Original German survey: Dörner and Naumann 1939. American excavations: Goell 1996. Recent historical study: Facella 2006. New excavations in Commagene: Wagner 2000; Winter 2008.

21. Ṭāq-e Bostān I, II, and III respectively. On the identification of the figures in Ṭāq-e Bostān I, see Trümpelmann 1975: 108–110; Azarpay 1982: 184; Shahbazi 1985: 181–185; Azarnoush 1986: 219–247; on the relationship to Sasanian relations with S. Asia, see Carter 1981; on the relief's relationship to Roman-Sasanian competition, see Canepa 2009: 108–109.

22. For debates regarding date and attribution, see Movassat 2005: 9–18.

23. On the problem of cross-cultural interaction, see Canepa 2010a.
24. See Canepa 2013 for bibliography on these reliefs.
25. Only the Qājār dynasty carved rock reliefs on a scale and in a number equal to the pre-Islamic dynasties, ironically often doing more harm to the Arsacid and Sasanian sites than the Arabs (Luft 2001; for the wider context, see Grigor 2009).

References

Alibaigi, Sajjad, Kamal-Aldin Niknami, and Shokouh Khosravi
  2012 The Location of the Parthian City of Bagistana in Bisotun, Kermanshah: A Proposal. *Iranica Antiqua* 47: 117–131.

Arvidsson, Stefan
  2006 *Aryan Idols.* University of Chicago Press, Chicago.

Azarnoush, Massoud
  1986 Šāpūr II, Ardašīr II and Šāpūr III: Another Perspective. *Archäologische Mitteilungen aus Iran und Turan n.s.* 19: 219–247.

Azarpay, Guitty
  1982 The Role of Mithra in the Investiture and Triumph of Šāpūr II. *Iranica Antiqua* 17: 181–187.

Bernard, Paul
  1980 Héraclès, les grottes de Karafto et le sanctuaire du Mont Sambulos en Iran. *Studia Iranica* 9: 301–324.

Bloch, Maurice
  1989 *Ritual, History and Power: Selected Papers in Anthropology.* Athlone, London.

Boehmer R.M., and Hubertus von Gall
  1973 Das Felsrelief bei Batas-Herir. *Baghdader Mitteilungen* 6: 65–77.

Bourdieu, Pierre
  1977 [1972] *Outline of a Theory of Practice.* Translated by Richard Nice. Cambridge University Press, Cambridge.

Boyce, Mary
  2000 Gotarzes Geopothros, Artabanus III, and the Kingdom of Hyrcania. In *Variatio delectat: Iran und der Westen. Gedenkschrift für Peter Calmeyer,* edited by Reinhard Dittmann, pp. 155–166. Ugarit-Verlag, Münster.
  2003 Gōdarz. *Encyclopaedia Iranica online,* www.iranica.com.

Canepa, Matthew
  2009 *The Two Eyes of the Earth: Art and Ritual of Kingship between Rome and Sasanian Iran.* The Transformation of the Classical Heritage 45. University of California Press, Berkeley.
  2010a Theorizing Cross-Cultural Interaction Among Ancient and Early Medieval Visual Cultures. In *Theorizing Cross-Cultural Interaction among the Ancient and Early Medieval Mediterranean, Near East and Asia,* edited by Matthew Canepa, pp. 7–19. Ars Orientalis 38. Smithsonian Institution, Washington D.C.

2010b Technologies of Memory in Early Sasanian Iran: Achaemenid Sites and Sasanian Identity. *American Journal of Archaeology* 114(4): 563–596.

2010c Achaemenid and Seleukid Royal Funerary Practices and Middle Iranian Kingship. In *Commutatio et Contentio: Studies in the Late Roman, Sasanian, and Early Islamic Near East in Memory of Zeev Rubin,* edited by Henning Börm and Josef Wiesehöfer, pp. 1–21. Wellem Verlag, Düsseldorf.

2013   Sasanian Rock Reliefs. *Oxford Handbook of Ancient Iran,* edited by Daniel T. Potts, pp. 856–877. Oxford University Press, Oxford and New York.

Callieri, Pierfrancesco

2006   Water in the Art and Architecture of the Sasanians. In *Proceedings of the 5th Conference of the Societas Iranologica Europæa,* edited by Antonio Panaino and Andrea Piras, Vol. 1, pp. 339–349, plates XXXIII–XXXVI. Mimesis, Milano.

Carter, Martha

1981   Mithra on the Lotus: A Study of the Imagery of the Sun God in the Kushano-Sasanian Era. *Acta Iranica* 21: 74–97.

de Waele, Eric

1989   L'Investiture et le triomphe dans la thématique de la sculpture rupestre Sassanide. In *Archaeologica Iranica et Orientalis: Miscellanea in Honorem Louis Vanden Berghe,* edited by Léon De Meyer and Ernie Haerinck, pp. 811–826. Iranica Antiqua, Ghent.

Duchesne-Guillemin, Jacques

1982   Ahriman. *Encyclopaedia Iranica* 1: 670–673.

Dörner Friedrich Karl, and Rudolf Naumann

1939   *Forschungen in Kommagene.* Istanbuler Forschungen 10. Archäologisches Institut des Deutschen Reiches, Berlin.

Downey, J. Glanville

1961   *A History of Antioch in Syria.* Princeton University Press, Princeton.

Erciyas, D. Burcu Arikan

2006   *Wealth, Aristocracy and Royal Propaganda under the Hellenistic Kingdom of the Mithradatids.* Colloquia Pontica 12. Brill, Leiden.

Facella, Margherita

2006   *La dinastia degli Orontidi nella Commagene ellenistico-romana.* Studi ellenistici 17. Giardini, Pisa.

Feldman, Marian

2007   Darius I and the Heroes of Akkad: Affect and Agency in the Bisitun Relief. In *Ancient Near Eastern Art in Context: Studies in Honor of Irene J. Winter by her Students,* edited by Jack Cheng and Marian H. Feldman, pp. 265–294. Brill, Leiden and Boston.

Fleischer, Robert

2009   The Rock-tombs of the Pontic Kings in Amaseia (Amasya). In *Mithridates VI and the Pontic Kingdom,* edited by Jakob Munk Højte, pp. 109–119. Aarhus Universitetsforlag, Aarhus.

Fukai Shinji, and Kiyoharu Horiuchi

1969–1972   *Taq-i Bustan.* Tokyo University Iraq-Iran Archaeological Expedition Reports 10 and 13 (2 vols.). Tokyo Institute of Oriental Culture, University of Tokyo, Tokyo.

Garrison, Mark B.

2009   Visual Representation of the Divine and the Numinous in Early Achaemenid Iran:
        Old Problems, New Directions. In *Iconography of Demons and Deities in the Ancient
        Near East,* edited by webmaster Jürg Eggler. A Research Project of the History of
        Religions Chair of the University of Zurich in co-operation with Brill Academic
        Publishers, Leiden.
        http://www.religionswissenschaft.uzh.ch/idd/prepublication.php (accessed Nov. 6,
        2010).

Ghasemi, Parsa

2009   The Sassanid Road between Bishapur and Borazjan in Ancient Fars Province, Iran.
        Antiquity 83.321. http://antiquity.ac.uk/antiquityNew/projgall/ghasemi321/

Ghirshman, Roman

1950   Notes iraniennes III: A propos des bas-reliefs rupestres Sassanides. *Artibus Asiae* 13:
        90–96.

1956   *Fouilles de Châpour: Bîchâpour.* Geuthner, Paris.

1971   *Fouilles de Châpour: Bîchâpour.* Vol. 1. Musée du Louvre, Département des
        antiquités orientales, Série archéologique 7. Geuthner, Paris.

Grenet, Frantz

2005   Découverte d'un relief sassanide dans le nord de l'Afghanistan. *Comptes rendus des
        séances des Académie des inscriptions et belles-lettres (2005)*: 115–134.

Grenet, Frantz, Jonathon Lee, Philippe Martinez, and François Ory

2007   The Sasanian Relief at Rag-i Bibi (Northern Afghanistan). In *After Alexander:
        Central Asia before Islam,* edited by Georgina Herrmann and Joe Cribb, pp.
        243–267. Proceedings of the British Academy 133. The British Academy, Oxford
        University Press, London and Oxford.

Grigor, Talinn

2009   Orientalism and Mimicry of Selfness: Archeology of the Neo-Achaemenid Style.
        In *Les orientalismes en architecture à l'épreuve des savoirs archéologiques, historiques,
        techniques et artistiques,* edited by Nabila Oulebsir and Mercedes Volait, pp.
        273–291. Picard, Paris.

Haerinck, Ernie

1975   Quelques monuments funéraires de l'île de Kharg dans le Golfe Persique. *Iranica
        Antiqua* 11: 44–167.

2005   Tang-e Sarvak. *Encyclopaeda Iranica online,* www.iranica.com.

Haerinck Ernie, and Bruno Overlaet

2009   The Sasanian Rock Relief of Bahram II at Guyum (Fars, Iran). *Iranica Antiqua* 44:
        531–558.

Hansman, John

1998   Elymaïs. *Encyclopaedia Iranica* 8: 373–376.

Herrmann, Georgina

1980   *The Sasanian Rock Reliefs at Bishapur I, Bishapur III, Triumph Attributed to Shapur
        I.* Iranische Denkmäler 9. Dietrich Reimer Verlag, Berlin.

1981   *The Sasanian Rock Reliefs at Bishapur 2: Bishapur IV, Bahram II Receiving a Delegation, Bishapur V, The Investiture of Bahram I, Bishapur VI, The Enthroned King.* Iranische Denkmäler 10. Dietrich Reimer Verlag, Berlin.

1983   *The Sasanian Rock Reliefs at Bishapur 3: Bishapur I, The Investiture/Triumph of Shapur I and Sarab-I Bahram, Bahram II Enthroned; The Rock Relief at Tang-I Qandil.* Iranische Denkmäler 11. Dietrich Reimer Verlag, Berlin.

Herrmann Georgina, and Rosalind Howell

1977   *Naqsh-i Rustam 5 and 8, Sasanian Reliefs Attributed to Hormuzd II and Narseh.* Iranische Denkmäler 8. Dietrich Reimer Verlag, Berlin.

Herrmann, Georgina, David Neil Mackenzie, and Rosalind Howell

1989   *The Sasanian Reliefs at Naqsh-i Rustam, Naqsh-i Rustam 6, The Triumph of Shapur I.* Iranische Denkmaler 13. Dietrich Reimer Verlag, Berlin.

Howard, Peter, Ian Thompson, and Emma Waterton

2013   *The Routledge Companion to Landscape Studies.* Routledge, London and New York.

Huff, Dietrich

1970   Zur Rekonstruktion des Turmes von Fīrūzābād. *Istanbuler Mitteilungen* 19/20: 319–338.

1972   Der Takht-i Nīshīn in Fīrūzābād. *Archäologischer Anzeiger* 87: 517–540.

1976   Survey and Excavation in Qal'eh Doxtor-Fīrūzābād. In *Proceedings of the 4th Annual Symposium on Archaeological Research in Iran 1975*, edited by Firouz Bagherzadeh, pp. 391–403. Iranian Center for Archaeological Research, Tehran.

2004   Archaeological Evidence of Zoroastrian Funerary Practices. In *Zoroastrian Rituals in Context*, edited by Michael Stausberg, pp. 593–630. Brill, Leiden and Boston.

2008   Formation and Ideology of the Sasanian State in Context with Archaeological Evidence. In *The Sasanian Era*, edited by Vesta Sarkhosh Curtis and Sarah Stewart, pp. 31–59. I.B. Tauris, London and New York.

Huff, Dietrich, and Phillipe Gignoux

1976   Ausgrabungen auf Qal'a-ye Dukhtar bei Firuzabad 1976. *Archäologische Mitteilungen aus Iran und Turan n.s.* 11: 117–150.

Isidore of Charax

[1914]   *Parthian Stations*, edited by Wilfred H. Schoff. Commercial Museum, Philadelphia.

Kawami, Trudy

1987   *Monumental Art of the Parthian Period in Iran.* Acta Iranica 26. Brill, Leiden.

Kleiss, Wolfram

1970   Zur Topographie des Partherhangs in Bisotun. *Archäologische Mitteilungen aus Iran* 3: 133–168.

1996   Der Sogenannte Partherhang. In *Bisutun: Ausgrabungen and Forschungen in den Jahren 1963–1967*, edited by Wolfram Kleiss and Peter Calmeyer, pp. 73–84. Mann Verlag, Berlin.

Koch, Klaus

2002   Persisch-hellenistischer Synkretismus am Beispiel Kommagene mit einem Seitenblick auf Israel. In *Religion und Religionskontakte im Zeitalter der Achämeniden*, edited by Reinhard Gregor Kratz, pp. 281–301. Chr. Kaiser, Gütersloh.

Levit-Tawil, Dalia
   1993   Re-Dating the Sasanian Reliefs at Tang-e Qandil and Barm-e Dilak: Composition
          and Style as Dating Criteria. *Iranica Antiqua* 28: 31–49.

Lincoln, Bruce
   1989   *Discourse and the Construction of Society: Comparative Studies of Myth, Ritual, and
          Classification.* Oxford University Press, Oxford.
   1999   *Theorizing Myth: Narrative, Ideology, and Scholarship.* University of Chicago Press,
          Chicago.
   2007   *Religion, Empire, and Torture: The Case of Achaemenian Persia, with a Postscript on
          Abu Ghraib.* University of Chicago Press Chicago.
   2012   *"Happiness for Mankind": Achaemenian Religion and the Imperial Project.* Leuven,
          Peeters.

Luft, J.Paul
   2001   The Qajar Rock-reliefs. *Iranian Studies* 34: 31–49.

Luschey, Heinz
   1974   Bisutun. Geschichte und Forschungsgeschichte. *Archäologischer Anzeiger* 114–49.
   1990   Bīsotūn ii: Archaeology. *Encyclopaedia Iranica* 4: 291–299.
   1996a Die Felsabarbeitung des Farhad ("Tarrash-e Farhad"). In *Bisutun: Ausgrabungen and
          Forschungen in den Jahren 1963–1967*, edited by Wolfram Kleiss and Peter Calmeyer,
          pp. 117–20. Mann Verlag, Berlin.
   1996b Taq-i Bostan. In *Bisutun: Ausgrabungen and Forschungen in den Jahren 1963–1967*,
          edited by Wolfram Kleiss and Peter Calmeyer, pp. 121–30. Mann Verlag, Berlin.

McGing, Brian C.
   1986   *The Foreign Policy of Mithridates VI Eupator, King of Pontus.* Brill, Leiden.

Messina, Vito, and Jafar Mehrkian
   2011a Iranian-Italian Joint Expedition in Khuzistan: 2nd Campaign. Laser Scanning of the
          Hung-e Azhdar, Hung-e Yaralivand, Hung-e Kamalvand Rock Reliefs, Topography
          of the Valley of Hung-e Azhdar and Trial Trenches near the Boulder of Hung-e
          Azhdar (February 9–March 2, 2009). http://www.parthia.com/khuzistan/2nd_
          campaign_photos.pdf [File updated June, 28, 2011].
   2011b Archaeological Researches at Hung-e Azhdar (Izeh, Khuzestan). Paper presented at
          the 7th European Conference of Iranian Studies, Krakow, Poland. Sept. 8, 2011.

Miller, Margaret
   2002   Greece ii: Greco-Persian Cultural Relations. *Encyclopaedia Iranica online*, www.
          iranica.com.

Mittag, Franz Peter
   2011   Zur Entwicklung des "Herrscher-" und "Dynastiekultes" in Kommagene. In *Studien
          zum vorhellenistischen und hellenistischen Herrscherkult: Verdichtung und Erweiterung
          von Traditionsgeflechten*, edited by Linda-Marie Günther and Sonja Plischke, pp.
          141–160. Verlag Antike, Berlin.

Mousavi, Ali
   2002   Persepolis in Retrospect: Histories of Discovery and Archaeological Exploration at
          the Ruins of Ancient Parseh. *Ars Orientalis* 32: 209–251.

Movassat, Johannah Domela

2005   *The Large Vault at Taq-i Bustan: A Study in Late Sasanian Royal Art*. Mellen Studies in Archaeology 3. Edwin Mellen Press, Lewiston.

Nelson, Robert, and Margaret Olin (eds.)

2003   *Monuments and Memory, Made and Unmade*. University of Chicago Press, Chicago.

Overlaet, Bruno

2009a   A Himyarite Diplomatic Mission to the Sasanian Court of Bahram II. *Arabian Archaeology and Epigraphy* 20.2: 218–222.

2009b   A Roman Emperor at Bishapur and Darabgird: Uranius Antoninus and the Black Stone of Emesa. *Iranica Antiqua* 44: 461–530.

2010   Flower and Fire Altar: Fact and Fiction on the Barm-i Dilak Rock Reliefs. *Iranica Antiqua* 45: 337–352.

2011   Ardashir II or Shapur III? Reflections on the Identity of a King in the Smaller Grotto at Taq-i Bustan. *Iranica Antiqua* 46: 235–250.

2013   And Man Created God? Kings, Priests and Gods on Sasanian Investiture Reliefs. *Iranica Antiqua* 48: 313–54.

Potts, Daniel T.

1999   *The Archaeology of Elam*. Cambridge University Press, Cambridge.

2004   Kharg Island. *Encyclopaedia Iranica online*, www.iranica.com.

Postgate, J. Nicholas, and Michael D. Roaf

1997   The Shaikhan Relief. *al-Rāfidān* 18: 143–156.

Renan, Ernest

1865   Note sur les sculptures colossales du mont Stavrin, à Antioche. *Comptes rendus des séances de l'Académie des inscriptions et belles-lettres (Paris)* 9: 307–310.

Robert, Louis

1963   Review of Peter M. Fraser, *Samothrace 2.1: Inscriptions on Stone*. *Gnomon* 35: 50–79.

Rodning, Chris

2010   Place, Landscape, and Environment: Anthropological Archaeology in 2009. *American Anthropologist* 112: 180–190.

Schippmann, Klaus

1971   *Die iranischen Feuerheiligtümer*. Religionsgeschichtliche Versuche und Vorarbeiten 31. De Gruyter, Berlin.

Schmidt, Erich F.

1940   *Flights over Ancient Cities of Iran*. University of Chicago Press, Chicago.

1953   *Persepolis*, Vol. 1. University of Chicago Oriental Institute Press Publications 68. University of Chicago Press, Chicago.

1957   *Persepolis*, Vol. 2. University of Chicago Oriental Institute Press Publications 69. University of Chicago Press, Chicago.

1970   *Persepolis*, Vol. 3. University of Chicago Oriental Institute Press Publications 70. University of Chicago Press, Chicago.

Schmidt, Rüdiger

1990   Bīsotūn i: Introduction. *Encyclopaedia Iranica online*, www.iranica.com.

Seidl, Ursula

1976   Ein Relief Dareios' I in Babylon. *Archäologische Mitteilungen aus Iran und Turan* n.s. 9: 125–130.

1999   Ein Monument Darius' I. aus Babylon. *Zeitschrift für Assyriologie und Vorderasiatische Archäologie* 89: 101–114.

Shafer, Ann

2007   Assyrian Royal Monuments on the Periphery: Ritual and the Making of Imperial Space. In *Ancient Near Eastern Art in Context: Studies in Honor of Irene J. Winter by her Students,* edited by Jack Cheng and Marian H. Feldman, pp. 133–59. Brill, Leiden.

Shahbazi, A.Shapur

1975   *The Irano-Lycian Monuments.* Institute of Achaemenid Research Publications 2. Kayhan Press, Tehran.

1985   Studies in Sasanian Prosopography II: The Relief of Ardašēr II at Ṭāq-e Bostān. *Archäologische Mitteilungen aus Iran* 18: 181–185.

Soudavar, Abolala

2009   The Vocabulary and Syntax of Iconography in Sasanian Iran. *Iranica Antiqua* 44: 417–60.

Summers, Geoffrey D.

1993   Archaeological Evidence for the Achaemenid Period in Eastern Turkey. *Anatolian Studies* 43: 85–108.

Tanabe, Katsumi (ed.)

1998   *Sculptures of Commagene Kingdom.* Tokyo: Ancient Orient Museum.

Thompson, Emma

2008   Composition and Continuity in Sasanian Rock Reliefs. *Iranica Antiqua* 43: 299–358.

Trümpelmann, Leo

1975   Triumph über Julian Apostata. *Jahrbuch für Numismatik und Geldgeschichte* 25: 108–110.

Tubach, Jean-Pierre

1995   Herakles vom Berge Sanbulos. *Ancient Society* 26: 241–271.

Vanden Berghe, Loius

1980   Lumière nouvelle sur l'interprétation de reliefs sassanides. *Iranica Antiqua* 15: 269–282.

1981–95   *Bibliographie analytique de l'archéologie de l'Iran ancien: Supplément.* 3 Vols. Brill, Leiden.

1983   *Reliefs rupestres de l'Iran ancien.* Musées Royaux d'Art et d'Histoire, Brussels.

1987   L'heritage Parthe dans l'art Sasanide. In *Transitional Periods in Iranian History: actes du Symposium de Fribourg-en-Brisgau (22–24 mai 1985),* edited by P.H. Gignoux, pp. 241–52. Studia Iranica, Cahier 5. Association pour l'avancement des études iraniennes, E. Peeters, Leuven.

Vanden Berghe, Loius, and Klaus Schippmann

1985   *Les Reliefs rupestre d'Elymaïde, Irān de l'époque Parthe.* Acta Iranica Supplement 3. Iranica Antiqua, Gent.

von Gall, Hubertus

1978 Die Kulträume in den Felsen von Karaftu bei Takab (West-Azarbaidjan). *Archäologische Mitteilungen aus Iran und Turan n.s.* 11: 91–112.

1988 Das Felsgrab von Qizqapan. Ein Denkmal aus dem Umfeld der achämenidischen Königstrasse. *Baghdader Mitteilungen* 19: 557–582.

1996a Die parthischen Felsreliefs unterhalb des Dariusmonumentes. In *Bisutun: Ausgrabungen and Forschungen in den Jahren 1963–1967*, edited by Wolfram Kleiss and Peter Calmeyer, pp. 61–71. Mann Verlag, Berlin.

1996b Der große Reliefblock am sog. Partherhang. In *Bisutun: Ausgrabungen and Forschungen in den Jahren 1963–1967*, edited by Wolfram Kleiss and Peter Calmeyer, pp. 84–88. Mann Verlag. Berlin.

2009 Karafto Caves. *Encyclopaedia Iranica online*, www.iranica.com.

Wagner, Jörg

2000 *Gottkönige am Euphrat: neue Ausgrabungen und Forschungen in Kommagene.* Philipp von Zabern, Mainz am Rhein.

Waldmann, Helmut

1973 *Die Kommagenischen Kultereformen unter König Mithradates I Kallinikos und seinem sohne Antiochos I.* Brill, Leiden.

Wiesehöfer, Josef

1995 *Ancient Persia from 550 B.C. to 650 A.D.* I.B. Tauris, New York and London.

2007 King, Court and Royal Representation in the Sasanian Empire. In *The Court and Court Society in Ancient Monarchies*, edited by Antony J.S. Spawforth, pp. 58–79. Cambridge University Press, Cambridge.

Winter, Engelbert (ed.)

2008 *Patris pantrophos Kommagene: neue Funde und Forschungen zwischen Taurus und Euphrat.* Asia Minor Studien 60. Habelt, Bonn.

— 6 —

Other Monumental Lessons

Ian Straughn

The varied Muslim polities and societies that would come to dominate much of the Near East and Mediterranean showed little enthusiasm for the monumental relief carving displayed by their various imperial predecessors, particularly that of the Sasanians. The "living rock" had lost its luster as a canvas on which to provide commentary about matters of authority, legitimacy, and power through its sculpted transformations. This is not to say that there was an absence of lithic appreciation in the emerging Islamic tradition. Indeed, two of its most important ritual monuments, the *kaaba* in Mecca that houses the sacred "black stone" (*al-hajr al-aswad*), and the Dome of the Rock in Jerusalem, testify to continued lapidary engagements. For these reflections on Canepa's article my plan is not to explain the general abstention within most Muslim societies from drawing on rocks. Nor will I examine the exceptions to this rule. Both would certainly be worthy projects. They are ones which other scholars have treated from a variety of angles, often from the perspective of the presumed aniconic, and often iconoclastic tendency within Islamic visual culture. Instead, I have chosen to investigate what happens to such monuments as they are inherited by a new civilizational tradition. My interest is to move beyond discussions of iconoclasm and to consider, instead, a number of arguments that have advocated leaving the stone alone. The potential for cultivating a physical disengagement with the material past lies in its ability to forge new lessons out of the complex interplay of remembrance and occlusion, presence and absence, action and avoidance.

The relationship between the fledgling Muslim imperial polity and its predecessor Sasanian Empire was marked by some particularly stony engagements that emerged from the conquest of the Persian state by the upstart Arab forces. One that is particularly instructive is recounted by the fourteenth-century Muslim philosopher of history Ibn Khaldūn in his landmark work *al-Muqaddimah* or "An Introduction to a Universal History." In a section where he reflects on the role of monuments as an important component of royal authority and the establishment of dynastic rule, he tells the story of how the early ninth-century Abbasid Caliph Harūn al-Rashīd attempted to tear down the monumental reception hall of the Sasanian King (*iwān Kisrā*). The caliph was himself a prodigious patron of large-scale building projects both within the capital, Baghdad, and elsewhere in the expanding Islamic Empire during a period often labeled as the golden age of early Islam (nearly a century and a half after the initial conquests). In this scenario we are told by Ibn Khaldūn that the caliph sought the advice from a former official, now imprisoned, on whether his intention to destroy this particular structure was a worthwhile endeavor. This jailed courtier, a certain Yahyā ibn Khālid whose offence cannot be detailed here, counseled that the caliph should refrain from this enterprise because such a monument demonstrated the glory of his ancestors who succeeded in its capture, thereby already appropriating the authority of the Sasanians who had built it in the first place. Not persuaded by the logic of this argument, and mistrustful of its purveyor, at least according to our narrator, Harun al-Rashid, nevertheless, gave orders for the demolition to take place. Despite the many efforts of his engineers, their attempts at leveling the building failed. Even vinegar, we learn, was no match for what the Sasanian monarch could erect from the ashlars his workmen had quarried and the bricks they had once manufactured.

The story, however, does not end there. The caliph returns to Yahyā hoping to salvage his disgrace and again seeks his advice about whether to persist in this affair. Al-Rashid is now told that he dare not quit lest he, the Commander of the Faithful and an Arab, demonstrate that he was powerless to obliterate that which the non-Arabs had built. Large portions of this structure still stand today at the site of Ctesiphon (medieval *Taysafūn*, modern *al-Mada'in*) and offer their testimony to caliphal impotence in the matter. As a preface to this account, Ibn Khaldūn put forward the claim that it is far easier and far less a demonstration of one's power and authority to destroy something than to have constructed it in the first place. Thus a monument that could have served as a marker for the strength of the Abbasid dynasty had now become a symbol of its weakness.

Ibn Khaldūn finds this episode of Harūn al-Rashīd and Khusraw's monument so illuminating for the workings of "royal authority" (*mulk*) that he discusses it in two separate sections. In its second and longer iteration, he offers several other examples of similar botched deconstruction jobs to make clear that this was not a historical anomaly, but rather a useful metric of dynastic power for the comparative historian. While Ibn Khaldūn will focus on the failings of the ruler, I want to analyze more closely the advice that he rejected. Yahyā Ibn Khālid, perhaps sitting cross-legged, smiling smugly on the dirt-packed floor of his rather dingy cell in some forgotten corner of the palace, advises to do nothing, to leave the monument untouched. To refrain, to stay one's hand, was the more powerful and authoritative act.

The former minister's counsel, put him at odds with a well-established, although variously practiced, Islamic iconoclasm. This form of engagement with the material past, one marked by erasure and absence, has often been understood as a means of silencing such monuments and enforcing a posture of forgetting. But is the work of the iconoclast necessarily the antithesis to the kinds of memory-making abilities for which Canepa has argued with the monumental Iranian rock reliefs analyzed in this volume? If this was the intention of our Abbasid caliph, then, indeed, he failed miserably. However, such destructive acts, be they the breaking of idols, the defacing of images, or the razing of monuments are far more effective in how they draw attention to the object whose absence is to be effected. Call to mind such recent examples as the Bamiyan Buddhas, the Babri Masjid, or Bahrain's Pearl Monument. If such monuments were not so worthy of remembrance, then they would not serve as useful canvases for the display of power by their destruction. Should we forget that they ever existed, it would hardly be worthwhile to have brought about their disappearance.

Harūn al-Rashīd's big mistake, then, was to have drawn attention to the monumental landscape of the once-vanquished Sasanian Empire. In so doing he thought to breathe new life into this structure, attributing to it a level of authority and power that he could then appropriate through its leveling. This was not an act of forgetting or occlusion, but of resuscitation and recognition. Ultimately it did backfire, and the lesson that was to be drawn never materialized.

Enter here another voice on the destruction of monuments as recorded by the thirteenth-century scholar al-Idrisī in his text on the Pyramids of Giza and their secrets. He records the following account from an earlier Muslim traveler to the Theban ruins who writes:

> Look, son, what the Pharaohs built and how it is being destroyed by these idiots. Nothing is more tragic and sad than the loss of what these ruins offer to those who would regard them and consider their lessons... What sort of wisdom preaches that these ruins should be removed from the face of the Earth? [cited in Colla 2007: 88].

This unnamed traveler calls upon his Muslim brethren to refrain from destroying these accretions of stone and, instead, to regard them as lessons (*'ibār* or, literally, "considerations"). Later he explains to his progeny that

they were specifically left unharmed by the Companions of the Prophet
Muhammad who passed through this region during the period of the early
Muslim conquests in order to serve those who would be seekers of knowledge.
How does this then compare to the advice of Yahyā ibn Khālid? Both support
a hands-off engagement with the material past – one that neither re-places
nor re-moves, but re-minds. However, their objects of remembrance are
quite different. For ibn Khālid the worldly machinations of "royal authority"
and imperial might are still an active lesson to be learned from the story of
Khusraw's reception hall and its status at that time as a captured landmark.
That the Caliph was unconvinced, and that this would then lead to his
disgrace would only prove the point. However, for our Theban visitor such
monuments of stone are valuable because their presence recalls the absence of
the Pharaonic kingdoms which created them. They are reminders that such
worldly things are no protection from the other-worldly fate which awaits
us all within the prevailing Islamic eschatological paradigm.

In each of these narratives there is a lesson to be learned from avoiding a
physical relationship with the stones of the past in favor of a contemplative
one. However, the lesson plan, as it were, is not the same. It is tempting
to read these accounts as evidence of vernacular forms of a preservationist
mentality that might serve to counter the destructive potential of iconoclastic
ideologies, nationalist and imperialist narratives, or the desire for material
resources. Yet such a set of agendas does not seem appropriate to either our
Upper Egyptian traveler or our incarcerated Abbasid minister. For the former
these particular acts of destruction are markers of ignorance, a failure to
recognize the potential of the divine to speak through material signs (āyāt)
that demand attention and reflection, while for the latter such efforts at
obliteration are neither efficacious nor sophisticated. The introduction of
brute force is not a necessary requirement for the continued legitimization
of authority. Rather, the advice is to let the monument speak for itself within
a particular discursive frame that has already become materially manifested
around it.

What are we to make of these other possible monumental lessons? What,
in fact, is the lesson that can emerge from material practices that advocate a
"do nothing" stance? This, of course, is a strategic misrepresentation on my
part. The deliberate absence of an action that would leave a physical trace, an
archaeological record as it were, is still something. Indeed, in both cases not
only is there a call for abstinence from destruction, but also the promotion
of an active cultivation of a disposition towards the material world whether
it tends toward a contemplative or more discursive engagement. Such
dispositions are not necessarily devoid of material consequences. They can
unleash the ravages of time, those taphonomic processes of ruination from

which Arab poets, Sufi mystics, religious scholars, and others have drawn inspiration and fashioned lessons. Similarly landscapes filled with the traces of past human efforts become a reservoir, a resource that might later become deployed in arguments that enfold the complex interplay of the historical, the political, the territorial, and the ideological dimensions of legitimacy.

Ultimately, I want to suggest that archaeologists do themselves a disservice when they become content to transform their objects of study into sites of memory, with the hope that this is a sufficient analysis. Memory strikes me as a much more valuable starting place than an end point. Such memories are the building blocks for a much richer story of the lessons that are supposed to be learned and the ones that are actually gained. Moreover this is not static. What is so exciting is that the monuments, rock reliefs, natural places, and others that serve as our teachers themselves mature and change with the world they inhabit. Their lessons are not always the same. At times they might be mute, while at other moments they can be quite vocal. Sometimes they might speak quite softly and it is incumbent upon us to listen carefully lest they truly become absent and forgotten. Here I might call our attention to those times, for instance, when the rock face is consciously not faced with the chisel of the sculptor and left unadorned. And then there are moments when our teachers are simply loud and overbearing and speak more like high-pressure salesmen. We, as archaeologists who are often in the position of authority (whether well-deserved or not is a matter of debate) to translate their words, might be well advised to close our ears to the propaganda, or at least attempt to analyze its agenda. Not all lessons will be equally valuable or desirable; however, there is certainly a need to consider just how to cultivate them and discuss our responsibilities for how and when to record them.

References

Colla, Elliott
    2007 *Conflicted Antiquities: Egyptology, Egyptomania, Egyptian Modernity*. Duke University Press, Durham, NC.

Rock-Reliefs of Ancient Iran:
Notes and Remarks

Ali Mousavi

Matthew Canepa's thoughtful article on the rock-reliefs of ancient Iran focuses on later periods of Iranian history in connection with the author's field of specialty, i.e., the Hellenistic, Roman, and early medieval periods. It provides a stimulating synthesis of the practice of carving monumental reliefs, but the author places less emphasis on two important aspects: the essentially Iranian character of this kind of art, and the history of studies on the rock-reliefs of ancient Iran.

The rock-reliefs of ancient Iran were visited first in the seventeenth century. Jean-Bapstiste Tavernier, the French businessman and traveler, was the first to mention the reliefs at Taq-e Bustan and at Barm Delak near Shiraz. Another Frenchman, the celebrated Jean Chardin, left us a substantial description of the Achaemenid and Sasanian monuments in Fars, including the rock-reliefs at Naqsh-e Rustam. Chardin's skillful painter, Grelot, produced the first reliable views of these monuments. As for the reliefs at Bisutun, Guillaume-Antoine Olivier was a pioneer in publishing, from his travels during 1792–98, sketches of the monumental reliefs of Darius the Great and also that of the Parthian ruler, Gotarz. The full history of the exploration and study of the Iranian rock-reliefs is yet to be written.

A glance at the multitude of rock-reliefs in Southwest Asia shows that the practice of carving rock-reliefs indeed originated in the mountains of western Iran. The four Lulubi reliefs at Sar-e Pol-e Zohab on the westernmost ridge of the Iranian Plateau are the earliest of their kind, going back to the third millennium B.C. These reliefs as well as the Elamite rock-reliefs in southern Iran served as prototype for later monumental reliefs until the sixth century B.C. A thorough examination of these early Zagros reliefs would have equipped both the author and the reader the better to tackle and understand the development of the practice of bas-reliefs and their function in ancient Iran.

The point of departure and inspiration for Canepa seems to be the relief of Darius the Great at Bisutun, carved sometime around 522/21 B.C. The reliefs and inscriptions of Darius the Great are the most important historical documents of the Achaemenid empire. According to the revisionist reassessment of the early phases of the history of the Achaemenid empire, Darius I is seen as a usurper who killed the second son of Cyrus, Bardiya, to seize the Achaemenid throne. The revisionist interpretation that questions the veracity of Darius's sayings in his inscriptions at Bisutun emanates from a distorted view that authentic ancient sources can be discarded for sensationalist reconstructions. The issue has been fully dealt with in some excellent publications by A. Shapur Shahbazi (2001).

The other issue, I think, is the relation between Achaemenid and Sasanian reliefs. A number of scholars have attempted to see continuity between the two. It should be made clear that the Achaemenid rupestral art and sculpture differs from preceding and succeeding rock-reliefs in both essence and form. The Bisutun relief is in line with the commemorative rock-reliefs of the Zagros region, namely the relief of Anubanini at Sar-e Pol-e Zohab. With the foundation of royal centers at Susa and Persepolis, the art of carving in relief departs from the previous tradition in that it became an integral part of the architecture. The reliefs carved on the jambs of the great stone door-frames of the palaces depict either the royal hero fighting fantastic creatures or the unnamed king walking with attendants. Even the audience scenes found in the Treasury showing the seated king and his crown prince do not bear any inscription or identification.

In contrast to Achaemenid reliefs, the Sasanian art of sculpture is temporal, highly personalized. The kings are either named or easily recognized by the form of their crowns. Some of the reliefs bear inscriptions. The other significant aspect of the Sasanian reliefs is their location, which is outside or in the proximity of urban centers. Locations such as the lower part of the cliff at Naqsh-e Rustam, the gorge at Naqsh-e Rajab or the cliffs on the rivers banks of Tangab and Bishapur were favored because of their symbolic value. No Sasanian relief is ever associated with the buildings of that period. As Herzfeld rightly pointed out some 70 years ago, the painting was the constituent factor and source of inspiration for Sasanian rock sculpture. It is why the bas-reliefs stand independently from architecture. Another interesting question is that most of the Sasanian rock-reliefs belong to the first 75 years of the period. Then, there is a gap of some 70 years before Shapur III (383–388) placed the panel depicting the image of his father and himself at Taq-e Bustan, near Kermanshah. The last rock-reliefs were carved more than 200 years later at Taq-e Bustan by Khosrow II (610–628). The reasons for this hiatus are unclear but it seems that crucial political events such as royal investiture or military victories occasioned the realization of rock reliefs. No major relief was carved after Shapur II, whose reign was marked with military prowess and victories. Surprisingly enough, no bas-relief is known from the reign of Kavad or Khosrow Anushirawan, whose reigns were also full of political turmoil and military exploits.

To sum up, Matthew Canepa's contribution provides an anthropological approach to the study of ancient Iranian rock-reliefs, which can be considered as the beginning of a new methodology for the one of the most extraordinary artistic accomplishments in ancient Iran.

References

Shahbazi, A. Shapur
    2001 Early Sasanians' Claim to Achaemenid Heritage. *Nāme-ye Irān-e Bāstān: The International Journal of Ancient Iranian Studies* 1: 61–74.

The Significance of Place: Rethinking Hittite Rock Reliefs in Relation to the Topography of the Land of Hatti

Lee Z. Ullmann

As to the pillars that Sesostris, king of Egypt, set up in the countries, most of them are no longer to be seen. But I myself saw them in the Palestine district of Syria, with the aforesaid writing and the women's private parts on them. Also, there are in Ionia two figures of this man carved in rock, one on the road from Ephesus to Phocaea, and the other on that from Sardis to Smyrna. In both places, the figure is over twenty feet high, with a spear in his right hand and a bow in his left, and the rest of his equipment proportional; for it is both Egyptian and Ethiopian; and right across the breast from one shoulder to the other a text is cut in the Egyptian sacred characters, saying: "I myself won this land with the strength of my shoulders." There is nothing here to show who he is and whence he comes, but it is shown elsewhere. Some of those who have seen these figures guess they are Memnon, but they are far indeed from the truth [Herodotus, Book 2.106.1–5].

Introduction

Sometime during the late 5th century B.C. Herodotus of Halicarnassus wrote that in Ionia he saw two figures carved on the natural rock, which he mistakenly attributed to Sesostris, King of Egypt. Although it has been known for over a century that the image Herodotus described is actually not of an Egyptian king but rather Hittite in nature, only recently was the hieroglyphic Luwian inscription that accompanies the image deciphered; it reads, "Tarkasnawa, King of Mira," a vassal of the Hittite Great King (Hawkins 1998). What is significant about Herodotus' observation is that people living in the Classical Greek world were cognizant that the land which they inhabited was marked with images of people and cultures that predated

Figure 8.1 Karabel, taken from *Voyage archéologique en Grèce et en Asie Mineure,*
by Philippe Le Bas, 1888, plate 59.

them by hundreds of years. From the passage one gets the sense that these monumental images were intended for propaganda and would have been visible to someone traveling on the road from Ephesus to Phocaea or from Sardis to Smyrna. If, however, one is to visit the monument today, despite the fact that the landscape has been altered since antiquity, it is rather difficult to see the carving from the road; the relief seems to be hidden in plain sight.

One can begin to deconstruct Herodotus' words and debate whether or not Herodotus actually *saw* the reliefs, or one could discuss whether the ancient and modern pass through the Tmolos mountain range (Boz Dağları) has changed over time. Yet such debate does not explain the simple fact that the relief, which is more than life-size, is not readily visible to the human eye from a short distance away.[1] This phenomenon of Hittite relief carvings being almost entirely hidden or meshed into the natural landscape is not unique to this relief in the Karabel pass; rather, it is a salient feature of Hittite rock-reliefs found throughout Anatolia. It is easy to be misled by the drawings of the early explorers to Anatolia, such as Le Bas and Texier, who portrayed the reliefs in an Orientalist romanticized manner with the images in clear view (Figure 8.1). However as early as 1890 Perrot and Chipiez report that:

...the mass of grayish white stone forms a bold foreground, and agreeably contrasts with the dark green of the forest-clad range of the Mahmoud Dagh, against which it leans. The rock upon which the carving occurs is perpendicular to the ravine; but as the figure stands in a recess it cannot be seen from the path immediately underlying it. To obtain the view of the annexed woodcut, it is necessary to walk to the southward until about to turn the corner of the rock [Perrot and Chipiez 1890: 227–228].

This pattern of portraying the reliefs in full view holds true even today with modern color publications that print photographs of the reliefs taken at an optimal time of year and day, with the carving taking up much of the viewing field (e.g., Ehringhaus 2005). These kinds of publications obfuscate both the function and the intended audience of the Hittite relief carvings. In the following discussion, I posit that the Hittites conceptually merged the natural landscape with images of their rulers and gods and thus established an imaginary network of lines that linked the settlements with places of ritual. I suggest that the monumental rock-cut images of the Hittites functioned in tandem with the natural environment as waypoints to demarcate the locations where specific rituals were performed.

The Hittite World

Since the rediscovery of the Hittites in the late 1800s, there has been a great deal of fascination with Hittite monumental rock carvings. In the preface to his book *The Hittites: The Story of a Forgotten Empire*, A.H. Sayce quotes W. Wright, who suggested a Hittite attribution for the Hama inscriptions as early as 1872 (Jean 2001: 162). In the quote, Wright laments the fact that we are unable "to unloose the dumb tongue of these inscriptions," and therefore we are unable to unlock their mysteries (Sayce 1890: 6). Though it is more than a century since the Hieroglyphic Luwian inscriptions, which accompany the reliefs, were deciphered, we are no closer in understanding what role the monumental images played. One factor that hinders our ability fully to comprehend the reliefs is our limited knowledge of Hittite geography. The Hittite archives provide hundreds of names of places, yet very few of these geographical names can be identified with the sites to which they belonged in the past. Although there have been many advances in the area of Hittite geography in the last two decades (for an overview, see Ullmann 2010), only a handful of sites can now be placed on a map unequivocally. In order to understand the function of the rock reliefs, I argue that we must first understand how the Hittite Kingdom was constructed spatially within the natural and cultural landscape of ancient Anatolia. The Hittites did not inhabit a previously unsettled environment; hence it needs to be emphasized that a process of selection occurred, whereby specific locales were chosen for habitation and others were not. Furthermore, the Hittites did not adhere to the purposeful distribution of site placement, conducive to trade, that was created in the Middle Bronze Age (Barjamovic 2005; 2008).

The constructed space of the Hittites was contingent on the natural environment of the Land of Hatti; this meant that the use of space was a reflection of how the Hittites saw themselves, as part of a larger triad that encompassed the gods, the human realm, and the natural environment. The Hittites were an agrarian and pastoral society, as much of Anatolia remains today, in which an undeniable relationship existed between the land and the people that depended on it for their survival. The majority of Hittite culture can be interpreted as having to do, in one way or another, with the environmental framework in which the lives of the Hittites unfolded (Gorny 1989: 81). Religion was one major aspect of Hittite culture based on the sheer amount of texts discovered related to cult, rituals, and/or festivals. Gary Beckman explains that:

> At its base, Hittite religion was concerned with the central preoccupation of peasant life on the central plateau: the fertility of the crops, domestic animals, and people... The chief deity retained the unmistakable features of a growth-sustaining storm god, even while presiding over the political structure of the Hittite Empire [1989: 99].

Amongst the "Thousand Gods of Hatti" many were directly linked to nature, such as the sun goddess, mountain gods, and river gods. The land was crucial to the Hittites of Anatolia and it permeated almost every aspect of their life.

For the human realm, we know that the king and the royal family acted as the intermediary between the gods and man. The king was given the Land of Hatti by the gods and it was his role to maintain order and see to its well-being. The king was the representative of the Sun God on earth and spent much of his year performing rituals and attending festivals in an attempt to appease the gods. Neither the king nor the people of Hatti could neglect the gods as they depended greatly on the good will of the gods for the fecundity of the land and the livestock and for precipitation to irrigate their fields. It is no coincidence that the major festivals took place during the beginning of the autumn and spring months, the crucial times of the agricultural calendar. The human and the godly realm are further connected. Upon his death the king himself became a god (Van den Hout 1994: 38). Thus, the godly, earthly, and natural zones are interconnected along a continuum without a strict separation between the zones. The gods were dependent on humans for sustenance, and humans were dependent on the gods to control nature in their favor – both thereby interdependent on the environment.

Hittite Locales as Defined by the Landscape:
A Note on the Methodology

To elucidate on the complex relationship between the Hittites and the environment in which they lived, the ancient textual record and Geographic Information Systems (henceforth GIS) may be employed. For a majority of the sites, only the foundations upon which the Hittites built their structures remain, yet through the landscape and the ancient texts one can begin to conceptualize the past. GIS allows one to model, visualize, and recreate the ancient landscape to provide a finite place for the imagined ancient space. However, it has its limitations. For example, GIS is only as good as the data sets being entered, which is difficult to assess when trying to account for changes in the landscape for such a large area and over a long span of time. Another limitation is that GIS is built on models and theories that apply to our modern western world. As Julian Thomas eloquently states:

> [t]he implication is that through our objective, high-tech methodologies we have access to a stratum of reality which was unavailable to people in the past. Their perceptions of these landscapes would necessarily have been distorted and impoverished versions of a reality which we can more fully grasp [2001: 171].

To understand the landscape through computer-generated models only and to make conclusions based on these models is inherently flawed. GIS has to be used as a tool to aid one's research, neither as a panacea for all problems nor as a system to create a reality that did not exist in the past (Gaffney 2006: 37–53). Thus, the rationale for implementing GIS in this study is to assist in the documentation of all of the distinct Hittite locales and to record them based on their spatial and topographic features. The application is necessary because of the large expanse of land that is being analyzed and the need to incorporate geographic data. Without such a program it would be extremely difficult to conceptualize such an enormous terrain holistically. Finally, with GIS the Land of Hatti can be studied in a 3-dimensional realm more similar to the manner in which the Hittites would have envisioned their homeland, rather than on a 2-dimensional map, which is a scholarly convention.

This discussion then begs the issue of how the Hittites envisaged Anatolia and its immediate surroundings. It goes without saying that their perception was significantly different from our modern abstract idea of what encompasses ancient Anatolia, thanks in part to satellite and aerial photography. However, this is not to say that the Hittites had no sense of the natural terrain. From the Hittite texts it is clear that they were cognizant of both the natural barriers and the foreign lands that surrounded them. A perfect example is the Sunashshura Treaty between Tudhaliya II and Sunashshura of Kizzuwatna

(CTH 41).[2] The treaty reads, "[I]n the direction of the sea the city of Lamiya belongs to His Majesty and the city of Bitura belongs to Sunashshura. The border district will be surveyed and divided between them. His Majesty may not fortify Lamiya" (CTH 41 Col. IV 40–42; translation from Beckman 1999: 24). The text continues to demarcate the frontiers based on mountains, rivers, and cities.

The corpus of Hittite treaties with vassal states is an excellent place to find descriptions of boundaries and at the same time to get insight on the manner in which the Hittites conceived of their own landscape; yet there are relatively few treaties that provide such detailed descriptions (Bryce 1986: 99). Although we will never be able to see the landscape entirely through the eyes of the Hittites, certain features and aspects of the terrain have not been wholly altered since the Late Bronze Age. Therefore, with the help of ancient texts, GIS, and archaeological survey and excavation as crutches, we are able to envision the Hittite landscape.

People are directly tied to the landscape. The conception of landscape needs to be understood as a network of related places that become significant to people through habitual activities and interactions. The affinity that has developed for some locations, through important events, festivals, rituals, and ceremonies, draws others to these same places, causing them to be remembered and incorporated into the lore of the land (Thomas 2001: 173; Harmanşah 2007: 180). Both GIS and ancient texts have been employed by other scholars to help reveal the past, though these studies have looked at the Hittite sites in isolation, often ignoring the relationship among settlements, shrines, relief carvings, and the natural topography.[3] Instead, one must consider the monumental images and settlement patterns as part of an ensemble of sites purposefully placed within the Hittite landscape. This comprehensive approach aims to identify correlations between the placement of the carvings and a greater imperial network of shrines and settlements connected to these rock reliefs.

One of the first comprehensive surveys of the ancient Hittite landscape was undertaken by a young British archaeologist, John Garstang, who set out on an expedition in 1907 across what is now the Republic of Turkey and subsequently published *The Land of the Hittites: An Account of Recent Explorations and Discoveries in Asia Minor, with Descriptions of the Hittite Monuments* (1910). This publication was among the first all-encompassing accounts of the geographical, philological, and art historical evidence about the Hittites. Garstang understood from the very outset that the problem of the reliefs was directly related to Hittite historical geography, an enormous problem to be faced by scholars interested in the new field of Hittitology. More recently Kay Kohlmeyer (1983), Dominik Bonatz (2007), Claudia

Glatz (2009), and Jürgen Seeher (2009) have all examined the reliefs as an interrelated corpus and have emphasized the need to examine the monumental images within a geopolitical context. The present study, which is an extension of my dissertation (Ullmann 2010), proposes to address the Hittite landscape by revisiting a statement made by John Garstang on the first page of his 1910 publication, where he poetically enumerates the difficulty of working within the context of the Hittite world. Yet he also inadvertently offers a solution:

> We must rely on the evidence afforded by the disposition of the Hittite monuments themselves. These cannot fix for us any certain boundaries, nor does the area throughout which they have as yet been found coincide with any great natural landmarks such as are wont to form the frontiers of nations [Garstang 1910: 1].

By focusing on the monuments themselves and their methodically chosen locations one can shed new light on the Hittite conception of natural and constructed space. That is to say, the location of the Hittite monumental rock reliefs needs to be understood as deliberate interventions in the landscape that were purposefully placed within the natural environment.

In total there are approximately 25 sites that contain Hittite monumental carvings, of which a little more than half are rock-cut reliefs that are hewn onto the natural terrain (Figure 8.2). These images are located throughout Anatolia, as far west as the mountains that rise over the Aegean coast to the Ceyhan River in the east, spanning an area of more than 800 km. The dating of the carvings is both unclear and controversial, yet one can argue with a great degree of certainty that they all date approximately to what has been dubbed the Hittite Empire period (c. 1350–1180 B.C.). These images and their inscriptions make up roughly a fourth of the known Hittite sites.[4] Hittite sites are defined as settlement sites, forts, dams, shrines, mountain passes, cemeteries, and any other location that has produced sufficient Hittite cultural material to warrant identification as Hittite.[5]

After visiting almost all of these sites and recording and mapping them with ArcGIS, a robust GIS program, one begins to see a standardization or a pseudo-standardization in site placement. Standardization is to be understood in accordance with Michael E. Smith's (2007) analysis of ancient urban planning that sees standardization in terms of coordination among places and spaces, focusing on formality and monumentality, access and visibility, and orientation. There are clear patterns in the location of the sites that indicated to me a sense and significance of placement. Moreover, the location of the sites cannot merely be attributed to utilitarian or practical purposes, such as being located on paths, as boundary markers, or for propagandistic reasons alone, as has been theorized up until present.

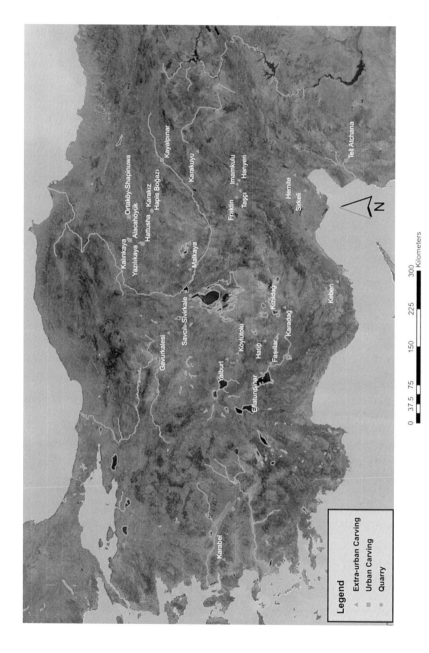

Figure 8.2 Map of Hittite rock reliefs, Fixed Stone Carvings, and Quarries (map generated by Lee Ullmann using ArcGIS).

Landscape Illuminated in the Textual Evidence

For the Hittites, landscape and ritual go hand-in-hand, whereby the concept of a Hittite landscape is rooted and contingent upon the natural terrain. It has been widely maintained that the rock-cut reliefs had some sort of cultic or ritual function. Thus to decode the true fabric of the Land of Hatti the carvings need to be examined in close relation to Hittite rituals as a way to elucidate the constructed landscape and vice versa. There is a great deal of Hittite textual material, much of which comments on the features of the landscape. Although few texts deal directly with the issue of the natural topography, enough can be extracted from the texts to get a sense of the Hittites' conception of their environment.

The description of various features of the landscape can be found in several of the textual genres, such as treaties, rituals, festivals, itineraries, and literature, to name but a few. Two examples that bear witness to the way in which the landscape was perceived by the Hittites and the importance of the natural terrain are Bo 86/299 and Bo 2004/1. Tablet Bo 86/299 is the only surviving example of a bronze tablet ever discovered in the Hittite world; it was found in 1986 during the course of German excavations of Hattusa, the Hittite capital, under a paved area just inside the Sphinx Gate:

> ...Up behind the city of Kusawanta, his frontier is the Stone Monument of the Dog. In the direction of the city of Ussa, his frontier is the city of Zarata, but Zarata belongs to the land of the Hulaya River. In the direction of the city of Wanzataruwa, his frontier is the city of Harazuwa, but Harazuwa belongs to the land of Ussa. In the direction of Mount Kuwakuwaliyatta, the city of Suttasna was made his frontier on my father's first treaty tablets, but it happened that later my father himself made the city Santimma the frontier. But Santimma belongs to the land of the Hulaya River. In the direction of the cities of Wanzataruwa and Kunzinasa, his frontier is Mount Arlanta and the city of Alana. Alana belongs to the land of the Hulaya River, but the water which is upon Mount Arlanta belongs jointly to Hatti and the land of the Hulaya River. In the direction of the city of Sinnuwanta, his frontier is Mount Lula and the Sphinx mountains, but the city of Ninainta belongs to the land of the Hulaya River. However, the service estate of the golden charioteer, which is behind (the city), belongs to My Majesty [translation from Beckman 1999: 115].

The excerpt is from a Hittite treaty between Tudhaliya IV (1237–1209 B.C.), the Hittite King, and Kurunta of Tarhuntassa, a Hittite Prince, and it illustrates that the Hittites were cognizant of their natural surroundings and used topographical features as markers or waypoints to demarcate their frontiers. Another aspect that is revealed in this text is that the Hittites are rather keen in distinguishing the mountain and the water which emanates from it.

In the second text, which does not fit precisely within any of the established genres, the utilization of features in the landscape as waypoints is even more evident. The tablet was found at Hattusa in 2004, in the area known as Sarıkale. Philologists have dated the text to the middle Hittite period. The text is 34 lines in length, including the colophon, and reads:

§ 1 Auf dem Weg der Stadt Shashshuna rechts:
Ein alter Turm.
Ein Ofen, *tittapaluant-*:oben (gelegen).
Der Berg Muranhila: der Berg ist rund (und) "gesalbt": oben (gelegen).

§ 2 Hirschhorn: eine krankheitbringende, trügerische Quelle.
Eine *shinahtura-*.
Sie sind drin im *Huuashi*-Heiligtum, behauene Steine.
Ihm ist ein Kornfeld (zugeordnet): oben (gelegen).

§ 3 In den Tiefen aber vier Quellen:
darunter (die Quellen) der bitter –süssen Münder der vier Frauen: vorne.

§ 4 Im *Huuashi*-Heiligtum aber sind sie drinnen, ein kleines (Quell-?)Gewässer
ein Ofen, *ashaliia-*.
Der Berg *Akkanhila*.
Der Weg [der Stadt *Sh*]*uuanzana*.
[Das –a]*lki* [des/r (-)]*hargasashshana-*.
Das *Huuashi*-Heiligtum der Stadt *Shalma*, [gr]oss??: rechts.
Das x-*ashkueshshar* der Stadt *Ukkiia*.
In einem Steinbruch: dunkle Steine.
Das *Huuashi*-Heiligtum der Stadt *Hupandahshuwa*.
Es ist (alles) hinter der Stadt.

§ 5 An grossen Steilhängen: *pandukishsha*, Buckel ein Turm.
Ein *Huuashi*-Gelände aber: nasse Feuchtgebiete?, mondförmiges kleines (Quell-?)Gewässer, *huuazzarani-*:vorne.
Ein Turm, der Berg *Tamuriia*, die Schleuse des Hirsches:
(alles) auf dem Weg der Stadt *Shashshuna* links.

§ 6 Diese Tafel schrieb *Ashkaliia*, der Schreiber, in *Hatti* vor *Labarna*, dem "Grossen" [Lorenz and Rieken 2007: 469].

We do not know where exactly the person that is describing the landscape is standing. However, the narrator of the text is presumably standing at some vantage point, all the while describing the natural features of the landscape in relation to cities and paths. This text shows that the Hittites had a good sense of not only the micro-landscape (the landscape in their immediate surroundings), but also the macro-landscape (the area they could not see). It can be gleaned from the description that the Hittites were able to think abstractly about their environment. In other words they were able to understand visually where cities and/or shrines were located in the landscape. The text is also interesting because of the amount of detail it provides to describe the terrain and the manner in which the information is provided. For instance, we are told the location of the city based on topographic features in the landscape such as mountains (Mount *Muranhila*, Mount *Akkanhila*, Mount *Tamuriia*), springs, monuments and stone features (*Huuashi*, quarry). The tablet is significant because it illustrates the Hittite manner of perceiving the landscape as a space comprised of markers to navigate and orient one's self.

Through an examination of the textual evidence it becomes apparent that the Hittites had an affinity for the environment in which they dwelled. This affinity goes beyond the pure fact that they lived in the picturesque highlands of Anatolia, as opposed to the lowlands of Mesopotamia. What can be deduced from the texts is that the natural features of Anatolia were being employed as a way for the Hittites to connect to their gods through ritual, and simultaneously as a tool to navigate through the landscape. In effect, the Hittites peopled their landscape with their gods. This is not to say that the Hittites were the only culture to make reference to the landscape. In the annals of the Assyrian King Shalmaneser I (1273–1244 B.C.), the language portrays the Assyrian army's advance in terms of the rugged terrain of the mountains, and differentiates between the varying schemes of both the topography and the cultural groups that they encountered (Ponchia 2004: 144). However, Shalmaneser I marks the introduction of this system of detailed geographical description for the Assyrians, whereas this style of painting an overtly descriptive picture of the landscape had already been established by the Hittites for over a century. In the earlier Assyrians texts the kings are boastful of their military achievements, yet devote very little effort to describing the areas which they have conquered.

Locating the Hittite Sites

In the following section, I review a representative corpus of textual evidence that discusses the manner in which the Hittites perceived their landscape. Although it is unclear from the texts which Hittite term or terms correspond directly to the monumental rock carvings, the rich archival textual material from Hittite sites, in conjunction with the images carved onto the living rock of Anatolia, allow one to investigate the interconnectivity and function of these monuments.[6] The similarities and patterns in the placement and topographical features of the landscape, not only among the sites but also between them, are telling. First, the majority of the sites, especially those that are located in the Hittite homeland, are all at or around the same elevation.

Based on data from British Naval Intelligence, the Anatolian plain is on average at an elevation of 1000 m (Great Britain Naval Intelligence Division 1942: 21), and many of the Hittite sites fall above 1000 m, with the majority located between 1100 and 1300 m. The Hittite locales all seem to lie on ridges or mountain flanks overlooking the plains below (Ökse 2007: 41). Also, many of the sites seem to be set back from the main pathways and are nestled into the surrounding topography, where the mountains serve to shield and limit the accessibility and visibility of the constructed space.

Secondly, when one begins to calculate "path," the distance between sites, it becomes evident that they are all located within a day's, if not two days', walk from one another. Most studies of Hittite sites have measured the distance between sites "as the crow flies" and neglected to deal with the topographic features of the landscape, which in Anatolia are crucial. This is one of the most difficult tasks to complete, because we do not have enough information on where the Hittites would have traveled, and on which paths. The least-cost path or pathway function is limited and makes assumptions based on our own perceptions of the way the Hittites would have traveled. Yet did the Hittites travel for the purpose of efficiency, for the purpose of security, or for the best route for wheeled vehicles (Bellavia 2006: 187)? Or did they travel based on the significance of place and the monuments associated with these places?

Several studies have been conducted to calculate/assess the distance one could travel in a one-day journey in the Late Bronze Age. Albrecht Goetze (1957) proposed rather early on that, from the description of the *nuntariyashas*-festival, the king's yearly journey, he could travel up to 80 km a day. This calculation is a bit too high for a pre-modern society. It is possible to suggest that an average day's travel was closer to 20–25 km, with a maximum of 30 km on consecutive days, coinciding with Tuba Ökse's (2007: 41) findings for the distance between sites in the upper Kızılırmak region. In the spring of 2007, in an attempt to test the average distance one could walk in the hilly terrain of central Anatolia and simultaneously to retrace one segment of the *nuntariyashas*-festival, "the festival of speed," a small group of scholars from Ankara and myself embarked on a short journey from Kerkenes Dağ, possibly ancient Mt. Daha, to Hattusa.[7] According to the festival text, on the 12th day the king leaves Hattusa through the Zippalanda Gate and travels to HARranašši and feasts there (Nakamura 2002: 102). On the following day 13, the King leaves with his entourage to Zippalanda where he spends the night. KBo 13.214 [CTH 635.5] informs the reader that the King descends from his wagon and makes two offerings to the Weathergod of Zippalanda and Daha. On the same day he gets back into his wagon and goes to Katapa, where he also makes an offering. Based on the assumption that Kerkenes Dağ was the sacred Mt. Daha, associated with the ancient city of Zippalanda, the trip should take approximately 2+ days, 2 days to get from Hattusa to Zippalanda and some extra time to make an offering on the mountain.[8]

Maciej Popko has argued that the use of festival texts to estimate distances between towns is limited, because the texts inform us only about the towns as places of ceremonies and of overnight rests. He continues to explain, "since at each town elaborate rituals were performed, each journey of the king and his retinue must have been much shorter than a full day" (Popko 2000: 445). Although elaborate rituals had to be performed at each town, the king and his retinue still had to travel from one place to the next and there is only so much one can travel in a day.

In two rather long days we were able to complete this proposed segment of the festival route, from Mt. Daha to Hattusa, totaling 72 km. On the first day we walked for 12 hours, and on the second for 17 hours. However, we lost a significant amount of time and some kilometers by starting the walk from the south side of Kerkenes Dağ ascending and descending the mountain on the first day. Thus, traveling from Kuşakli Höyük (possibly Zippalanda) to Hattusa in two days is plausible; yet traveling 36 km on consecutive days in the hilly terrain of central Anatolia is an almost unrealistic feat. Moreover, we were carrying just the bare minimum we needed to survive. One would imagine that for this festival voyage the king and the queen would have traveled in a wagon, as mentioned in the festival texts, with all of their regalia and certain units of the army to defend them. We know that there were certain units from the Hittite military and a specific formation that would have accompanied the king on his travels (see Beal 1992: 528 for the Chart of the Royal Procession). Additionally, one has to take into consideration the limited hours of daylight. This does not mean that they did not travel at night. But it is a fact that night brings many more dangers and risks – in the Annals of Hattusili I, for example, there is a description of military action taken at night (Houwinck ten Cate 1984: 68) – and these were not likely taken with the king and queen in tow.

Another method one can utilize to go about calculating the per diem distance in the Anatolian terrain for a large group (e.g., the army, or the king and his entourage) is based on historical documents, both from the Late Bronze Age and in subsequent periods. The Hittite material that offers information about movement in the landscape is predominantly festival texts and letters regarding the military. As mentioned earlier, although we know a large number of Hittite city-names and the amount of time it took to go from city X to Hattusa, unfortunately we only know a handful of locations of these cities.

Yet we are lucky to have the travel-time from Maşat Höyük (ancient Tapikka, both an administrative center and military outpost), approximately 100 km to the north east of Hattusa. Based on a text unearthed at Maşat, we believe that it can be traveled on foot with haste in three days. In a letter from the king to one of the local military commanders, we learn of the peremptory summonses such as: "Say to Kassu and Zilapiya: 'As soon as this letter reaches you, come in three days before His Majesty with the troops mustered there and also the chariots which are there with you'" (*HKM* 50, translation from Bryce 2003: 180). From Ortaköy-Sapinuwa, an important Hittite city that is also thought to be a military base of sorts, "where troops from the surrounding areas were mustered for the defense of the homeland's northern frontier" (Bryce 2003: 170–171; Süel 2002: 157–166), we can surmise that it was approximately a two-day walk to Hattusa, approximately 35 km away.[9] And if the Hittite name for the classical site of Tavium, modern-day Büyüknefes, is correct (for the identification of ancient Tawiniya with Tavium, see Garstang and Gurney 1959: 11–13; Bittel 1942: 6, 28), we then also know from the itinerary undertaken for the *nuntariyashas*–festival that Tawiniya can be reached in an easy day from Hattusa, about 20 km distant.

Aside from festivals, another major aspect of Hittite life that is dependent on timed movement within the landscape is the military. Warfare and the military are rooted in spatial operations, which are contingent upon accurate timing (Gaffney 2006: 37). It should be emphasized that the movement of a military force is something very complex and specific, unlike non-military movement: it is dictated by numerous factors, such as the ability to forage and feed themselves, water supply, safety, visibility (or lack thereof), weather, slopes, space for prayers, and a consistency in rate. If not for all these factors, the military would never get to where it needs to be within a certain time-frame. With the use of GIS-generated data on site location, in conjunction with Richard Beal's extensive work (1992) on the organization of the Hittite military, I was able to determine that the daily distances traveled by the armies of Alexander the Great, the Romans, and the Crusaders in Anatolia were the same as those between many of the Hittite sites (Engels 1978; Haldon 2006; Krentz 2007). This does not imply that all of the Hittite sites, either settlements or reliefs, are necessarily military in nature, but one cannot ignore the fact that the military was central to the Hittite Kingdom and the Kingdom's expansion was a direct result of continuous military campaigns each year.

Zamantı Su Valley and its Rock Reliefs

One example that illustrates the military's movement in relation to the rock-cut reliefs is found in the Zamantı Su valley. I will focus on three monumental rock carvings: Fıraktın (Figure 8.3), Imamkulu (Figure 8.4), and Hanyeri (Figure 8.5).[10] Normally, these monumental reliefs have been seen as border-stones or landmarks on the fringe of the Hittite Empire, a

Figure 8.3   Fıraktın rock relief (photo by Lee Ullmann).

Figure 8.4   Imamkulu rock relief (photo by Lee Ullmann).

Figure 8.5   Hanyeri rock relief (photo by Klaus-Peter Simon, taken in 1995; from
http://commons.wikimedia.org/wiki/file:Hanyeri.jpg, accessed 15
December 2013).

form of royal propaganda to exhibit the king's power and control over a
foreign land (Huot 1999: 33). Although propaganda and aggrandizing might
have been one facet of the reliefs, one should not see them only in such a
limited guise. The idea that Hittite rock reliefs functioned in the same way
as the monumental reliefs of Egypt in the Late Bronze Age, as propaganda to
validate their wars, is not a well-founded argument. This notion of marking
the extent of one's territory for propagandistic purposes does not seem to be
characteristic of the Hittites. Furthermore, this theory also does not explain
the location of many of the carvings and the lack of carvings in other areas.
For instance, the northern and northeastern frontier was an obvious threat
for the Hittites, due to its proximity to the capital of Hattusa and because of
the well-known continuous raids and attacks by the Kaska tribes throughout
Hittite history. For that reason one would imagine that, if the images served
as propaganda, this area would be littered with monumental images of the
Hittite gods and rulers. However, the results of a five-year survey project led
by Roger Matthews in the Paphlagonia region in north-central Anatolia, are
described by Glatz and Matthews as follows:

A notable feature of the Late Bronze Age landscape of Paphlagonia is the complete absence, as it so far seems, of Hittite carved rock monuments, such as occur in the core region and in areas to the south of Hattusa. The landscape of Paphlagonia is dotted with countless rock outcrops suitable for the carving of highly visible relief scenes, and their absence in the region is not likely to be an accident but rather an indication of the unsettled nature of this volatile border zone [Glatz and Matthews 2005: 62].[11]

Furthermore, the misconception in both the notion of the reliefs making up a boundary of sorts and Matthew's assertion about visibility is that it does not acknowledge the often hidden nature of the reliefs.

These rock carvings are not readily visible. Even when they are located on an assumed route, it is possible to walk right by them without even knowing they are there. The reliefs are entirely meshed into the natural surroundings. GIS viewshed analyses of the reliefs indicate that they can be seen from kilometers away, yet ground-truthing the projection shows something completely different. Even if color was added to the monuments, the reliefs do not stand out in the landscape; they are totally blended into the natural rock.[12] Moreover, when dealing with this area scholars seem to neglect the fact that the Hittite border was closer to Elbistan in this period (14th–13th centuries B.C.), and between the monuments and Elbistan-Karahöyük (possibly Hittite *Lauazantiia* [Forlanini 1979: 170 n.22]) there is a rather formidable mountain, the Alaylıdağ, that acts as its own natural boundary. It seems that at the end of the Late Bronze Age the borders with both *Ishuwa* and *Kizzuwadna* posed no serious threat to Hittite security after the collapse of the Mitannian Kingdom (Bryce 1986: 85–102).

Thus, I propose an alternative reading of the three reliefs: the carvings functioned as markers to indicate where the military would stop and camp after a day's march when they left the Hittite homeland for their southern and eastern campaigns towards northern Syria and Mesopotamia. That is to say, originally (pre-carving) these locales must have been noted and important for their natural attributes and/or location, and only later on did the Hittites intervene in the landscape by adding images of their rulers and gods. One aspect about the carvings that has been noted and relatively well documented is their connection to springs or natural watercourses.[13] The monuments are situated at approximately the distance for a pre-modern army's one-day march while on campaign.[14] The assumed path taken from Fıraktın to Imamkulu is c. 30 km and that from Imamkulu to Hanyeri is c. 15 km.[15]

Although 15 km seems to be a half of what can be traveled in a day by a pre-modern army (one marching day of approximately 25–30 km, with a maximum of 35 km), one need not forget that to go from Imamkulu to Hanyeri one must cross the Gezbel pass that is uphill with a steep gradient reaching an elevation of approximately 1,990 m.[16] From later texts we learn that, according to the Byzantine Emperor Nikephoros II of Phokas, a march of approximately 24 km was both long and tiring for men and horses in the mountainous and broken terrain of the Taurus and anti-Taurus region (Haldon 2006: 143; cf. discussion in McGreer 1995: 340–341). Furthermore, it is worth noting that the Hittite army was a rather large war machine. According to Ramesses II, the Hittites had 47,500 men at the battle at Qids (Kadesh) (Beal 1992: 296). This sizeable number might have been inflated by the pharaoh, yet one can assume that the Hittite army had at its disposal well in excess of 10,000 men for a major expedition to northern Syria or beyond in this time period (Beal 1992: 277–296; Houwink Ten Cate 1984: 73). Again it is unclear where exactly the mustering points for all of these troops were located. However, if we are to hypothesize that the mustering point was within the confines of the Kingdom and that at least 10,000 men were to meet in the area surrounding Imamkulu, that would mean that the column of soldiers needed to pass through the anti-Taurus mountain range would have been strung out for at least 8 km. If we take into account established ratios of movement of space between soldiers and units, not considering baggage or animals, the rearmost ranks would not be able to leave the camp before more than three hours after the first ranks started marching (Haldon 2006: 143; Engels 1978: 131–133, 154–155).

Additionally, the placement of these three monuments, and several others, is perfect for a military encampment. There are three chief requirements for a suitable military camp: a defensible location, a good supply of water and fodder, and adequate space for all of the different units (Haldon 1999: 152–153). Later textual sources reveal that there were two main ways of going about the selection of a camp: Polybius (*Histories* 6.42) comments that Greeks, in contrast to Romans, are concerned with security rather than the natural advantages of the position – wood, pasturage, and water (Krentz 2007: 147–185). Two of the sites, Fıraktın and Imamkulu, are found near open fields that can be easily defended and they are in areas where there is no danger of an enemy surprise attack from above. Hanyeri is somewhat different, because the mountains continue to rise above the site; however, just beyond and above the monument there is sufficient room to allow the military to rest. Moreover, each of these locales has a water source and large expanses of woodland, suitable for making fires.[17] The monuments are not located on the main branch of the river, but on its tributaries. Thus, there seems to be a sufficient amount of moving water for drinking and it is better situated for defensive purposes. The notion of what constitutes a good military encampment seems to be rather standard over time and one can see that the three Hittite sites mentioned adhere to both the Greek and Roman standards for suitable military camps.

Returning to the Hittite texts, we are told that the Hittites were concerned with the safety and security of their camps. There were specific rituals and magical incantations used by the military to rid them of any harm (Beal 1995: 63–76). One ritual, known as "When the soldiers go away from the land to campaign and [they go] to the enemy land to fight," was intended to protect the army and hand them a victory (Beal 1995: 66). Another speaks directly to the issue of army camps more specifically, ridding the army of devastating diseases and passing them to the enemy. Parts of both of these rituals needed to take place in open fields (Beal 1995: 71). One has to imagine that rituals were performed on a frequent, if not daily, basis by the army during their campaigns, most probably requesting that the gods hand them a victory and that they have a safe return home, which in turn makes the placement of the monuments an ideal location to camp for the night. The notion of camping near the monuments might be likened to what occured with the Greeks camping in sanctuaries for *asylia* (sacred immunity). Lastly if Itamar Singer's theory is correct that a considerable part of the Hittite army consisted of men originating from western Anatolia, presumably Luwian speakers, then the use of monuments with Luwian inscriptions makes even more sense, because it catered to a military force that both recognized and possibly understood the script (Singer 2005: 447–451).

Conclusion

In short, I would argue that the monumental rock-cut reliefs were intentionally carved in places that had significance even before the images were added to them. The constructed was added to a landscape already imbued with symbolic importance, as evidenced by the texts. The addition of the images only took place in a finite period towards the end of the Kingdom, probably beginning in the middle of the fourteenth century B.C.[18] This coincides with Suppiluliuma I's territorial expansion of the Kingdom and also parallels a change in the literature: according to Harry Hoffner, "new with Mursili II (approx. 1322 B.C.) there is the concern to describe the terrain of some of the battle sites. In at least one instance the author even assumes that his statements about the terrain can be checked by the reader" (Hoffner 1980: 315). In terms of function, it seems reasonable to assume that the monuments were used for ritual or cult; however the issue is who, when, and why someone would make use of these monuments. We live in a world full of signs and images, where traveling 30 km in a day is common. Yet in a world that was dominated by nature, where the average person did not travel great lengths on a daily basis, who would have seen or made use of these locales?

Figure 8.6 Obscured nature of Karabel relief with arrow pointing to location
of the monument (photo by Lee Ullmann).

When considering the sites where these carvings and others (e.g., Eflatun
Pınar, Fasıllar, and Hatip) are located in relation to their setting and the
natural environment, it seems difficult to interpret the monuments as
boundaries or attempts at displaying hegemony. Alternatively, these sites and
several others can be interpreted as places at which the Hittite military would
gather, and thus the images served an internal function for the Hittite soldiers
and accompanying elite. Returning to the Hittite rock-relief carving in the
Karabel Pass, the monument is poorly situated to attract the attention of
travelers or armies heading in either direction (Figure 8.6). There are several
other rock faces in close proximity that would allow for a more prominent
viewing. Thus, the relief must have been a place of significance that was
dependent on the local topography (i.e., the mountains and the springs), and
must have been a place that was known to whoever was intent on visiting it.
Similarly, Hasan Bahar, the scholar who discovered the Hittite monument
at Hatip, argues that the large rock outcrop above the monument shows
evidence of being a fortress (Bahar et al. 2007).

The Hittite rock reliefs and the rituals that took place in front of them
reside in a distinct space and time, outside of daily life. Zainab Bahrani

(2008: 212–215) has shown that this too is the case with the ancient war machine of Mesopotamia, where the military and war belong to a space and time that can be likened to that of ritual and festival. These places exhibit an intersection between the military and ritual. It is undeniable that military force was a tool of the Hittite rulers, and simultaneously the military cannot be disentangled from ritual. The gods had to be consulted to justify war and to secure the upper hand. The carvings, whether because of the proximity to a spring or the view offered of a particular mountain (from the vantage point of the figures in the images, not the viewer), offered a direct conduit to the gods. The monuments were situated in liminal zones that were chosen based on the natural environment. These places were marked by a distinct change in the topography and/or the landscape, either at the site of the monument or just beyond it. The significance of these places, due to their relationship with the surrounding environment, was the crucial factor in their selection. It is not fortuitous that the monuments were carved onto the rock. This style of representation prevents the transporting or movement of the monument from its intended location, which is an aspect of the Hittite relief carvings that is often overlooked. The simple fact that they are one with the natural terrain in which they were fashioned implies that first and foremost it was the placement of the image that was crucial. For most of Hittite history, the borders and boundaries of the Kingdom were continuously expanding and contracting, and the Hittites were mindful of this. Thus it seems somewhat illogical for them to have hewn several images so close to one another, because the distances are not substantial enough for a king to gain glory by adding a second or third marker within 30 km of the previous one.

The ancient textual material, in conjunction with GIS modeling, begins to shed light on the interconnections between Hittite sites and the landscape of Anatolia. In particular, it becomes evident that the relief carvings were used as places that served to tie the Hittites directly to their gods. Features of the natural topography of the Land of Hatti served as waypoints to navigate through and demarcate the landscape. The Hittite monumental reliefs ostensibly merged the natural and constructed spaces of the Land of Hatti and created a place for ritual to be performed. The most likely candidate to be performing rituals at these places of significance was the king and his army on their campaigns, when they were leaving their homeland to fight the enemy.

Notes

1. There is some speculation that the Hittite reliefs would have been painted (Alexander 1986: 28–29), but to date there is no evidence supporting this assertion. At Yazılıkaya there are remnants of a patina covering the relief carvings. It is unclear what effect paint would have played on the visibility of these monuments.
2. For further discussion of the Hittite king associated with this treaty see Wilhelm 1988.
3. The most recent study that has attempted to look at the reliefs with the aid of GIS (Stokkel 2005) did not take into account the more phenomenological aspects of the monuments, such as the complex features of the natural topography that cannot be detected from satellite imagery at certain resolutions and by computer-generated models.
4. Enumeration and explanation of how sites were identified can be found in the author's dissertation (Ullmann 2010). For an earlier list of known Hittite sites, see Forlanini and Marazzi 1986. The two lists are similar, but some additions and subtractions have been made in my dissertation.
5. At time of writing and research the author was a Ph.D. candidate and thus, according to Turkish law, was only permitted to visit sites that have a publication devoted to them or are mentioned in a published article.
6. For articles dealing with the debate concerning the terms NA$_4$ *hekur* and *Huuwasi/ Huuashi*, see Stokkel 2005; Bonantz 2007; van den Hout 2002.
7. There is a rather lengthy bibliography on the city of Zippalanda and Mt. Daha: see, e.g., Gurney 1995; Gorny 1997, 2006; Popko 1994, 2000. The walk was not intended to prove or disprove whether Kerkenes Dağ was indeed Mt. Daha, but came about more as a result of circumstances (Prof. Geoffrey Summers was kind enough to provide the group with a place to stay there before we set out).
8. It is assumed that, regardless of which direction one walks (either to or from Hattusa), the number of days it takes to make the journey should be approximately the same.
9. Much of what is known about the mustering of troops comes from the tablets unearthed at Maşat Höyük (ancient Tapikka) and Ortaköy-Shapinuwa (possibly the second capital of the Hittites). The textual evidence about the mustering of troops and of army staging areas are not very specific about these mustering points (i.e., the places where the soldiers actually gathered), though it is clear that these were sites that were able to provide sufficient provisions for an army of sizeable proportions.
10. It is unclear exactly how Taşçı fits within the path of the other three monuments. Taşçı is thought to be on a route from the Byzantine period (Kohlmeyer 1983: 74). It is located almost equidistant from Fraktin and Imamkulu, though to the south of both sites. Also, Taşçı was incised, rather than hewn in relief, and this might indicate a difference in function. One possibility is that it could have been a node along a different path for soldiers coming from the south, rather than those from the north, the core of the Hittite kingdom, heading south. This is in contrast to the path created by Stokkel (2005), based on the data he entered into the GIS program; he assumed that the four nodes all had to be connected on one single path and that there were no alternative ways to connect the monuments.
11. The authors in the proceeding sentence, however, state: "It is also likely that the Hittites realized that the Kaska were not likely to be a receptive audience for their rock-cut propagandistic scenes." As I have argued above, I do not think that propaganda is the primary function for these monuments and therefore the way in which the Kaska would have understood these reliefs is not relevant.

12. Similar inquiries on Phrygian rock reliefs have shown that there is only one known example of a rock-cut façade with traces of painted decoration. For a more detailed analysis of the Phrygian material, see Berndt-Ersöz 2006.
13. For a new analysis on the association between Hittite sites and water, see Erbil and Mouton 2012.
14. "Speed of movement for large forces varied according to a range of variables from 11–12 kilometers per day to 29 or 32" (Haldon 2006: 141).
15. These measurements have been calculated by using GIS modeling for assumed pathways. Although we do not know the exact path taken by the Hittites, it was created by taking the monuments as points and then running least-cost path and other functions to attempt to model the route that might have been taken by the Hittite army in antiquity.
16. In terms of elevation, one starts at c. 1471 m at Imamkulu, then crosses the Gezbel Pass at c. 1990 m, and then drops to 1723 m at Hanyeri – a gain of 500 m and then a decline of more than 250 m, all within a short 10 km.
17. For the most part, the water sources are the same as in Hittite times. Although today there are wooded areas near the monuments, it is difficult to say whether the region would have been more heavily forested or less in antiquity. As far as I am aware there have been no published palaeoenvironmental studies within the general area of any of the monuments. Because of strong regional environmental contrasts across Anatolia, studies that have been conducted elsewhere (e.g., at Çadır Höyük) would have no bearing on the area discussed here.
18. What is accepted as the earliest datable rock relief, based on the *terminus post quem,* is the Sirkeli relief of Muwatalli II with an accompanying Luwian inscription, which has provided the evidence for the relative date. The argument, as it stands now, is that all other reliefs are either contemporaneous or post-date the one from Sirkeli. Yet there is very little evidence to substantiate this theory and the dating of many of the reliefs remains elusive.

References

Alexander, Robert L.
    1986 *The Sculpture and Sculptors of Yazılıkaya.* University of Delaware Press, Newark.
Bahar, H., T. Çay, and F. Iscan
    2007 The Land and City of Tarhuntassa: Geodetic Researches Around It. Paper read at the XXI International CIPA Symposium, 1–6 October, 2007, Athens, Greece.
Bahrani, Zainab
    2008 *Rituals of War: The Body and Violence in Mesopotamia.* Zone Books, New York.
Barjamovic, Gojko
    2005 A Historical Geography of Ancient Anatolia in the Assyrian Colony Period. Unpublished Ph.D. dissertation, University of Copenhagen.
    2008 The Geography of Trade: Assyrian Colonies in Anatolia c. 1975–1725 BC and the Study of Early Interregional Networks of Exchange. In *Anatolia and the Jazira during the Old Assyrian period,* edited by Jan G. Dercksen, pp. 87–100. Nederlands Instituut voor het Nabije Oosten, Leiden.
Beal, Richard
    1992 *The Organisation of the Hittite Military.* Carl Winter Universitätsverlag, Heidelberg.

1995   Hittite Military Rituals. In *Ancient Magic and Ritual Power,* edited by Marvin W. Meyer and Paul A. Mirecki, pp. 63–76. Brill, Leiden.

Beckman, Gary

1989   The Religion of the Hittites. *The Biblical Archaeologist* 52: 98–108.

1999   *Hittite Diplomatic Texts.* 2nd edition. Scholar's Press, Atlanta.

Berndt-Ersöz, S.

2006   *Phrygian Rock-cut Shrines: Structure, Function, and Cult Practice.* Brill, Leiden.

Bittel, Kurt

1942   Kleinasiatische Studien. *Istanbuler Mitteilungen,* Beiheft 5. Hakkert, Amsterdam.

Bellavia, Gino

2006   Predicting Communication Routes. In *General Issues in the Study of Medieval Logistics: Sources, Problems and Methodologies,* edited by John F. Haldon, pp. 185–198. Brill, Leiden.

Bonatz, Dominik

2007   The Divine Image of the King: Religious Representation of Political Power in the Hittite Empire. In *Representations of Political Power: Case Histories from Times of Change and Dissolving Order in the Ancient Near East,* edited by Marlies Heinz and Marian H. Feldman, pp. 111–136. Eisenbrauns, Winona Lake, IN.

Bryce, Trevor

1986   The Boundaries of Hatti and Hittite Border Policy. *Tel-Aviv* 13–14: 85–102.

2003   *Letters of the Great Kings of the Ancient Near East: The Royal Correspondence of the Late Bronze Age.* Routledge, New York.

Ehringhaus, Horst

2005   *Götter, Herrscher, Inschriften: die Felsreliefs der hethitischen Grossreichszeit in der Türkei.* Phillip von Zabern, Mainz am Rhein.

Engels, Donald W.

1978.   *Alexander the Great and the Logistics of the Macedonian Army.* California University Press, Berkeley.

Erbil, Yiğit, and Alice Mouton

2012   Water in Ancient Anatolian Religions: An Archaeological and Philological Inquiry on the Hittite Evidence. *Journal of Near Eastern Studies* 71: 53–74.

Forlanini, Massimo

1979   Appunti di geografia Etea. In *Studia Mediterranea Piero Meriggi dicata,* edited by Onofrio Carruba, pp. 165–186. Aurora Edizioni, Pavia.

Forlanini, Massimo, and Massimiliano Marazzi

1986   *Anatolia: l'impero hittita.* Università degli studi di Roma, "La Sapienza", Dipartimento di scienze storiche, archeologiche e antropologiche dell'antichità, Roma.

Gaffney, Vincent

2006   Who's in Command Here? The Digital Basis of Historical, Military Logistics. In *General Issues in the Study of Medieval Logistics: Sources, Problems and Methodologies,* edited by John F. Haldon, pp. 37–68. Brill, Leiden.

Garstang, John

1910   *The Land of the Hittites: An Account of Recent Explorations and Discoveries in Asia Minor, with Descriptions of the Hittite Monuments.* Constable, London.

Garstang, J., and O.R. Gurney
    1959   *The Geography of the Hittite Empire.* British Institute of Archaeology at Ankara,
           London.

Glatz, Claudia
    2009   Empire as Network: Spheres of Material Interaction in Late Bronze Age Anatolia.
           Journal of Anthropological Archaeology 28: 127–141.

Glatz, Claudia, and Roger Matthews
    2005   Anthropology of a Frontier Zone: Hittite-Kaska Relations in Late Bronze Age
           North-central Anatolia. *Bulletin of the American Schools of Oriental Research* 339:
           47–65.

Goetze, Albrecht
    1957   The Roads of Northern Cappadocia. *Revue Hittite et Asianique* 15/61: 91–103.

Gorny, Ronald L.
    1989   Environment, Archaeology, and History in Hittite Anatolia. *The Biblical
           Archaeologist* 52: 78–96.
    1997   Review: Zippalanda and Ankuwa. The Geography of Central Anatolia in the Second
           Millennium B.C. *Journal of the American Oriental Society* 117: 549–557.
    2006   The 2002–2005 Excavation Seasons at Çadir Höyük: The Second Millennium
           Settlement. *Anatolica* 32: 29–54.

Great Britain Naval Intelligence Division
    1942   *Turkey*, Vol. 1. Naval Intelligence Division Geographic Handbook Series BR507.
           Naval Intelligence Division, London.

Gurney, O.R.
    1995   The Hittite Names of Kerkenes Dağ and Kuşaklı Höyük. *Anatolian Studies* 45:
           69–71.

Haldon, John
    1999   *Warfare, State, and Society in the Byzantine World, 565–1204.* University College
           London Press, London.
    2006   Roads and Communications in the Byzantine Empire: Wagons, Horses, and
           Supplies. In *Logistics of Warfare in the Age of the Crusades: Proceedings of a Workshop
           held at the Centre for Medieval Studies, University of Sydney, 30 September to 4 October
           2002,* edited by John H. Pryor, pp. 131–158. Ashgate, Burlington, VT.

Harmanşah, Ömür
    2007   Source of the Tigris: Event, Place and Performance in the Assyrian Landscapes of
           the Early Iron Age. *Archaeological Dialogues* 14: 179–204.

Hawkins, John D.
    1998   Tarkasnawa King of Mira, "Tarkondemos", Boğazköy Sealings and Karabel.
           Anatolian Studies 48: 1–31.

Hoffner, Harry A.
    1980   Histories and Historians of the Ancient Near East: The Hittites. *Orientalia* 49:
           283–332.

Houwink ten Cate, Ph. H.J.
    1984   The History of Warfare according to Hittite Sources: The Annals of Hattusilis II.
           Anatolica 11: 47–83.

Huot, Jean-Louis

1999   The Archaeology of Landscape. In *Landscapes: Territories, Frontiers and Horizons in the Ancient Near East. Papers presented to the XLIV Rencontre Assyriologique Internationale, Venezia, 7–11 July 1997,* edited by Lucio Milano, S. de Martino, F.M. Fales, G.B. Lanfranchi, Vol. I, pp. 29–35. Sargon, Padova.

Jean, Eric

2001   *Boğazköy'den Karatepe'ye: Hititbilim ve Hitit Dünyasının Keşfi [From Boğazköy to Karatepe: Hittitology and the Discovery of the Hittite World].* Yapi Kredi Yayıncılık, Istanbul.

Krentz, Peter

2007   War. In *The Cambridge History of Greek and Roman Warfare,* Vol. 1: *Greece, the Hellenistic World and the Rise of Rome,* edited by Philip Sabin, Hans van Wees, and Michael Whitby, pp. 147–185. Cambridge University Press, New York.

Kohlmeyer, Kay

1983   Felsbilder der hethitischen Großreichszeit. *Acta Praehistorica et Archaeologica* 15: 7–153.

Le Bas, Philippe

1888   *Voyage archéologique en Grèce et en Asie Mineure.* Firmin-Didot, Paris.

Lorenz, J., and E. Rieken

2007   Auf dem Weg der Stadt Sassuna. In *Tabularia Hethaeorum: Hethitologische Beiträge. Silvin Košak zum 65. Geburtstag,* edited by Detlev Groddek und Maria Zorman, pp. 467–486. Harrassowitz, Wiesbaden.

McGreer, Eric

1995   *Sowing the Dragon's Teeth: Byzantine Warfare in the 10th Century.* Dumbarton Oaks Research Library and Collection, Washington, D.C.

Nakamura, Mitsuo

2002   *Das hethitische nuntarriyašha-Fest.* Nederlands Instituut voor het Nabije Oosten, Leiden.

Ökse, A. Tuba

2007   Ancient Mountain Routes Connecting Central Anatolia to the Upper Euphrates Region. *Anatolian Studies* 57: 35–46.

Perrot, Georges, and Charles Chipiez

1890   *History of Art in Sardinia, Judaea, Syria, and Asia Minor.* Translated by I. Gonino. A.C. Armstrong, New York.

Ponchia, Simonetta

2004   Mountain Routes in Assyrian Royal Inscriptions. *Kaskal* 1: 139–178.

Popko, Maciej

1994   *Zippalanda: ein Kultzentrum im hethitischen Kleinasien.* Universitätsverlag C. Winter, Heidelberg.

2000   Zippalanda and Ankuwa Once More. *Journal of the American Oriental Society* 120: 445–448.

Sayce, Archibald H.

1890   *The Hittites: The Story of a Forgotten Empire.* The Religious Tract Society, London.

Seeher, Jürgen
2009 Der Landschaft sein Siegel aufdrücken – hethitische Felsbilder und Hieroglyphen-inschriften als Ausdruck des herrscherlichen Macht- und Territorialanspruchs. *Altorientalische Forschungen* 36: 119–139.

Singer, Itamar
2005 On Luwians and Hittites. *Bibliotheca Orientalis* 62: 430–451.

Smith, Michael E.
2007 Form and Meaning in the Earliest Cities: A New Approach to Ancient Urban Planning. *Journal of Planning History* 6: 3–47.

Stokkel, Peter J.A.
2005 A New Perspective on Hittite Rock Reliefs. *Anatolica* 31: 171–188.

Süel, Aygül
2002 Ortaköy-Shapinuwa. In *Recent Developments in Hittite Archaeology and History: Papers in Memory of Hans G. Güterbock*, edited by K. Aslihan Yener and Harry A. Hoffner Jr, pp. 157–166. Eisenbrauns, Winona Lake, IN.

Texier, C.
1839 *Description de l'Asie Mineure faite par ordre du Gouvernement Français, de 1833 à 1837, et publiée par le Ministère de l'Instruction publique. Ouvrage Dédié au Roi. Beaux-arts, monuments historiques, plans et topographie des cités antiques, gravures de Lemaitre.* Firmin-Didot, Paris.

Thomas, Julian
2001 Archaeologies of Place and Landscape. In *Archaeological Theory Today*, edited by Ian Hodder, 165–186. Blackwell Publishers, Malden, MA.

Ullmann, Lee Z.
2010 Movement and the Making of Place in the Hittite Landscape. Unpublished Ph.D. Dissertation, Columbia University.

van den Hout, Theo
1994 Death as a Privilege: The Hittite Royal Funerary Ritual. In *Hidden Futures: Death and Immortality in Ancient Egypt, Anatolia, the Classical, Biblical and Arab Islamic World*, edited by Jan M. Bremer, Theo P.J. van den Hout, and Rudolph Peters, pp. 37–77. Amsterdam University Press, Amsterdam.

2002 Tombs and Memorials: The (Divine) Stone-House and Hegur Reconsidered. In *Recent Developments in Hittite Archaeology and History*, edited by. K. Aslihan Yener and Harry A. Hoffner Jr, pp. 73–92. Eisenbrauns, Winona Lake, IN.

Wilhelm, Gernot
1988 Zur ersten Zeile des Sunassura-Vertrages. In *Documentum Asiae Minoris Antiquae: Festschrift für Heinrich Otten zum 75. Geburtstag*, edited by Erich Neu and Christel Rüster, pp. 359–370. Harrassowitz, Wiesbaden.

Places in the Political Landscape
of Late Bronze Age Anatolia

Claudia Glatz

The landscape monuments of Late Bronze Age Anatolia comprise a diverse range of rock reliefs and architectural carvings associated with the storage and ritual use of water, and the guarding of topographic boundaries and communication routes in extra-urban contexts. An intriguing, and, until the Late Bronze Age (LBA), a rare practice among the complex societies of the ancient Near East, Anatolian landscape monuments have seen a recent resurgence in scholarly interest, as well as discovery (Dinçol 1998; Hawkins 1998; Emre 2002; Ehringhaus 2005; Stokkel 2005; Bonatz 2007; Seeher 2009, 2012). Despite new information and research, however, interpretations have remained largely conservative and inspired primarily by Hittite textual sources. As a group, landscape monuments are invariably seen as generic expressions of Hittite imperial ideology and power, which they are thought to reproduce through ritual practice, symbolic content, and a range of practical and military functions.

An overhaul of traditional perceptions of state and imperial societies as monolithic entities, and of imperial relationships as driven solely by an omnipotent center, is long overdue in Anatolian studies. So too are perceptions of material culture as merely reflective of socio-political relationships, and political dominance as inevitably resulting in cultural uniformity. To break down past generalisations and to do justice to the complexity of past social, political, and cultural relationships and practices, it is vital that their material media are re-examined in a bottom-up archaeological framework of analysis. Multi-scalarity and diversity in analytical method and interpretive approach are crucial in constructing a contextually rich narrative of the past; in this case, of the meanings, functions, and experiences of Anatolian landscape monuments and their wider socio-political context.

A phenomenology or ethnography of place, couched in Hittite textual accounts of landscape and GIS-based examinations of movement and visual access (Harmanşah 2010b; Ullmann, this volume), contributes to an understanding of the range of plausible past perceptions and experiences of particular places and associated activities. More importantly perhaps, this approach draws attention to the multiple layers of meaning and significance that naturally wondrous places may be imbued with and why they are appropriated by political elites (Harmanşah 2010a). Such archaeologies and ethnographies of place help write the local histories – or at least possible versions of it – that these monuments as yet lack. A purely particularistic approach, which downplays the significance of the interregional interaction network of which Anatolian landscape monuments without a doubt formed an integral part during the LBA, however, is flawed and in danger of perpetuating those generic and unproblematized perceptions of empire that it aims to challenge (Harmanşah 2010b). It is where local agency and histories of place intermesh with, challenge, or contradict imperial practices in, and narratives of, landscape that some of the most fruitful advances in the study of these monuments will be made.

For instance, despite Ullmann's criticism – and as his own conclusions about monument function later demonstrate – there is no escaping the political context and territorial significance of Anatolian landscape monuments in their LBA incarnations at least. With few exceptions, monument iconography is royal, male, and often military in nature, as are most of the inscriptions forming either the focus of a monument or accompanying pictorial representations. All LBA Anatolian documentary sources, whether ritual or otherwise, derive exclusively from state-related contexts. The perception of landscape conveyed in these sources, while perhaps indirectly offering insights into more widely held cultural attitudes, are expressed in the conventions and suffused with the ideology of the Hittite state apparatus, whose agendas and interest they served.

The practice of inscribed or architectural landscape monuments, moreover, appears to be closely connected with the emergence of expansive states in the Near East and the new challenges of large-scale territorial integration and competition encountered by them (Glatz and Plourde 2011). Anatolian landscape monuments are not the earliest material manifestations of strategic appropriations of parts of the landscape in this way (Börker-Klähn 1987), but the practice proliferates during the LBA in tandem with the expansion of large-scale, and to varying degrees politically integrated, interaction spheres.

A geopolitical approach to these monuments can contribute to a bottom-up perspective of imperial relationships, by highlighting the active role and significance of local or non-imperial agents in the shaping of these relationships and the climate and nature of interaction networks more generally.

The LBA practice of monument production served the construction and appropriation of a political landscape. But of what sort of political landscape were these monuments constitutive? Recent approaches to early states have emphasized the tensions that exist between the technologies of domination available to early elites and the scope and degree to which spatial control can be affected with them. In addition to a more active role accredited to those affected by state or imperial control, this renders state power subject to continuous challenges and requires a perpetual re-production of practices and symbols of control (e.g., Smith 2003). Monumental display forms part of the repertoire of techniques of domination through which early elites project their ideologies, but also negotiate and compete with their rivals. This is because the media of socio-political competition can be wielded not only by the dominant elite, but by anyone who possesses the necessary resources to do so. From this perspective, the mere fact that monument construction occurs indicates an unsettled political environment in which re-affirmative statements of strength are required (Glatz and Plourde 2011).

Two important aspects of LBA Anatolian landscape monuments have been rather astonishingly neglected in the past. The first is the fact that the majority of LBA landscape monuments bear not the names and titles of Hittite rulers, but those of princes, dignitaries, vassals, and rivals, or lack declarations of patronage entirely. The second concerns the neglect of the chronological dimension of monument production. The first oversight produces a spatially monolithic perspective of unchallenged Hittite control over much of Anatolia, whilst the latter renders a dynamic process of monument construction, re-use, destruction, and perhaps also abandonment – one that took place over several generations – ahistoric and static.

If LBA landscape monuments were a centrally orchestrated expression of Hittite imperial power and functioned to facilitate the exertion of this power in ritual and/or military ways, as most commentators have suggested, why not engrave royal *aediculae* rather than the names of vassals, princes or officials? This multivocality in monument authorship is matched by rather stark contrasts in the quality of workmanship between monuments commissioned and inscribed by Hittite great kings and those of other patrons. Examples for this are the reliefs at Taşçı and Suratkaya, which are carved and scratched onto the rock rather than fashioned in the typical relief of Hittite royal representations and inscriptions. The construction of landscape monuments was a practice with which a range of different socio-political players engaged with, to the best of their abilities and the resources at their disposal. Not all of these were perhaps constructed directly in defiance of Hittite political power, but the textually well attested struggle between Tudhaliya IV and his cousin Kurunta of Tarhuntassa, both of which engaged in the construction of landscape monuments, suggest that at least some of them were. In concert, these different strands of evidence would suggest a much more diverse, as well as unsettled, political landscape in LBA Anatolia than conventionally inferred from these monuments.

Even a tentative chronological reconstruction brings into focus the fact that monument construction was a long-term process over at least 100 years, or four generations of Hittite rulers. We are, thus, dealing with a palimpsest of monuments on the Anatolian landscape, not all of which may have been "in (political) use" at the same time. In several cases, the monuments themselves bear inscriptions by multiple – and most likely sequential – claimants to power. There also appears to be a chronological shift of imperial monument construction from east to west, suggestive of changing geopolitical concerns. The monuments of earlier Hittite great kings, for instance, concentrate in Cilicia and along communication routes through the Taurus. In the final decades of the Hittite empire, Tudhaliya IV appears to concentrate his efforts on the western fringes and the south-central plateau, where his rival, Kurunta, also placed a monument proclaiming himself great king.

Perhaps most interesting of all is the possibility – based on the traditional syncretizations proposed for individuals mentioned on landscape monuments and in contemporary textual and glyptic sources – that landscape monuments may have originated not as an imperial strategy, but one of princes and officials. If the identification of prince Ku(wa)lanamuwa of the Akpınar 1, İmamkulu and Hanyeri A inscriptions with a high official of the transitional period between Suppiluliuma I and Mursili II is permissible, LBA landscape monuments, rather than primarily a sign of central imperial appropriation, commenced as a strategy of provincial power or resistance. Hittite imperial landscape monuments first appear in the reign of Muwatalli II and it took another three generations until Tudhaliya IV, his rival Kurunta, and another powerful western vassal adopted landscape monuments in a vibrant dialogue of territorial power. No landscape monuments of Hittite great kings are known from the final years of the LBA. The monuments of Hartapu on Kızıldağ and Karadağ, however, could represent the claims of a southern rival in the transitional phase leading up to and following the fall of the Hittite empire over the south-central Anatolian plateau (for a more detailed discussion see Glatz and Plourde 2011).

Brief and therefore incomplete, the above discussion serves to illustrate that much is still to be learnt about LBA Anatolian landscape monuments; as places with local histories and as material expressions of interaction at a much wider, interregional scale. It also demonstrates that the monuments themselves can tell us much about their patrons, the spatial scope of their political and ideological claims, and the general political climate in LBA

Anatolia. The diversity in patronage encountered in this way and the hints this provides for a dynamic and ongoing process of territorial negotiation is a first step in the direction of a more differentiated and less imperial-centric understanding of these monuments at the interregional level of inquiry, but should also prove significant in the exploration of place and place-making in the Anatolian countryside, while reconciling, I hope at least in part, overstated theoretical oppositions.

Acknowledgements

I would like to thank Ömur Harmanşah for the kind invitation to contribute to this volume.

References

Bonatz, Dominik

2007　The Divine Image of the King: Religious Representation of Political Power in the Hittite Empire. In *Representations of Political Power: Case Histories from Times of Change and Dissolving Order in the Ancient Near East*, edited by Marlies Heinz and Marian H. Feldman, pp. 111–36. Eisenbrauns, Winona Lake.

Börker-Klähn, Jutta

1982　*Altvorderasiatische Bildstelen und vergleichbare Felsreliefs*, Band I–II. Baghdader Forschungen 4. Philip von Zabern, Mainz.

Dinçol, Ali M.

1998　Die Entdeckung des Felsmonuments in Hatip und ihre Auswirkungen über [sic] die historischen und geographischen Fragen des Hethiterreichs. *TÜBA-AR* 1: 27–35.

Ehringhaus, Horst

2005　*Götter, Herrscher, Inschriften: Die Felsreliefs der hethitischen Grossreichszeit in der Türkei*. Philip von Zabern, Mainz.

Emre, Kutlu

2002　Felsreliefs, Stelen, Orthostraden: Großplastiken als monumentale Form staatlicher und religiöser Repräsentation. In *Die Hethiter und ihr Reich: Das Volk der 1000 Götter*, edited by Kunst- und Ausstellungshalle der Bundesrepublik Deutschland GmbH, pp. 218–233. Theiss, Stuttgart.

Glatz, Claudia

2009　Empire as Network: Spheres of Material Interaction in Late Bronze Age Anatolia. *Journal of Anthropological Archaeology* 28: 127–41.

Glatz, Claudia, and Aimée M. Plourde

2011　Landscape Monuments and Political Competition in Late Bronze Age Anatolia: An Investigation of Costly Signaling Theory. *Bulletin of the American Schools of Oriental Research* 361: 33–66.

Harmanşah, Ömür

2010a　Rock Reliefs and Sacred Springs: Towards an Archaeology of Place in Anatolia.

Paper presented at the 7th International Congress for the Archaeology of the Ancient Near East, London, 12th–16th April 2010.

2010b Archaeology of Place and Place-making: Re-orienting Ancient Anatolian Rock Reliefs and Spring Monuments. http://proteus.brown.edu/harmansah/8396 (last accessed 14 January 2011).

Hawkins, J. David

1998 Tarkasnawa King of Mira, Tarkondemos, Boğazköy Sealings and Karabel. *Anatolian Studies* 48: 1–31.

Kohlmeyer, Kay

1983 Felsbilder der hethitischen Großreichszeit. *Acta Praehistorica et Archaeologica* 15: 7–135.

Seeher, Jürgen

2009 Der Landschaft sein Siegel aufdrücken – hethitische Felsbilder und Hieroglyphen-inschriften als Ausdruck des herrscherlichen Macht- und Territorialanspruchs. *Altorientalische Forschungen* 36(1): 119–139.

2012 Natürliche und künstliche, unbewusste und beabsichtigte Landmarken: Menschliche Wahrnehmung und herrscherliche Betonung der Besetzung von Landschaft und Territorien. In *Manifestationen von Macht und Hierarchien in Stadtraum und Landschaft*, edited by Felix Pirson, pp. 25–42. Byzas 13. Ege Yayınları, Istanbul.

Smith, Adam T.

2003 *The Political Landscape: Constellations of Authority in Early Complex Polities*. University of California Press, Berkeley.

Stokkel, Peter J.A.

2005 A New Perspective on Hittite Rock Reliefs. *Anatolica* 31: 171–188.

Living Rock and Transformed Space

Betsey A. Robinson

> ... if we think of space as that which allows movement, then place is pause; each pause in movement makes it possible for location to be transformed into place [Tuan 2001: 6].

The carvings of deities and rulers that enliven rocky landscapes across rural Anatolia are among the most charismatic monuments of the Hittite empire, and perhaps the most enigmatic. About a dozen exist; most are dated from the mid-14th through the 13th centuries, though few with any real certainty. Carved into the "organic" rock, otherwise pristine outcrops and cliff-faces alongside major throughways, the reliefs are monumental yet inconspicuous, merging into their surroundings and difficult to see from afar, or even close by. They hover above the open terrain, as if it were important to their makers that they, and people who would gather before them, should have clear views.

The purpose of the reliefs has long been debated. In this volume, Lee Ullmann argues against the common notion that they served as boundary markers addressed to foreigners. He notes that most occur in uncontested territory, far from frontiers, but overlooking easily defensible points with one or more sources of water, plentiful food, and room for encampment. He proposes that they mark the sites of certain rituals, particularly those enacted where Hittite armies camped en route to foreign wars, and on their return.

Ullmann's research illuminates relationships among gods, humans, and nature, through the lenses of ancient texts, rupestral reliefs, and modern survey methods projected back on the Anatolian landscape. For him landscape is "a network of related places that become significant to people through habitual activities and interactions," (p. 106) and by applying GIS modeling he makes significant strides in conceptualizing Hittite rock carvings as a dynamic ensemble. His work builds upon recent scholarship in humanistic geography, which has emphasized that landscape is never simply scenic or purely natural, but that it is a socio-cultural construct, always changing in response to human action and, in turn, actively impacting human experience. The landscape is thus a co-producer of experience, identity, memory, and belief. My goal in this short contribution is to harmonize with Ullmann's paper, by engaging with his main themes and expanding on several minor points. In particular, I believe that further reflection on medium and iconography can enrich Ullmann's conceptual and spatial analysis.

Ullmann adduces several archival documents to demonstrate that the Hittites were not only cognizant of geographical features, but had an affinity for the land around them. This thinking recalls Yi-Fu Tuan's (1990: 4) invention of the term *topophilia* to describe affective bonds between some peoples and places. Such a connection is not an innate human response, and it cannot be assumed to be common to all cultures, all periods of a single culture, or all individuals within any social group; nor can it be assumed that a culture that does not explicitly represent natural features in its art lacks an affinity for its environment (see, e.g., Hurwit 1991: 36). Thus, for the modern scholar to recognize ancient *topophilia* can be challenging, but Ullmann effectively musters textual evidence to establish such a sensibility among the upper echelons of Hittite society and, moreover, to show that not only spatial relations but aesthetic responses to landscape are expressed in surviving documents.

For example, the treaty of Tudhaliya IV with his cousin, Kurunta of Tarhuntassa (Bo 86/229), references borders or frontiers with cities, rivers, and mountains, as well as unique features like a sacred dog stele (*ḫuwaši*). Rivers mark boundaries between Hittite holdings and others, such as the "land of the Hulaya River," probably a Tarhuntassa frontier-zone (Bryce 1998: 251–252, n.28). Mountains and cities serve as conspicuous points of reference. Besides describing political divisions, this treaty records servitude to natural resources, for instance, naming the joint beneficiaries of water-sources on Mount Arlanta.

Tablet Bo 2004/1 is richer in its engagement with landscape, while still fairly impressionistic. Ullmann reads this unusual document not as an itinerary of a journey or a territorial record, but as a catalog of landmarks visible from one central point, beginning and ending with the road of the unknown Shashshuna. The first section (§1) lists the road, then a tower, a city, a kiln, and a mountain above and/or beyond. The road appears again near the end, giving the impression of coming full-circle. Water-features, more highlands, and sanctuaries follow. There is practical information, such as the notice that one spring (§ 2) is unhealthy or contaminated. Four other springs are associated with a water-course, and beneath them are "the bittersweet mouths of the four ladies" (§ 3). To a classicist like myself, these evoke springs and their nymphs or *numina*, and perhaps the ladies were comparable minor deities. Other descriptors indeed help us to "see the landscape through the eyes of the Hittites," in Ullmann's words – for example, one distinctive mountain, "round and shiny," and what appears to be a "moon-shaped" wetland. The language is laconic, yet resonant.

Furthermore, despite artists' concentration on human form in Hittite art, natural and physical features make important appearances, as in reliefs carved into the basalt masonry walls of Alaca Höyük, in which scattered vegetation adds variety to hunting scenes (Macqueen 1986: 145–147, figures 136–141). Geographical references are also integral to many representations of the "apotheoses of elements and forces of nature" that were Hittite deities (Alexander 1986: 11). Written accounts imagine the Storm-god standing on two sacred peaks, and visual counterparts appear across media (Alexander 1986: 56, 65–66, 124–125, whose identifications of figures I follow; for the origins and symbolism of Hittite mountain-god representations, see Danrey 2006). In one relief panel within the sanctuary at Yazılıkaya, near Hattuša, a vegetation (grain) god stands on two stylized hillocks, while a Storm-god stands on the shoulders of two mountain gods, anthropomorphic figures with mountain-shaped skirts textured with scale patterns. Such imagery reflected the concept that all mountains were deities, or associated with them (Freu 2006: 237–239). Mountain rituals seem to have been geared to protecting the royal family, appeasing the gods, and preserving cosmic order, and they often required elaborate preparation (Birchler 2006; Mazoyer 2006). Conversely, mountains were moved into the city in the form of sacred images, housed in temples, and honored in festivals, through which city foundations and royal power were recapitulated (Mazoyer 2006).

Ullmann's three case-sites, Fraktın, İmamkulu, and Hanyeri provide a cross-section of characteristic relief subjects and a snapshot of Hittite cosmology. By the period in which the reliefs were carved, the Hittites had as many deities as regions, a "thousand gods of Hatti" representing the natural world and nurturing its human stewards (Singer 1994). Members of the royal family were the primary interlocutors for their people. They are outfitted for priestly and military roles in the reliefs. The relief at Fraktın is the largest outside Yazılıkaya, and appears to be unfinished (Alexander 1986: 24). There, King Hattušili III and Queen Paduhepa offer libations at altars to the Storm-god and Sun-goddess (Figure 8.2). At İmamkulu, a staff-wielding ruler is juxtaposed with a goddess borne aloft on a many-winged figure, as well as a Storm-god driving a chariot over the heads of three lesser gods on animal-headed demons (Figure 8.4). The "son of a king" dominates the carving at Hanyeri, a large figure wearing a tunic, cap, and shoes with curled-up toes, and bearing a bow, sword, and spear or staff (Figure 8.5). Above him to the left, at a smaller scale, the Storm-god's bull stands on the backs of two anthropomorphic mountain gods resembling those at Yazılıkaya.

Blending into the environment and seen only by those who know how to look, the reliefs must have been intended for a Hittite audience. Ullman's interpretation, that they marked places of pause on military itineraries, reminded me of the words of Yi-Fu Tuan, quoted at the beginning of this article. If we imagine military movements broken into day-long segments, each overnight encampment would have held strong potential for meaningful place-making. While physical features – proximity to road networks, distances and terrain, and availability of food and water – certainly played a part in determining stopping points, those places, in turn, would have become sacred through ritual performances and the eventual creation of the reliefs.

Whatever the initial impetus for their creation, the sacred images would remain through every season thereafter. Readings and responses must have been as diverse as their viewers, from troops in transit, to the rural elite who owed their land-ownership to the royals, to resident and transhumant farmers and herders. Some viewers may have simply seen gods, kings, and queens, while those able to read the hieroglyphic identifiers would have gained more specific information. Still others would have appreciated further nuances: monumental rock-carvings were state art, an extension of the imperial capital and its religion through its most distinctive artistic medium. Thus, a network of meaningful places extended across the Hittite homeland, connected through formal references and pious themes, as well as similarities of setting, roads, and timetables.

Although Ullmann clearly shows that most reliefs occur well within the Hittite homeland and can be ruled out as boundary markers, they are nonetheless transitional works. Current dating estimates place their creation in a period of tension and external hostilities for the Empire, during which country roads regularly would have carried military deployments, as well as couriers with news of border skirmishes and other hostilities. The creation of the reliefs ensured a continued physical presence of gods and rulers in the landscape, helping to safeguard residents and transients. While Ullmann deemphasizes possible propagandistic purposes, it seems clear to me that the images were powerful signs of imperial oversight. Just as mountains could be moved into the center as images and through ritual, imperial culture could be exported into the countryside, reinforcing contact with resident gods.

If only we had sculptors' signatures, better chronological control, or more extensive excavation results. Were the carvings created for a certain occasion in the reign of those pictured, or were they commissioned by descendants? Even if they marked military encampments, did other groups return on a festive schedule to reenact sacred rituals, or on their way to other venues? Were carvings accompanied by additional ritual architecture and other furnishings? At Sirkeli in southeast Turkey (Cilicia), where two cliff-side reliefs portray thirteenth-century Hittite royals, cuttings in the rock above have been identified as basins for libations, and a structure to their west may be a cultic building (Usshishkin 1975). For how many other, more isolated, sites would systematic study reveal such evidence?

Lee Ullmann's paper demonstrates how effectively GIS can serve as a platform for exploring "imagined ancient space," especially combined with philological research and sometimes grueling fieldwork. Carved into the living rock of highland landscapes, Hittite reliefs and their recently mapped relationships are offering new insights into one ancient culture's sense of space and place; relations among gods, rulers, and subjects; the mechanisms with which meaning may have been created in the countryside; and the ways location, ritual, and artistic imagery worked together to maintain order within the empire, despite mounting challenges at its edges.

Acknowledgments

I would like to thank Ömür Harmanşah for the invitation to participate in the "Drawing on Rocks" workshop, the Joukowsky Institute for Archaeology and the Ancient World of Brown University for its support of conference and travel expenses, and Lee Ullmann and other participants for fascinating discussion.

References

Alexander, Robert L.
  1986 *The Sculpture and Sculptors of Yazılıkaya*. University of Delaware Press, Newark, N.J.

Birchler, Anne
  2006 Quelques réflexions sur la montagne comme lieu de culte des Hittites. *Res Antiquae* 3: 165–177.

Bryce, Trevor
  1998 *The Kingdom of the Hittites*. Clarendon Press, Oxford.

Danrey, Virginie
  2006 L'homme-montagne ou l'itinéraire d'un motif iconographique. *Res Antiquae* 3: 209–217.

Freu, Jacques
  2006 Les montagnes dans l'historiographie et la géographie hittites. *Res Antiquae* 3: 219–243.

Hurwit, Jeffrey M.

1991   The Representation of Landscape in Early Greek Art. In *New Perspectives in Early Greek Art*, edited by Diana Buitron-Oliver, pp. 33–62. Studies in the History of Art 32. National Gallery of Art, Washington, D.C.

Macqueen, James G.

1986   *The Hittites and their Contemporaries in Asia Minor*. Revised ed. Thames and Hudson, London.

Mazoyer, Michel

2006   Quand la montagne se rend à la ville. *Res Antiquae* 3: 261–270.

Singer, Itamar

1994   "The Thousand Gods of Hatti": Limits of an Expanding Pantheon. In *Concepts of the Other in Near Eastern Religions*, edited by Ilai Alon, Ithamar Gruenwald, and Itamar Singer, pp. 81–102. Israel Oriental Studies 14. Brill, Leiden.

Tuan, Yi-Fu

1990   *Topophilia: A Study of Environmental Perception, Attitudes, and Values*. Morningside Edition, New York.

2001   *Space and Place: The Perspective of Experience*. University of Minnesota Press, Minneapolis.

Usshishkin, David

1975   Hollows, "Cup-Marks," and Hittite Stone Monuments. *Anatolian Studies* 25: 85–103.

Event, Place, Performance:
Rock Reliefs and Spring Monuments in Anatolia

Ömür Harmanşah

Why start with place? ... Because place continues to be an important source of culture and identity; despite the pervasive delocalization of social life, there is an embodiment and emplacement to human life that cannot be denied ... because scholarship of the past two decades in many fields (geography, anthropology, political economy, communications, and so on) has tended to deemphasize place and to highlight, on the contrary, movement, displacement, traveling, diaspora, migration, and so forth. Thus, there is a need for a corrective theory that neutralizes this erasure of place, the asymmetry that arises from giving far too much importance to the "the global" and far too little value to "place" [Escobar 2008: 7].

Introduction: Documenting Places?

If Arturo Escobar is correct about the broader trends in humanities and social sciences of the last two decades, one could also point out that there is a remarkable, though relatively modest, interest in places as culturally meaningful locales and micro-geographies of lived experience, in fields such as archaeology, anthropology, sociology, and art. This may be understood as a conscious or unconscious reaction to the popular interest in macro-scale perspectives on human geographies, transnationalism, and global movements that has characterized the late twentieth and early twenty-first centuries. Speaking of place has visibly become a political discourse, moving away from homogenizing, ambivalent macro-perspectives, standing for the decolonization of "Places of the Other" and for the postcolonial safeguarding of locality (Bhabha 1994; Dirlik 2001; Dirlik and Prazniak 2001; Hamilakis and Duke 2007; Escobar 2008). Powerfully written theories of place and locality have appeared in the fields of geography, critical theory, anthropology, postcolonial studies, political ecology, and cultural studies, as critiques of the modernist conceptualization of Cartesian space.[1] There has been, however, much less interest in the *"ontological* nature of place itself" – the material substratum of cultures of place (Merrifield 1993: 516, emphasis in the original). Few attempts have been made so far to tackle the question of place in empirical research, especially for articulating new methodologies of fieldwork to gain access to biographies of places. Such a goal can be taken further to seek a new ethics of doing fieldwork with a sensitivity to local practices, not with a nostalgic structuralism of attempting to document or conserve what is now being lost under the conditions of globalism or destructive modernity, but rather with an interest in the hybrid and continuously changing nature of places.[2] In the conduct of archaeological fieldwork, the question of place is also being posed: how does one go about investigating, documenting, and understanding places of cultural practice and political discourse, archaeologically, in the field? Is it possible to trace the material *and* discursive genealogies of places, while being politically engaged and ethically responsible to their historicity, without reducing or restricting places to colonial notions of the "traditional" and the "vernacular", and without reducing them to dots and abstract numbers on archaeological/historical maps? What I attempt here in a preliminary way is to answer that question.

Between the good old archaeological practice of excavating large sites and cities, on the one hand, and the rather impressive developments in extensive and intensive archaeological survey projects in the Mediterranean world during the last 30–40 years,[3] one aspect of landscapes always seems to fall between the cracks of our field methodologies, having received relatively little interest in a conscientious and rigorous manner. I am speaking about those unorthodox localities that escape our overarching site typologies, resist our methods of scientific quantification, make a mockery of our systemic approaches to land use and settlement patterns, and defy obsessive inquiries such as the "thermodynamic explanation of symbolic behaviour" (Trigger 1990). I am speaking of *places* where our tidy nature-culture categories collapse. "More than unusual dots in the map", *places* gather a complex and heterogeneous set of human practices around them (Alcock and Rempel 2006) – their materiality is a coming-together of things, rocks, soils, plants, waters, animals, humans, and the myriad of ways in which they interact. Localities are often fragile and ephemeral entities, as Arjun Appadurai (1996) has elegantly argued. Vulnerable to forgetting and silencing, *places* are hosts for situated practices, associated human imaginations, and deeply embedded material residues. They are significantly difficult to grasp through standard archaeological field techniques. They most frequently run deep in their temporality, however, where multiple pasts coexist in very odd combinations and serendipities.

In recent years, regional survey projects in the archaeology of both the Mediterranean world and the Near East increasingly focussed on methodologies that make possible macro-scale analysis, especially with the advances in the use of declassified satellite imagery, geographical information systems, analytical spatial distribution and predictive models, and comprehensive-coverage fieldwalking. The disciplinary focus, therefore, is increasingly shifting to aim at imperial settlement systems, long-distance movements, migrations, and diasporas, sweeping environmental histories, "transregional economic and political processes", and the like (Kouchoukos and Wilkinson 2006: 16; cf. Smith 2001). An alternative to such quantification-based, macro-scale methodologies are those phenomenological approaches to landscape that highlight the experience of the world through the body and its senses (David and Thomas 2008). In neither of these two major currents in archaeological study of landscapes, does *place* feature as a significant unit of analysis, for it requires in-depth, personally engaged, politically charged, and historically nuanced study of its genealogy, its socio-symbolic associations, and accumulated material forms and residues. Methodologically, it calls for disciplinary collaborations, especially among archaeologists, anthropologists, geologists, environmental scientists, ethnohistorians, and heritage specialists in most unusual ways. The *archaeology of place* that is proposed here combines their methodologies with a sustained interest in the long-term biography and contemporaneity of places.

Rock reliefs and spring monuments of pre-classical antiquity in the Near East and the Anatolian peninsula offer a rare opportunity for investigating places and testing new fieldwork methodologies for an explicitly archaeological approach to locality. I use archaeology in two different meanings here, not only in the common disciplinary understanding of studying the stratified material remains at a place, site, or a landscape, but also referring to the broader, social-scientific concept of *archaeology* in the Foucauldian sense of tracing the genealogies of discourses and local narratives produced about a place and around that place (Foucault 2002). The research project I am undertaking on Late Bronze and Early Iron age rock-cut monuments and spring sanctuaries in Anatolia seeks to understand the poetics and politics of places at mountainous landscapes, caves, springs, river sources, sinkholes, and other such odd geological formations, while attempting to articulate an archaeology of place and place-making that derives from this very particular historical context.

In the following sections, I unpack my understanding of the concept of *place* in relation to questions of event, performance, and bodily practice, with reference to three specific places, before returning to a broader discussion of the rock reliefs and spring sanctuaries of Anatolian antiquity. The first is an almond grove at the village of Ayanis in Eastern Turkey where I worked in recent years; the second, the Source of the Loue river in Franche-Comté, West of the Jura Mountains in France, via Gustave Courbet's paintings; and, finally, the Source of the Tigris River in Southeastern Turkey, by virtue of the Assyrian monuments on its cave walls. Such a multi-sited look at the concept of place becomes possible in the ways that the three places are constituted through their unique geological character, place-based associations and cultural representations, as well as the site-specific performance of various historical actors.

Almond Trees of Ayanis: Place, Imagination, Deep Time

Since 2001, I have been involved intermittently with the Turkish-American archaeological project at the site of Ayanis, a seventh-century B.C. Urartian city on the eastern shore of Lake Van in eastern Turkey (Harmanşah 2009; Çilingiroğlu and Salvini 2011). I had been primarily studying architectural technologies at this site, until a few years ago, when I was invited to participate in an ethnoarchaeological project at the adjacent village of Ayanis, specifically to explore the architectural development and the building practices at the contemporary village[4]. The village of Ayanis (current name Ağartı) was built on top of a good portion of the southern half of the Urartian Lower town (Figure 11.1). It is a former Armenian-Turkish village, re-settled by Turkmen families from Northern Iraq and Kurdish families from the region throughout the twentieth century following the foundation of the modern Turkish Republic. Its economy depends heavily on animal husbandry, grain agriculture, fruit orchards, and cheese-making. Although I had spent several seasons at the project earlier, I had little contact with the families at Ayanis. This distance from local inhabitants of the archaeological study area is still typical of many archaeological projects in the Middle East, despite the genuine efforts of an increasing number of projects emphasizing the importance of public and community-based archaeology (Atalay 2012). Only with this new opportunity, once I started long conversations with the villagers, asking about their houses, the history of the village and the immediate landscape around it, did I became aware of a small but precious grove of almond trees on the steep western slopes of the citadel mound, overlooking the lake (Figure 11.2). Almond trees are rare in this region, and according to the villagers, unattested in the surrounding landscape.[5] However, this unusual grove of scraggly almonds seems to have been inhabiting the citadel mound for quite some time, well beyond the collective memory of the village. The trees are spread over the surface remains of the stepped foundations of the Iron Age citadel wall, as well as the rock outcrops that support them. Inhabitants of Ayanis consider the almond trees sacred,

Figure 11.1. The village of Ayanis and the Iron Age fortress (author's photograph).

Figure 11.2. Almond grove in Ayanis (author's photograph).

cutting or carrying away dried branches from them is considered a taboo, and several stories exist among the villagers about the dire consequences of such acts. Those who disturb the almond trees in any way are haunted by ancestors in their dreams.[6]

The almond grove perched on the steep rocky slopes of the ancient mound is a *poetic landscape*. It is a powerful place in the cultural imagination of the people at Ayanis, rooted deeply in the past. The past in the almond grove is made alive with the material presence of ancient ruins, and the close association of almonds with the pre-World War I Armenian presence in the area. The almond trees of Ayanis fit well with my understanding of "place", both miraculous and mundane, richly layered in its materiality, deep historicity, and the body of very specific stories, practices, shared memories, and contingent meanings that are associated with it. The almond grove at Ayanis is on the one hand relatively marginal to the spaces of everyday life in the village, yet it is an important aspect of the rural landscape that gives definition to Ayanis's unique identity as a rural place. As an "environment" of lived memory, to borrow Pierre Nora's concept (1989) of *milieux de mémoire,* the grove connects the everyday practices and beliefs of the villagers to a shared past.[7] In the next section, I turn to the question of representation of place in the context of a cave spring, a geologically performative place that becomes the subject-matter of a series of nineteenth-century paintings by Gustave Courbet.

Source of the Loue: Place, Presence, Performance

Imagine the mouth of a dark cave, cut into a rocky cliff, from which a river flows towards you. Darkness envelops the scene to such an extent that only nearby patches of stone and stream offer any light to guide your way, and as the cave approaches even these illuminated forms begin to lose their shape, mutating into amorphous clumps at the periphery of your visual field. It is the image of a landscape about to swallow you whole [Galvez 2003: 17].

This paragraph is a quote from art historian Paul Galvez (2003), writing about Gustave Courbet's 1864 painting the Source of the Loue (Figure 11.3), very successfully bringing out the visceral, bodily impact of the painting on the viewer that he characterizes as "an uncertain plunge into the abyss".[8] This well-known realist artist of nineteenth-century France painted a series of landscapes in the 1850s and 60s around his hometown of Ornans in the region of Franche-Compté, West of the Jura mountains.[9] These landscapes concern a number of powerful, evocative places, with high looming rocky cliffs, meandering river gorges, dark caves and lush springs, abandoned beaches and monumental ruins, which appear as the primary subject matter of his thickly applied, materially distinct paintings that brought about the tactile, bodily immediacy of the places he was depicting.[10] Each of these pre-modernist works, predating the aesthetic ambitions of modernism, such as "The Stream of the Puits Noir" (the Black Well), focuses on a highly specific locus "out there" in the countryside. Yet these are not anonymous, idyllic, natural landscapes, but in fact firmly located *real places* painted with Courbet's ubiquitous earthy textures. As the meticulously place-specific titles of the paintings suggest, they tell their own story and have their own intrinsic dynamic. As Linda Nochlin (2007) notes, Courbet's painting "has insisted upon the ungeneralized, unidealized configuration of his gnarled,

Figure 11.3. Source of the Loue, Gustave Courbet (1864). Oil on Canvas 39¼ × 56 in. (99.7 × 142.2 cm). Metropolitan Museum of Art. Acquired Permission by Images for Academic Publishing.

unclassical, rocky countryside, the Franche-Comté, as a basic ingredient in his construction of a sense of place."

Such is a curious series he painted at the Source of the Loue, the river that runs through the middle of Ornans. In his letters, Courbet mentions several visits to the source of the Loue, especially in 1864, to paint numerous landscapes (Chu 1992: 243). The karstic, porous limestone geology of the Jura plateau allows the Doubs River, and its tributaries like the Loue, to flow through impressive deep gorges and over waterfalls, while they disappear and reemerge from deep caves. The source of the Loue is probably one of the most spectacular of such cave-spring sites. Repeatedly engaging with this powerful place, Courbet depicted the source in a series of dense and dark paintings, occasionally bringing human elements into the scene. The material qualities of his paintings were particularly important in constructing this extraordinary sense of place. It has been pointed out that his unorthodox use of the palette knife to obtain pictorial effects was especially innovative, such as his use of "the shavings of pigment which give the cliff of Ornans its dry and chalky aspect, imitating in an almost indexical manner the mineral structure so characteristic of the Jura relief."[11]

The source of a river, a place with the shiny transparent water pouring out of a dark mouth of a cave, is an *evocative landscape*, a place of geological wonder, always alluding to the fecundity of the earth and the origin of the world, which Courbet evoked in the titles of his later paintings focusing on the nude female body (Nochlin 1986: 82). The source of a river is an eventful landscape, which performs itself with the gushing water. It is this performativity of the place to which Courbet was attracted. His landscapes demonstrate his intimate experience and deep knowledge of the landscapes around Ornans, if not his obsession with them, while the making of his paintings can be understood as his performative interaction with such powerful places. Significantly, the representation of a landscape here is no longer a disembodied exercise of depicting the world, but the immersion of the body into the lush matter of the earth, both for the painter and the viewer. I would like to suggest that Courbet was an ethnographer of place and landscape, ethnographer of a spatial culture, of which he was a part.[12] As Desbuissons (2008: 260) suggests, "Courbet's body had the particular function of materialising the organic attachment of his works to his native region."

This is why Courbet's Realism was so often understood as an excrescence of his person, in turn seen as an extension of the material world. His paintings transported the local bodies of place-knowledge in Ornans to the broader world of pictorial representation in the salons of Paris.

Source of the Tigris: The Event of Place

The time has come to move back to more familiar territories and introduce my third and last place. Like the Jura mountains in eastern France, the landscapes of southern Anatolia offer extensive regions of karstic formations composed of Mesozoic and Tertiary limestones, covering as much as one third of the peninsula (Atalay 1998; 2003). In these areas with copious underground drainage, particularly the region of the central, western and eastern Taurus plateaus, one finds a wealth of "karstic features such as karrens, dissolution dolines, collapse dolines, blind valleys, karstic springs, swallow holes, caves, unroofed caves, natural bridges, gorges and poljes" (Doğan and Özel 2005: 373). Among these features, particularly significant are springs, natural "tunnels" or caves through which rivers and streams flow briefly, as well as poljes or "sinkholes" where surface-flowing streams disappear underground. The human engagement with this mineral world has varied dramatically through history, but such sites where the geological landscape performs its spectacles engaged the cultural imagination deeply. There is a fairly recent interest among archaeologists to take up these cultural

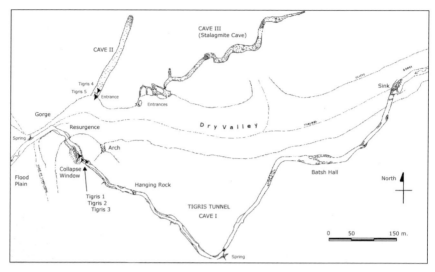

Figure 11.4. Plan of the Tigris Tunnel area and environs at Birkleyn Çay
(after Waltham 1976; reproduced by courtesy of Tony Waltham)

perceptions of the mineral world. The significance of rocks, caves, and watery places, especially among prehistoric societies, is now not only eradicating the long-held Cartesian split between nature and culture, but also opening up a new territory of archaeological research.[13]

One fascinating place that has always provoked the imagination of locals, travelers, and political actors since antiquity is the site known to geologists, archaeologists, and Assyriologists as the *Tigris Tunnel*, or the "Source of the Tigris". The site features multiple caves, rock outcrops, and gorges, known as the Birkleyn cave system, located to the north of the Diyabakır Plain, northwest of the modern town of Lice in southeastern Turkey (Figure 11.4).[14] Dibni Su, one of the tributaries of the Tigris, emerges at the end of a 1018 m-long natural tunnel under the Korha Mountain, and flows southwest through a spectacular, incised valley. Its "palaeovalley" (i.e., ancient river-bed) is surrounded by four other resurgence caves.[15]

The caved river source has a rich archaeological history in the Early Iron Age. Assyrian kings Tiglathpileser I and Shalmaneser III, in the early eleventh and mid-ninth centuries B.C., repeatedly visited the site of the Tigris Sources during their military expeditions. The site was located in the midst of a politically contested region immediately north of the Upper Tigris River basin, where the Assyrians carried out an active frontier settlement program in the Early Iron Age and controlled agricultural production as well as mining through their regional

Figure 11.5. Relief image of Tiglath-pileser I on the Lower Cave (Cave I) walls, with Tigris 1 cuneiform inscription to his left (author's photograph).

capital at Tušhan (modern Ziyarettepe) in the Upper Tigris valley.[16] The Tigris Source was astoundingly at the heart of the Hurrian kingdom of Šubria; at that time, it lay only 24 km from Lice, a town usually identified with Upūmu/Uppumu, the Early Iron Age Hurrian-speaking capital of that kingdom (Desző 2006). Dibnu Su valley was also well connected both to the Urartian Lake Van Basin and to the Ergani Maden (ancient Arqania), one of the most important copper sources for northern Mesopotamia to the west. During their visits to the Source of the Tigris, the Assyrian kings performed sacrificial rituals, held sumptuous feasts, received tribute and gifts from the submissive local rulers, and had their craftsmen carve commemorative inscriptions and "images of kingship" on the bedrock at the mouth of multiple caves (Figures 11.5, 11.6). The details of these commemorative and ritual events are known from multiple sources, from the pictorial representations of the events on the Balawat Bronzes and from textual accounts in Assyrian annals and monumental inscriptions. In the Assyrian narrative accounts of military expeditions, the Source of the Tigris, like the Source of the Euphrates or the Sea of Nairi, appears as an important geographic locale and a poetic expression that denotes a particularly distant and fecund landscape at the very edge of the imperial territories. Shalmaneser III boasts, for instance, that he "subjected [the territory from] the source of

Figure 11.6. Tigris Tunnel-Birkleyn Çay Upper Cave mouth, with Shalmaneser III's relief
and inscriptions (author's photograph).

the Tigris to the source of the Euphrates, from the Sea of Inner Zamua to
the Sea of the land of Kaldu" (Grayson 1996: 95). In the Assyrian annalistic
narratives, these places become symbolically charged, holy landscapes in the
geographical imagination of Assyrians. However, I have also tried to show that
these are *real places*, as they are repeatedly visited by the Assyrian kings, and
some site-specific ritual activities are carried out at those locales.

Seven years ago, I presented a detailed discussion of the Source of the
Tigris site as an evocative Assyrian frontier landscape in relation to the ways
in which the specific commemorative events at the site were represented on
Assyrian urban monuments of the imperial center (Harmanşah 2007). In
that article, I suggested that the Assyrian state's practices of raising or carving
monuments at frontier landscapes appropriated and/or took over places that
were already symbolically charged, as sites either of cult practice or political
contestation. The physical act of carving of rock monuments itself, and the
political statements that accompany it, propagated a discourse of *terra nullius,*
claiming a take-over of wilderness, of untouched or virgin rocks/landscapes.
In the specific case of the Tigris Sources, I pointed to the Hurrian-Anatolian
practice of associating caves, sinkholes, and river-gorges with the underworld,
the world of ancestors, and noted that Assyrian kings visiting the Tigris

Sources subscribed to the Hurro-Anatolian cult of the DINGIR.KAŠKAL.KUR ("Divine Road of the Earth") (see discussion below). It has been shown from textual evidence that the land of the kingdom of Šubria had constituted a landscape of long-term Hurrian presence since the mid-second millennium B.C. and housed several sacred sites by the beginning of the first millennium B.C. (Desző 2006: 38).

What is striking about the commemorative performances and image-making events at this symbolically charged landscape is that they were then re-presented on the pictorial narrative monuments and royal annals of the state, back in Assyria, transporting this frontier place and its exotic symbolisms to the imperial center. Just as is the case in Courbet's paintings of the Source of the Loue at Ornans, a powerful place and its cultural meanings were transported to larger audiences through the act of visual and textual representation. A fascinating example of the transportation of this landscape commemoration comes from the series of bronze strips from the gates of Tell Balawat, in northern Iraq, dated to the time of King Shalmaneser III in the ninth century B.C. The episode on Relief Panel 10, which narrates the king's seventh-year campaign, culminates with a ceremonial scene, understood as one of Shalmaneser's visits to the Source of the Tigris (Figure 11.7). From various annalistic accounts, it is known that, at the Tigris Sources, the king had received the submission of local kings, made offerings to the gods, celebrated a banquet, and had his craftsmen carve his images and inscriptions on the rock faces during his seventh- and fifteenth-year campaigns.[17]

In the outstanding scene on the Balawat Bronzes, the cultic and ceremonial activity is depicted in great detail, while the rock faces, the river, and the caves from which the Tigris emerges are represented in an articulate spatial specificity. In the upper register a sacrifice takes place, while within a large cave-like space the image of the king is carved, attended by a high Assyrian official standing on a raised platform. In the lower register, while a series of sacrificial animals are being led to the scene from the left, the stele-shaped image of the king is carved by the artisan on the rock face. The spatial representation on the Balawat bronze bands is remarkably commensurate with the topography of the Birklinçay caves. Furthermore, Balawat Bronze Band 10 carries a fascinating summary inscription above the scene, revealing very well the sacred, performative function of the event: "I entered the opening of the river, made offering to the gods (and) set up my royal image" (Yamada 2000: 281). The Assyrian king directly communicates with the cults of the place or the cave. We do not have to assume that the Assyrian deities are being referred to here, but more appropriately the cults of the locale.

Place-making practices of ancient states appropriated places of cultural significance through such commemorative ceremonies, various acts of

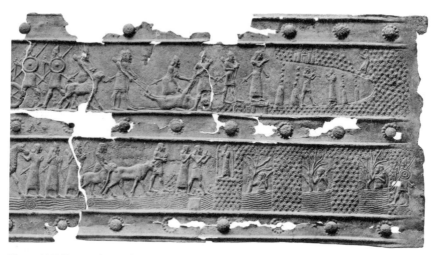

Figure 11.7. Bronze door reliefs of Shalmaneser III. Tell Balawat (Imgur-Enlil),
Relief Panel 10 (King 1915: plate LIV).

inscription, and monumentalization. One could argue that, at these sites, spectacles and performances of the state merged with existing local practices that had a much longer-term presence at such locales, but perhaps in materially much less ostentatious ways. In a recent conversation, Nick Shepherd memorably described this process as colonial practice "eating up" such local practices: it both destroys those situated practices but was also nurtured by them. The carving of rock reliefs and the raising of landscape monuments at geologically "eventful" places such as springs and sinkholes already testifies to the long-term human engagement with these sites. The carving of rock-relief monuments, setting up monumental stelae or commemorative monuments such as the very popular "weapons of Aššur," at river sources and lakes for commemorative spectacles of the state, were important, contemplative moments during the so-called Assyrian "military" expeditions (Harmanşah 2012). In the present line of thinking outlined above, I suggest that we must understand these acts as taking place at already locally powerful places that are hosts for a multiplicity of cultural meanings and symbolisms. In this way, such powerful landscapes were woven into narratives of the state. These political narratives might hinder or mask such rich layers of human interaction in generating rhetorics of kingship and official histories. It is the task of the archaeologist to "excavate" such place-palimpsests that the elite-dominated representational record of the past usually obfuscates. It is archaeological fieldwork that can offer some hope of recovering these subtle materialities.

I propose that if archaeology is a discipline of memory and material culture and must be rescued from traditional historiography, as Laurent Olivier (2008) has recently argued, it can offer a rigorous methodology and a critical framework for investigating places. Archaeology is advantaged with its refined field methodologies and extraordinary sensitivity to document diachronically the almost ephemeral traces of material practices that constitute places that are not necessarily monumentalized, or before they are monumentalized. My project intends to contribute to landscape archaeology, and the broader fields of the humanities and social sciences, by developing an archaeology of place with a fine-grained understanding of located practices and the long-term biography of regional landscapes.

"Divine Road of the Earth": Event, Place, Performance

In 1988, in Hattuša, the capital city of the Hittites, two curious stone-built structures were excavated in the area now known as the Südburg or "Southern Citadel", the site of a major Iron Age fortress.[18] The stone-built chambers were later understood to belong to an extensive ceremonial pool-complex in the eastern part of the city, known as the Eastern Ponds, which both served as a water reservoir for the city and had a ritual function (Seeher 1999: 344; Wittenberg and Schachner 2012), and was most likely associated with Temple 31, built on the northern part of the Südburg. These two stone chambers had vaulted roofs which were constructed of large, finely shaped, limestone ashlar blocks immediately underneath the northern corner of one of the two well-built artificial lakes which were fed by several springs. Chamber 1 is not decorated; however the western wall of the four-meter deep Chamber 2 to the north is covered with a lengthy six-line hieroglyphic Luwian inscription of the late thirteenth-century king Šuppiluliuma II (1207–? B.C.), along with reliefs of the Sun God and the king himself. The inscription, published by J. David Hawkins with a detailed commentary (1995), commemorates the king's military successes and foundation of new cities in the lands of Wiyanawanda, Tamina, Masa, Lukka and Ikkuwaniya, and Tarhuntašša. These are the western and southwestern frontiers of the Hittite Empire, where the majority of the political diplomacy and military campaigns focused in the thirteenth century B.C. More significantly for the present argument, the inscription ends with the following phrase:

18. zi/a+a-ti DEUS.*202 pa-ti-' ANNUS i(a)-zi/a
18. Here a Divine Road of the Earth in that year (I) constructed.

Working on the inscription, David Hawkins noticed that DEUS.*202 should be read DEUS.VIA+TERRA, which corresponds to the sign-by-sign rendering of the well-known cuneiform expression DINGIR.KAŠKAL.KUR of the Hittite and Hurrian texts. Hawkins translates this ambiguous term as "The Divine Road of the Earth" or "Divine Earth-Road"[19]. In Hittite and Hurrian texts, DINGIR.KAŠKAL.KUR is associated with the geological features of springs, natural tunnels, river gorges, or caves, as well as poljes or potholes, those features that clearly link the circulation of water above and below the earth (Gordon 1967). These are considered liminal spaces, entrances to the underworld, places where ritual communication with the dead ancestors could be established. Occurrences of this phrase in the Late Bronze Age texts appear overwhelmingly in the descriptions of Hittite frontiers, but these ritually significant places were also listed among divine witnesses to inter-polity treaties, along with a multiplicity of Hittite divinities, mountains, and rivers, as is well known from the Bronze Tablet from Hattuša. They are also frequently portrayed as recipients of cultic libations. For the first time, in the case of the Hieroglyphic chamber, a "Divine Road of the Earth" was associated with a specific monument, strongly suggesting that Hittites may have built artificial tunnels to access the underworld, with a mimetic link to the geological features such as caved springs, and a semantic relationship to the ritual significance of karstic springs, river tunnels, and sinkholes as cult places. In Hattuša and elsewhere, then, "Divine Road of the Earth" took the form of sacred pools or rock monuments, accompanied by rock-cut reliefs, monumental inscriptions, and other ritual features. I have earlier suggested that the Assyrian imperial interest in visiting the Source of the Tigris caves, the carving of reliefs and inscriptions at this site, and feasting there, was a form of appropriating the Anatolian practice of venerating the "Divine Road of the Earth" (Harmanşah 2007). In ritualizing powerful sacred topographies associated with water sources, the Assyrian kings were settling their political disputes with the local polities at a frontier site, as we learn from the Assyrian annals and the Balawat gate pictorial narratives. The Assyrian king's carved images at the Tigris Tunnels are indeed engaging with the divinities of the Underworld, at a sacred, god-filled landscape.

Rock Reliefs in the Zamantı Su Valley

Using a similar multi-sited approach to address the complexity of cultural associations and the layered materiality that places possess, I have been working on Hittite and Early Iron Age landscape monuments in Anatolia, with a specific focus on sacred springs and rock relief monuments (Harmanşah 2011a; 2014). Hittite rulers of Hattuša, as well as their contemporaries in Anatolia, and several rulers of the Syro-Hittite that rose to power in Anatolia and Upper Mesopotamia in the aftermath of the Hittite Empire's collapse, favored the construction of cultic installations at prominent rocky landscapes and sacred springs, where commemorative inscriptions and visual representations are displayed, linking the state's official discourse with the divine beings of places. What is most challenging is to understand such monumentalized sites as already symbolically charged, culturally saturated places with intricate human associations, where state ideology and local social practices merge, rather than assuming that such sites were simply transformed by the state apparatus from a "natural place" to a "socialized space". A critical mass of scholarly work has been published in recent years on rock reliefs, sacred springs, and other extra-urban monuments, where macro-scale perspectives have been emphasized and the role of the monuments in the territorial spread of the empire has been clearly articulated (e.g. Ehringhaus 2005; Bonatz 2007; Seeher 2009; Glatz 2009). Represented on a single large map of the Hittite Empire covering the highlands of the Anatolian peninsula, this heterogeneous set of landscape monuments (rock reliefs, sacred pool-complexes, and earthen dams) give us the impression of marking or even controlling or surveying the political frontiers of the Empire. This politically-charged colonial function of rock monuments at the borders, as politically-charged sites of state spectacles and official discourse, has been argued for Assyrian reliefs as well (Shafer 1998; 2007). While I agree with the significance of these sites as imperial interventions, I intend to push this dominant paradigm further with site-specific study of each monument. In many cases, archaeological, and epigraphic evidence suggests that these monuments should be seen as appropriations by the elite of already existing places of significance, human practice, and collective memory, while also pointing to their site-specific relationship with local geologies, their immediate context within regional settlement geographies, and the historically-nuanced circumstances of their making. Several seasons of reconnaissance work at rock-relief sites in Turkey and, specifically, in the regional survey project I direct in the vicinity of the Yalburt Yaylası Mountain-Spring Monument, suggest that meticulous archaeological study of those monuments may indeed lead to significant revisions to our understanding of the cultural meaning and historical significance in a micro-regional, geological, and settlement context. Below, I present a small sample of that preliminary fieldwork in south-central Anatolia.

One cluster of rock monuments of relevance here is a series of Hittite reliefs, situated along the Zamantı Su valley in the province of Kayseri, possibly within the territory of ancient Kizzuwatna. Zamantı Su and its tributaries flow through a semi-volcanic landscape, through a deep limestone-ignimbrite gorge walled-in by lofty precipices, eastwards from the fertile Develi plain, at the foothills of the colossal mountain Erciyes, which constituted one of the

Figure 11.8. Fıraktın Hittite rock relief site and Zamantı Su valley
(author's photograph).

Figure 11.9. Fıraktın Hittite rock relief (author's photograph).

most important routes linking the Land of Hatti to Syria. Extremely rich with
abundant springs, the entire valley seems to be heavily settled during the Late
Bronze and Iron Ages, and especially in the Roman period. The rock relief at
Fıraktın is situated on such a volcanic bedrock façade, immediately above one
of the tributaries of the Zamantı Su, overlooking a very green plain, with a
spectacular view of Erciyes Mountain, and immediately below an ignimbrite
pumice-flow platform (Figures 11.8, 11.9). Walking on the bedrock plateau

immediately above the relief, one comes across several cup-marks and circular basins, and extensive quarrying activity. On a prominent rock promontory to the northeast of the riverbed, only a few hundred meters north of the relief, one can observe a dense artifact cluster and surface remains of a monumental building, at least 30 × 28 m. Cup-marks and circular basins also cluster near this building, suggesting its affiliation with the rock monument. Fıraktın Höyük, an impressive settlement mound, is located about 1.5 km to the west/northwest of the rock relief and in the floodplain of the Kara Su, a tributary of Zamantı (Stokkel 2005: 172; Ehringhaus 2005: 59–65; Ullmann 2010: 220–221). The rock relief is located close to the confluence of the two rivers.

The thirteenth-century B.C. relief itself depicts the royal couple, Hittite Great King Hattušili III and Puduhepa, in the act of pouring libation in front of the Storm God Tarhunzas and the seated Hepat respectively, as the hieroglyphic inscription indicates. The hieroglyphic inscription on the rock relief refers to Puduhepa as "great queen, daughter of Kizzuwatna, having become god," which is a well-known Hittite euphemism for being deceased (Ehringhaus 2005: 64; Bonatz 2007: 112–114). Similar associations of various rock-relief monuments of the Hittites may suggest that at least some of them should be associated with the "Divine Stone House," (É NA$_4$) or *hekur* (NA$_4$.*hekur*. SAG.UŠ), monuments that are frequently mentioned in the texts. Theo van den Hout (2002: 91) has argued that monuments such as the NA$_4$.*hekur*. SAG.UŠ probably represent a funerary monument to dead royal ancestors; however, he adds that they were not simply tombs in the modern sense of the term, but "large self-supporting institutions employing cultic, administrative, and other personnel, and mostly enjoying some kind of tax exemption." These institutions are well known from the cult inventories (Hazenbos 2003).

The topographic settings of each of the other rock-relief sites in the region are dramatically different from each other, despite the fact that they are chronologically and functionally interrelated (see also Ullmann 2010: 217–226). Two sets of Taşçı carvings (referred in the literature as Taşçı A and Taşçı B, about 100 m apart) are on quite a modest and non-monumental setting in a narrow river gorge (Şamaz Dere) on a rather low surface on the rock, and they can be more accurately characterized as graffiti, based on the style of carving. One of the reliefs has a brief inscription translated by Hawkins as "Manazi, daughter of Lupaki the Army-Scribe (son of ?) Zida the MEŠEDI-man, servant of Hattušili" (Ehringhaus 2005: 68; Glatz and Plourde 2011: 47). A number of caves and caverns are attested in the immediate vicinity of these reliefs. Moving about 10 km to the east of the Taşçı reliefs, one finds the Imamkulu monument, which is carved on a free-standing, boulder-like rock, very close to an abundant spring, overlooking a spectacular plain, and in front of a bedrock cliff-façade, similar to that of Fıraktın and Taşçı

(Ehringhaus 2005: 70–76). On top of the cliff above the İmamkulu relief, one also can observe plenty of circular cuttings associated with this relief, again reminiscent of Fasıllar's context. The Luwian hieroglyphs identify the sponsor of the monument as "Prince Ku(wa)lanamuwa" or "Ku(wa)lamuwa" (Ehringhaus 2005: 73). The pictorial scene features and honors the Weather God. Finally, the Hanyeri monument is located on the southern side of the Gezbel pass over the Bey Dağı Mountain range. This is a route not frequently used these days, while the relief overlooks yet another river gorge, and it is also located by a spring (Ehringhaus 2005: 70, 76, 80). The relief is carved relatively quite high on the rock (c. 4 m up) and was clearly intended to be seen from a distance, unlike the earlier three monuments. The iconography is a familiar one of a warrior figure holding a bow and spear, well known from other Hittite rock monuments, such as Karabel near Manisa, and Hatip near Konya. The Luwian inscription identifies him as "Prince Ku(wa)lanamuwa," just as the İmamkulu monument, and here he is confronting/having an encounter with a mountain god, identified as Šarruma.

It is quite likely that three of these sets of rock reliefs – namely Fıraktın, Taşçı (A and B), and İmamkulu – are associated with the specific geological context of the deeply-gorged river in the Zamantı Su valley and have been carved in close association with spectacular trachyte/ignimbrite/pumice rock façades of the gorge, or near it. All of the reliefs tend to come as part of an assemblage of rock cuttings, building and settlement remains, and other archaeological features, which suggests long-term ritual use and repeated visits to the sites. Not all the monuments seem to be directly sponsored by the Hittite Great Kings who were resident in the state capital Hattuša-Boğazköy, but one can assume that local rulers and elites were responsible for the making and upkeep of these monuments. In their iconographic details, and more discursively in the hieroglyphic Luwian inscriptions, they lay claim to imperial Hittite iconographies and titles, and connect themselves with the central power in the empire. Perhaps equally significantly, these monuments constitute and appropriate sites where ritual practices are housed within a special geological context that has associations with the underworld, the ancestor cult, and divinities.

Conclusion: Towards an Archaeology of Places

Caves, rock reliefs, and architectural monuments that alter, imitate, or recreate geological orifices to the underworld are places where the cultural imagination of local communities met the bedrock of Anatolian landscapes. These sites had significant everyday and extraordinary functions as sources of drinking water, ritual grounds for communicating with deities and ancestors, witnesses to political events, practices of imagemaking and inscription, and the construction of commemorative monuments. What I propose here is a nuanced approach to rock reliefs and water monuments of the Anatolian countryside, an archaeologically rigorous and critical approach to *places*. The archaeology of place pays close attention to the site-specific character of cultural practices, socio-symbolic associations, and multi-layered materiality of places.

There is a long and very rich scholarly tradition of writing about so-called "landscape monuments," for the simple reason that they have been some of the most visible features of the Anatolian landscape since antiquity. They have duly drawn a significant amount of interest among travelers and antiquarians, as well as archaeologists, of the eighteenth, nineteenth, and early twentieth centuries. In those great centuries of Romanticism and adventure, these ruins were always the most fascinating places to which the imagination of the Western and Eastern antiquarians was drawn. In mapping the historical geographies of the ancient world, rock-relief sites were important anchoring points for classically-trained scholars, while the decipherment of the cuneiform script itself was performed with the help of rock inscriptions. Sparked by this long-term scholarly interest in reconstructing ancient geographical regions, the reading of monumental inscriptions and the iconographic analysis of the rock reliefs have become normative field practice around the rock reliefs. The meaning and function of rock monuments that emerge from these readings appear to be religious representations of political power, and this view reduces them to an administrative technology for projections of imperial, territorial power.

I argue here that precisely such a prioritization of imperial interventions to places has the danger of adhering to Orientalist colonialisms of early modernity and has to be scrutinized. In contrast, here I advocate seeing these monuments as elite appropriations of places of power that already existed in a web of significance prior to such interventions. Based on available archaeological evidence, it is possible to suggest that a critical archaeological study of rock-relief sites and spring sanctuaries reveals their deeper histories and more intimate stories within local landscapes of cultural memory. A responsible archaeological project, therefore, will investigate place genealogies and biographies, not only through an archaeological investigation of their making in antiquity, but also engaging with ethnohistorical sources and ethnographic methodologies, in order to reflect on their afterlife as places of lived heritage and social memory. This emphasis on the afterlife of monuments can also be read as a gesture to return sites of archaeological heritage to their contemporary publics who have long been denied this heritage, due to the scientific prioritization of the "most ancient" episodes and "original" making of monuments.

Places are significant locales for communities around the world for anchoring their identities and senses of belonging. In the globalizing world of aggressive development projects and neo-liberal interventions, places are often defended by local communities, ecological or human rights activists, and heritage specialists, and archaeological places are included in such place-based struggles. Much work falls in the hands of archaeologists to take part in this debate, mobilizing archaeology's extraordinary tools to trace deep histories and place genealogies. The time is ripe for such a critical turn in studies of archaeological landscapes.

Notes

1. The literature on place that has appeared in recent decades is large. Some of the outstanding examples are Entrikin 1991; Casey 1993, 1997; Auge 1995; Basso 1996; Massey 2005; Malpas 2006.

2. Having said that, I must point to some significant exceptions of deep place histories such as Davis 1998; Cruikshank 2005; Forbes 2007; Scandura 2008. The recent edited volume entitled *The Archaeology of Meaningful Places* (Bowser and Zedeño 2009) is perhaps the first rigorous attempt to bring the discussion of "place" into archaeology and archaeological fieldwork.

3. See e.g. discussion in Anschuetz et al. 2001 and Cherry 2003, with some excellent collections such as Frankovich and Patterson 1999; Alcock and Cherry 2004; Athanassapoulos and Wandsnider 2004.

4. The project was funded by TÜBİTAK, The Institute of Scientific Research of Turkey, and the results of the two seasons of fieldwork are being prepared for publication in a volume edited by Altan Çilingiroğlu and Özlem Çevik.

5. In fact the almond is one of the oldest cultivated nuts in the Near East: its cultivation from wild species goes back to the Early Bronze Age in the Eastern Mediterranean world (Clement 2005: 134; Ladizinsky 1999). Almonds are a lot more common in the steppe forest environments of Upper Mesopotamia, Armenia, and Azerbaijan, and along the borderlands between Turkey and Syria, east of the Euphrates in the provinces of Gaziantep and Urfa (Van Zeist 2008: 38).

6. I also determined during the ethnographic interviews that the nearby village of Panzis (Özyurt), which also was an Armenian village in the nineteenth and early twentieth century, had a major mulberry plantation in and around the village, which was cut down by the villagers who settled in the abandoned village in 1950s. This partly helps us understand the contemporary perception of the landscape through the particular clustering of special trees and groves, and the way they are associated with the pre-World War Armenian culture in the area. Abdülkadiroğlu (1992: 425–29) mentions several sacred tree sanctuaries in the area of Van. Most of these sacred trees had healing qualities for various sicknesses.

7. Pierre Nora (1989) differentiates between real "environments" of memory (i.e., *milieux de mémoire*, where lived shared pasts are materialized) versus the sites of memory (i.e., *lieux de mémoire*, which refer to discursively formed, designed sites of commemoration with reference to historical events). However, this definition suggests some form of a "death" of collective memory, which may be objected to for its nostalgic view of pre-industrial and/or "traditional" societies; see especially discussion in Alcock 2002: 21.

8. Galvez 2003: 20. Also, Bois and Krauss (1998: 37) make a phenomenological comparison of Cézanne's paintings with Courbet's landscapes, and suggest that the "sense of touch" in Cézanne's paintings owed a lot to Courbet's paintings such as the "Source of the Loue". On Courbet's intimate connection to physical reality or "materialism", see Debuissons 2008.

9. On Courbet's landscapes, see also Fried 1990: 238–254; Galvez 2003; Nochlin 2007.

10. Fried 1990: 213. Courbet "used thick impasto, overtly applying the pigment in heavy layers where he left visible not only the strokes of the paintbrush but – even more crudely – the marks of the palette knife" (Desbuissons 2008: 251).

11. Desbuissons 2008: 256. A similar argument has been made by Galvez (2003: 17), who suggested that "the palette knife is used to model forms as weighty as an encrusted rock..."

12. It is well known that Courbet never lost his heavy Franche-Comté accent. Desbuissons (2008: 259) points out that he spoke "like a countryman from the Jura: the system of this earthy speech, which bears the stamp of its geographical and social origins, is a necessary signpost to his identity (an index)."

13. See for instance excellent contributions in Boivin and Owoc 2004; Bradley 2000; Cruikshank 2005; Brady and Prufer 2005; Holmberg 2005.

14. On the geology of the Birkleyn cave system, see Waltham 1976; Doğan 2009. See Schachner 2009: 1–6 and Harmanşah 2007: 185–186 for detailed geographical context.

15. Doğan 2009: 24; see also map of the Birkleyn Caves in Doğan 2009: fig. 20.

16. Parker 2001. On excavations at Ziyarettepe, see Matney et al. 2003; MacGinnis and Matney 2009.

17. For a detailed documentation of the annals related to the Source of the Tigris, see Yamada 2000: 281–283. Shalmaneser III writes: "I went as far as the Source of the Tigris where the origin of the water is located. I washed therein the weapon of Ashur, made offering to my god(s) and held a ceremonial banquet. I fashioned a splended royal image of myself, inscribed thereon the praise of Ashur, my lord (and) all the heroic deeds which I achieved in the ends (and) set (it) up therein." (Ann. 13.II.69–72. and Ann. 14. ll40–44; see Yamada 2000: 281).

18. See Hawkins 1995, and Neve's preliminary archaeological report in Hawkins 1995: 9–12 and Neve 1993: 67–80, as well as Seeher 1999, 2006. The area is called Südburg ("Southern Fort") due to the Iron Age/Phrygian fortress that overlaid the Hittite sacred pool complex.

19. Hawkins 1995: 44, commentary on line 18. See also discussion in Harmanşah 2011b: 636 and Erbil and Mouton 2012: 58–60. According to Hawkins, the sign *202 appears twice on the Karahöyük (Elbistan) hieroglyphic Luwian stele as a ligature OF VIA+TERRA. On the Karahöyük stele and its archaeological context, see Harmanşah 2011a.

References

Abdülkadiroğlu, Abdülkerim (ed.)
  1992 *Van Kütüğü*. Yüzüncü Yıl Üniversitesi Yayınları, Van.

Alcock, Susan E.
  2002 *Archaeologies of the Greek Past: Landscape, Monuments, and Memories*. Cambridge University Press, Cambridge.

Alcock, Susan E., and John F. Cherry (eds.)

2004 *Side-by-Side Survey: Comparative Regional Studies in the Mediterranean.* Oxbow
Books, Oxford.

Alcock, Susan E., and Jane E. Rempel

2006 The More Unusual Dots on the Map: "Special-Purpose" Sites and the Texture of
Landscape. In *Surveying the Greek Chora: The Black Sea Region in a Comparative
Perspective,* edited by Pia Guldager Bilde and Vladimir F. Stolba, pp. 27–46. Aarhus
University Press, Aarhus.

Anschuetz, Kurt F., Richard H. Wilshusen, and Cherie L. Scheick

2001 An Archaeology of Landscapes: Perspectives and Directions. *Journal of Archaeological
Research* 9: 157–211.

Appadurai, Arjun

1996 *Modernity at Large: Cultural Dimensions of Globalization.* University of Minnesota
Press, Minneapolis.

Atalay, İbrahim

1998 Paleoenvironmental Conditions of the Late Pleistocene and Early Holocene
in Anatolia, Turkey. In *Quaternary Deserts and Climatic Change,* edited by
Abdulrahman Sultan Alsharnan, Kenneth W. Glennie, Gregory L. Whittle, and
Christopher G. St.C. Kendall, pp. 227–239. Balkema, Rotterdam.

2003 Effects of the Tectonic Movements on the Karstification in Anatolia, Turkey. *Acta
Carsalogica* 32(2): 196–203.

Atalay, Sonya

2012 *Community-based Archaeology: Research with, by and for Indigenous and Local
Communities.* University of California Press, Berkeley.

Athanassapoulos, Effie, and LuAnn Wandsnider (eds.)

2004 *Mediterranean Archaeological Landscapes: Current Issues.* University of Pennsylvania
Museum of Archaeology and Anthropology, Philadelphia.

Auge, Marc

1995 *Non-places: Introduction to an Anthropology of Supermodernity.* Verso, London and
New York.

Basso, Keith H.

1996 *Wisdom Sits in Places: Landscape and Language among the Western Apache.* University
of New Mexico Press, Albuquerque.

Bhabha, Homi K.

1994 *The Location of Culture.* Routledge, London and New York.

Bois, Yve-Alain, and Rosalind Krauss

1998 Cézanne: Words and Deeds. *October* 84: 31–43.

Boivin, Nicole, and Mary Ann Owoc (eds.)

2004 *Soils, Stones and Symbols: Cultural Perceptions of the Mineral World.* UCL Press, London.

Bonatz, Dominik

2007 The Divine Image of the King: Religious Representation of Political Power in the
Hittite Empire. In *Representations of Political Power: Case Histories from Times of*

Change and Dissolving Order in the Ancient Near East, edited by Marlies Heinz and Marian H. Feldman, pp. 111–136. Eisenbrauns, Winona Lake.

Bowser, Brenda J., and María Nieves Zedeño (eds.)
2009   *The Archaeology of Meaningful Places.* The University of Utah Press, Salt Lake City.

Bradley, Richard
2000   *An Archaeology of Natural Places.* Routledge, London and New York.

Brady, James Edward, and Keith Malcolm Prufer
2005   *In the Maw of the Earth Monster: Mesoamerican Ritual Cave Use.* University of Texas Press, Austin.

Casey, Edward S.
1993   *Getting Back into Place: Toward a Renewed Understanding of the Place-World.* Indiana University Press, Bloomington.
1997   *The Fate of Place: A Philosophical History.* University of California Press, Berkeley.

Cherry, John F.
2003   Archaeology Beyond the Site: Regional Survey and its Future. In *Theory and Practice in Mediterranean Archaeology: Old World and New World Perspectives*, edited by John K. Papadopoulos and Richard M. Leventhal, pp. 137–160. Cotsen Institute of Archaeology, UCLA, Los Angeles.

Chu, Petra ten-Doesschate
1992   *Letters of Gustave Courbet.* The University of Chicago Press, Chicago.

Çilingiroğlu, Altan, and Mirjo Salvini (eds.)
2001   *Ayanis I: Ten Years' Excavations at Rusahinili Eiduru-kai 1989–1998.* CNR Istituto per gli Studi Micenei ed Egeo-Anatolici, Roma.

Clement, Charles
2005   Nuts, Seeds and Pulses. In *The Cultural History of Plants*, edited by Sir Ghillean Prance and Mark Nesbitt, pp. 133–152. Routledge, New York.

Cruikshank, Julie
2005   *Do Glaciers Listen? Local Knowledge, Colonial Encounters and Social Imagination.* University of British Columbia Press, Vancouver.

David, Bruno, and Julian Thomas (editors)
2010   *Handbook of Landscape Archaeology.* Left Coast Press, Walnut Creek, CA.

Davis, Jack L. (ed.)
1998   *Sandy Pylos: An Archaeological History from Nestor to Navarino.* University of Texas Press, Austin.

Desbuissons, Frédérique
2008   Courbet's Materialism. *Oxford Art Journal* 31(2): 253–260.

Deszö, Tamás
2006   Šubria and the Assyrian Empire. *Acta Antiqua* 46: 33–38.

Dirlik, Arif
2001   Place-based Imagination: Globalism and the Politics of Place. In *Places and Politics in an Age of Globalization*, edited by Roxann Prazniak and Arif Dirlik, pp. 15–51. Rowman and Littlefield, Lanham, MD.

Dirlik, Arif, and Roxann Prazniak

    2001   Introduction: Cultural Identity and the Politics of Place, In *Places and Politics in an Age of Globalization*, edited by Roxann Prazniak and Arif Dirlik, pp. 3–13. Rowman and Littlefield, Lanham, MD.

Doğan, Uğur

    2005   Land Subsidence and Caprock Dolines Caused by Subsurface Gypsum Dissolution and the Effect of Subsidence on the Fluvial System in the Upper Tigris Basin (Between Bismil–Batman, Turkey). *Geomorphology* 71: 389–401.

    2009   The Geomorphology of the Birkleyn Caves (Diyarbakır-Türkiye): Preliminary Results. In *Assyriens Könige an einer der Quellen des Tigris: Archäologische Forschungen im Höhlensystem von Birkleyn und am sogenannten Tigris-Tunnel*, edited by Andreas Schachner, pp. 20–31. Istanbuler Forschungen 51. Wasmuth, Tübingen.

Doğan, Uğur, and Sadettin Özel

    2005   Gypsum Karst and its Evolution East of Hafik (Sivas, Turkey). *Geomorphology* 71: 373–388.

Ehringhaus, Horst

    2005   *Götter, Herrscher Inschriften: Die Felsreliefs der hethitischen Großreichzeit in der Türkei.* Philipp von Zabern, Mainz am Rhein.

Entrikin, J. Nicholas

    1991   *The Betweenness of Place: Towards a Geography of Modernity.* Macmillan, London.

Erbil, Yiğit, and Alice Mouton

    2012   Water in Ancient Anatolian Religions: An Archaeological and Philological Inquiry on the Hittite Evidence. *Journal of Near Eastern Studies* 71: 53–74.

Escobar, Arturo

    2008   *Territories of Difference: Place, Movements, Life, Redes.* Duke University Press, Durham and London.

Forbes, Hamish A.

    2007   *Meaning and Identity in a Greek Landscape: An Archaeological Ethnography.* Cambridge University Press, Cambridge.

Foucault, Michel

    2002   *The Archaeology of Knowledge.* Translated by Alan M.S. Smith. Routledge, London and New York.

Francovich, Riccardo, and Helen Patterson (eds.)

    1999   *Extracting Meaning from Plough Soil Assemblages.* Archaeology of the Mediterranean Landscape, Populus Monograph 5. Oxbow Books, Oxford.

Fried, Michael

    1990   *Courbet's Realism.* The University of Chicago Press, Chicago.

Galvez, Paul

    2003   Courbet's Touch. In *Soil and Stone: Impressionism, Urbanism, Environment,* edited by Frances Fowle and Richard Thomson, pp. 17–32. Ashgate, Burlington, VT.

Glatz, Claudia

    2009   Empire as Network: Spheres of Material Interaction in Late Bronze Age Anatolia. *Journal of Anthropological Archaeology* 28: 127–141.

Glatz, Claudia, and Aimée M. Plourde
  2011 Landscape Monuments and Political Competition in Late Bronze Age Anatolia: An
        Investigation of Costly Signaling Theory. *Bulletin of the Schools of Oriental Research*
        361: 33–66.

Gordon, Edmund I.
  1967 The Meaning of the Ideogram ᵈ KASKAL.KUR = "Underground Water-Course"
        and its Significance for Bronze Age Historical Geography. *Journal of Cuneiform
        Studies* 21: 70–88.

Grayson, A. Kirk
  1996 *The Royal Inscriptions of Mesopotamia/Assyrian Periods, Vol. 3: Assyrian Rulers of the
        Early First Millenium B.C. II (858–745 B.C.).* University of Toronto Press, Toronto.

Hamilakis, Yannis, and Philip Duke (eds.)
  2007 *Archaeology and Capitalism: From Ethics to Politics.* Left Coast Press, Walnut Creek,
        CA.

Harmanşah, Ömür
  2007 Source of the Tigris: Event, Place and Performance in the Assyrian Landscapes of
        the Early Iron Age. *Archaeological Dialogues* 14(2): 179–204.

  2009 Stones of Ayanis: New Urban Foundations and the Architectonic Culture in
        Urartu during the 7th C. BC. In *Bautechnik im Antiken und Vorantiken Kleinasien:
        Internationale Konferenz 13–16. Juni 2007 in Istanbul*, edited by Martin Bachmann,
        pp. 177–197. Byzas 9. Ege Yayınları, Istanbul.

  2011a Moving Landscapes, Making Place: Cities, Monuments and Commemoration at
        Malizi/Melid. *Journal of Mediterranean Archaeology* 24(1): 55–83.

  2011b Monuments and Memory: Architecture and Visual Culture in Ancient Anatolian
        History. In *Oxford Handbook of Anatolian Studies (8000–323 B.C.)*, edited by
        Sharon R. Steadman and Gregory McMahon, pp. 623–651. Oxford University
        Press, Oxford.

  2012 Beyond Aššur: New Cities and the Assyrian Politics of Landscape. *Bulletin of the
        American Schools of Oriental Research* 365: 53–77.

  2014 Stone Worlds: Technologies of Rock-Carving and Place-Making in Anatolian
        Landscapes. In *Cambridge Handbook of the Bronze and Iron Age Mediterranean*,
        edited by A. Bernard Knapp and Peter van Dommelen. Cambridge University Press,
        Cambridge, forthcoming.

Hasluck, Frederick W.
  1929 *Christianity and Islam under the Sultans*, edited by Margaret Hasluck. Oxford
        University Press, Oxford.

Hawkins, J. David
  1995 *The Hieroglyphic Inscription of the Sacred Pool Complex at Hattusa (SÜDBURG).*
        Studien zu den Bogazköy-Texten Beiheft 3. Harrassowitz, Wiesbaden.

Hazenbos, Joost
  2003 *The Organization of the Anatolian Local Cults during the Thirteenth Century B.C.: An
        Appraisal of the Hittite Cult Inventories.* Brill/Styx Holmberg, Leiden and Boston.

Holmberg, Karen
  2005 The Voices of Stones: Unthinkable Materiality in the Volcanic Context of Western

Panamá. In *Archaeologies of Materiality*, edited by Lynn Meskell, pp. 190–211. Wiley-Blackwell, Malden MA.

Kouchoukos, Nicholas, and Tony Wilkinson

2006 Landscape Archaeology in Mesopotamia: Past, Present, and Future. In *Settlement and Society: Essays Dedicated to Robert McCormick Adams*, edited by Elizabeth C. Stone, pp. 1–18. Cotsen Institute of Archaeology, UCLA, Los Angeles.

Ladizinsky, Gideon

1999 On the Origin of the Almond. *Genetic Resources and Crop Evolution* 46: 143–147.

Mellaart, James

1962 The Late Bronze Age Monuments of Eflatun Pınar and Fasıllar near Beyşehir. *Anatolian Studies* 12: 111–117.

MacGinnis, John, and Timothy Matney

2009 Archaeology at Frontiers: Excavating a Provincial Capital of the Assyrian Empire. *Journal of Assyrian Academic Studies* 23: 3–21.

Malpas, Jeff

2006 *Heidegger's Topology: Being, Place, World*. The MIT Press, Cambridge, MA.

Matney, Timothy, John MacGinnis, Helen McDonald, Katleen Nicoll, Lynn Rainville, Michael Roaf, Monica L. Smith and Diana Stein

2003 Archaeological Investigations at Ziyaret Tepe, 2002. *Anatolica* 29: 175–221.

Merrifield, Andrew

1993 Place and Space: A Lefebvrian Reconciliation. *Transactions of the Institute of British Geographers* 18(4): 516–531.

Neve, Peter

1993 *Hattuša – Stadt der Götter unde Tempel. Neue Ausgrabungen in der haupstadt der Hethiter*. Philipp von Zabern, Mainz am Rhein.

Nochlin, Linda

1986 Courbet's "L'origine du monde": The Origin without an Original. *October* 37: 76–86.

2007 *Courbet*. Thames and Hudson, London.

Nora, Pierre

1989 Between Memory and History: Les Lieux de Mémoire. *Representations* 26: 7–24.

Olivier, Laurent

2008 *Le sombre abîme du temps: mémoire et archéologie*. Seuil, Paris.

Özyar, Aslı

2006 A Prospectus of Hittite Art Based on the State of our Knowledge at the Beginning of the 3rd Millennium AD. In *Strukturerung und Datierung in der hethitischen Archäeologie/Structuring and Dating in Hittite Archaeology*, edited by Dirk Paul Mielke, Ulf-Dietrich Schoop, and Jürgen Seeher, pp. 125–148. Byzas 4. Ege Yayınları, İstanbul.

Parker, Bradley J.

2001 *The Mechanics of Empire: The Northern Frontier of Assyria as a Case Study in Imperial Dynamics*. The Neo-Assyrian Text Corpus Project, Helsinki.

Scandura, Jani
   2008 *Down in the Dumps: Place, Modernity, American Depression.* Duke University Press, Durham and London.

Schachner, Andreas
   2006 An den Ursprung des Tigris schrieb ich meinen Namen – Archäologische Forschungen am Tigris-Tunnel. *Antike Welt* 37: 77–83.

Schachner, Andreas (ed.)
   2009 *Assyriens Könige an einer der Quellen des Tigris: Archäologische Forschungen im Höhlensystem von Birkleyn und am sogenannten Tigris-Tunnel.* Istanbuler Forschungen 51. Wasmuth, Tübingen.

Seeher, Jürgen
   1999 Die Ausgrabungen in Boğazköy-Hattusa 1998 und ein neuer topographischer Plan des Stadtgeländes; mit einem Beitrag von Hans P. Birk und Jochen Görsdorf. *Archäologischer Anzeiger* 1999: 317–344.

   2006 Die Hethitischen Ostteiche. In *Boğazköy-Berichte 8: Ergebnisse der Grabungen an den Ostteichen und am mittleren Büyükkale-Nordwesthang in den Jahren 1996–2000,* edited by Jürgen Seeher, pp. 3–23. Philipp von Zabern, Mainz am Rhein.

   2009 Der Landschaft sein Siegel aufdrücken – hethitische Felsbilder und Hieroglypheninschriften als Ausdruck des herrscherlichen Macht- und Territorialanspruchs. *Altorientalische Forschungen* 36: 119–139.

Shafer, Ann Taylor
   1998 The Carving of an Empire: Neo-Assyrian Monuments on the Periphery. Unpublished Ph.D. dissertation, Harvard University, Cambridge, MA.

   2007 Assyrian Royal Monuments on the Periphery: Ritual and the Making of Imperial Space. In *Ancient Near Eastern Art in Context: Studies in Honor of Irene J. Winter by her Students,* edited by Jack Chang and Marian H. Feldman, pp. 133–59. Brill, Leiden and Boston.

Smith, Adam T.
   2001 On Landscapes in the Ancient Near East. *Journal of the Economic and Social History of the Orient* 44: 363–371.

Stokkel, Peter J.
   2005 A New Perspective on Hittite Rock Reliefs. *Anatolica* 31: 171–188.

Stone, Elizabeth C., and Paul E. Zimansky
   2003 The Urartian Transformation in the Outer Town of Ayanis. In *Archaeology in the Borderlands: Investigations in Caucasia and Beyond,* edited by Adam T. Smith and Karen S. Rubinson, pp. 213–228. The Cotsen Institute of Archaeology, UCLA, Los Angeles.

Trigger, Bruce
   1990 Monumental Architecture: A Thermodynamic Explanation of Symbolic Behaviour. *World Archaeology* 22: 119–132.

Ullmann, Lee Z.
   2010 Movement and the Making of Place in the Hittite Landscape. Unpublished Ph.D. dissertation, Columbia University, New York.

van den Hout, Theo

2002 Tombs and Memorials: The (Divine) Stone House and Hegur Reconsidered. In *Recent Developments in Hittite Archaeology and History: Papers in Memory of Hans G. Güterbock*, edited by Kutlu Aslıhan Yener and Harry A. Hoffner Jr, pp. 73–91. Eisenbrauns, Winona Lake, IL.

Van Zeist, W.

2008 Reflections on Prehistoric Environments in the Near East. In *The Domestication and Exploitation of Plants and Animals,* edited by Peter Ucko and G. Dimbleby, pp. 35–46. Transaction Publishers, New Brunswick, NJ.

Waltham, Anthony Clive

1976 The Tigris Tunnel and Birkleyn Caves, Turkey. *Bulletin of the British Cave Research Association* 14: 31–34.

Wittenberg, Hartmut, and Andreas Schachner

2012 The Ponds of Hattuša – Early Groundwater Management in the Hittite Kingdom. *Water Science and Technology: Water Supply* 13(3): 692–698.

Yamada, Shigeo

2000 *The Construction of the Assyrian Empire: A Historical Study of the Inscriptions of Shalmaneser III (859–824 B.C.) Relating to his Campaigns to the West.* Brill, Leiden.

Ruins within Ruins:
Site Environmental History and Landscape Biography

Ben Marsh and Janet Jones

Archaeologists love sites – they are drawn to the artifacts, the chronology, the architecture, and the connections to the historic record best found where human occupation was densest on the land. But a focus on the site makes it easy to forget that every archaeological site must exist within a landscape that nurtured it and absorbed its impact. Landscape-scale human activity is an emerging research focus in archaeology, as more researchers explore the complex links between cities and their hinterlands. We want to take this shift a step further, and focus on the evolution of the landscape itself, as having a history and value separate from its support of the site. The particular conception that will guide us is the idea of landscape biography, the archaeological history of the environment itself as it responds to evolving cultural needs, capacities, and perceptions over the millennia.

We suggest that the interpretation of archaeological landscapes can be strengthened by an understanding of them as ruins with continuing biographies. In this chapter, we will bring ideas from the geographical concept of cultural landscape to bear on archaeological landscapes. We will use the idea of ruin, as developed in history, literature, and landscape architecture, to support our adaption of object biography as a tool for understanding sites and landscapes. Landscape biography widens our perception of ancient environments to encompass the study of their own histories as they affected, and were affected by, the different people who occupied them. The landscape biography of ancient Gordion, where the authors have worked for many years, will be used to illustrate how a historical approach to the landscape itself can enrich our understanding of the site and of its environment, and of the complex interactions between the two.

Landscape Biography in Archaeology

Landscape-scale work in archaeology invites researchers to shift their view from a familiar anthropocentric perspective, with humans being the central actors in shaping the world, to an eco-centric worldview, in which humans share agency with the natural forces situated in the environment around a site. This is an important realignment, because it encourages scholars to see sites as parts of larger ecological wholes. Such research acknowledges that the environmental conditions that permitted an ancient city to thrive were located within the space around the city from which food and other resources come. The city was situated at its particular place because that hinterland was sufficient for its survival. Reciprocally, the impact of the city on the natural world is most evident in its immediate environs, in the area onto which the urban residents projected deforestation, soil erosion, pollution, sedimentation, water diversion, overgrazing, over-hunting, etc. The city gradually, but inevitably, ruined the environment that fed it and those environmental changes, in turn, altered the city's capacity to support itself from that landscape.

Landscape biography is a way to conceptualize the continuous and ongoing story that a cultural landscape presents to the observer, throughout its entire history. To approach archaeological landscapes by self-consciously thinking of them as environmental ruins allows the researcher to learn about human culture from the information that is borne within the alteration of the landscape itself. The researcher is thus carried beyond the conventional archaeological task of seeking the information that has been masked through environmental change, to examining the entire suite of processes that worked on the landscape over its history to bring it to its present state. Ruins are not an end-product of degradation; they continue to exist and evolve within the lived world, and continue to be acted on after they stop being used in their original roles. The environmental effects that worked during site occupation and after abandonment made an archaeological landscape into a ruin of an earlier form. But some later form will be a ruin of this one, with added effects from the archaeologists themselves. The study of a ruin, including a landscape-scale ruin, seeks to track this on-going biography of archaeological features as they continue to evolve in form and meaning.

In geography the term cultural landscape formalizes the task of understanding the world as it is altered by human groups through their activities and toward their goals. Cultural landscapes are hybrid spaces, affected by both human action and environmental process. They are "manifestations of culture's traffic with nature," as Mitchell (2000: 20) puts it, they are the most immediate locus of human-environment exchange. The cultural landscape directs environmental enquiry to the scale of individual humans' interactions with the world. The cultural landscape encompasses three complementary aspects of the human environment: this landscape is an altered natural system, reflecting human adaptation to the environment at this place; it is also the built environment, the set of physical constructions that support human lives; and it is a symbol system, a series of messages encoded – consciously or not – into the artifacts of the built world (Marsh 2010). All three of these aspects can be applied to the interpretation of archaeological landscapes, since the landscapes are simultaneously environmental, functional, and symbolic.

Formal conceptualization of landscape, of ruins, and of object biography guides the observer to understand a given site and its context, to interpret the information borne within the specific and ongoing history of that landscape. A landscape, like a site, is pushed toward ruination by specific processes taking place immediately after settlement begins. Like at a site, those particular processes happened in part because of the ways the landscape was understood and used by residents at subsequent stages – its landscape biography. Archaeological landscapes, as ruins, bear marks of the natural processes and human activities that acted upon them, and thus they demonstrate what values about the landscape were inherent in subsequent land use, they show what the most vulnerable landscape components are, and they illuminate the different ways that the archaeological features within them have been understood by subsequent occupants of the region.

Recognizing the magnitude and timing of anthropogenic impact upon the archaeological landscape is important for three reasons. First, any effort to understand an ancient human landscape must consider how that landscape was formerly different from its modern manifestation; that is, careful archaeological studies about a given period must be able conceptually to undo the alterations of a site's hinterland subsequent to that time. Second, most of the major changes were wrought upon the land by the actions of humans during and since antiquity. Thus the changes are artifactual, and they provide evidence of the ways humans have shaped that world over that time. The degradation of the landscape is an archaeological study in its own right; Wilkinson (2003) conceptualizes the landscape itself in the Near East as a human artifact. Finally, landscape changes that began in antiquity frequently engendered responses in antiquity. That is, many sites under excavation are structured in part as a response to the occupants' alteration of their own environment; human landscape degradation was itself a significant environmental stress for many settlements.

Ruin

Ruin, the noun, refers to remains of artifacts, structures, and features that have been degraded over time from their former complete state – either from abandonment or by intentional damage. Ruins represent one life-stage of a structure, like any other; they are not simply the inert product of uniform entropy defacing features. The concept of the ruin is explored in various fields, yet in archaeology – the study of actual ruins – the concept of ruin has not been examined to the same extent. Although archaeology explores in detail the ways temporality manifests itself in the existence of people and their goods, archaeologists have seldom approached the existential questions of ruin that attract much interest elsewhere.[1]

Ruins are the result of inevitable entropic processes. Time's arrow always points toward more entropy; the world is disintegrating and it always has been. Physics underlies physical ruin, finally. Mundane natural processes – oxidation, abrasion, fracture, collapse, and weathering – obliterate the work of the human hand that had crafted those things to be shiny, smooth, angular, or inscribed. A set of cultural processes also strips off or re-forms the meaning of human-made features. People physically assault sites and degrade them by robbing from them or reusing building materials. This recycling selects out the reusable parts and leaves the useless. Mental processes also degrade features. Meaning is lost to memory lapse at individual and cultural levels, leaving features in a cognitive vacuum: "If stones are not, meanings are perishable and mistakable, local to cultures which fade or undergo convulsive change" (Harbison 1991: 7). And meaning can be altered intentionally, as victors rewrite history. New meanings are appended to old features, by folk archaeology of evocative ruins or by misconstruing some lingering historic knowledge about the feature to situate it into more contemporary cultural forms.

Archaeological sites, like all landscapes, exhibit differential survival. The physically refractory is preserved – stone, fired brick, concrete – and the less sturdy – thatch, timber, mud brick – is degraded (Waters and Kuehn 1996). The more vigorously the processes of leveling act, the more uneven preservation will be. Incan structures in upland Peru were built within an architectural tradition that respected tectonic forces, and pre-European buildings frequently survived the subsequent earthquakes that shook off the frailer colonial structures built over them. Monumental architecture is designed to escape ruination or weathering within its intended environment, to withstand the attack of time better than other structures. Buildings of religion and power are usually constructed out of the most permanent materials, in explicit contrast to the ephemera of everyday items and architecture. Egyptian elites worked in stone so their tombs and temples would remain. The cultural goal was to build for perpetuity, since societal survival was deemed to depend on the continued functioning of the ceremonial structures. The most resistant of structures, such as the pyramids of Giza, mimic the stable and low-energy shape of a pile of dirt. New World pyramids, burial mounds, and ziggurats have that same form – they cannot fall down because, geomorphically, they already have.

Differential preservation is affected by ongoing human factors such as the potential economic value of artifacts on a site after they are used or deposited. Material will remain within a site if it has no other value. Sherds are common artifacts because they are physically resistant, but also because they have no ordinary value that would encourage their harvesting. Iron is rare in sites, because it had value and was recycled in antiquity. Gold artifacts are not only removed and melted down, but their presence, or their imagined presence, threatens the rest of the site by luring looters.

Archaeology emphasizes the skills of reading degraded objects and reconstructing degraded sites, but the ruins from which the archaeologist's knowledge of the past comes are only the most resistant of materials – ceramics, earth, tooth, pollen, charcoal: the ruins. More legible stuff – wood, paper, flesh, fabric – is the first to go. Preservation – non-ruin – is a gift of unusual circumstances. Very few natural conditions protect organic material well. The same circumstances that humans use to preserve food – as dried food, frozen food, canned food, or pickled food – are the conditions that preserve bodies, artifacts, or structures in archaeological contexts. Dry sites, frozen sites, waterlogged sites, and salty sites all store their archaeological information especially well. Because the absence of degrading influences is so unusual, the best-preserved sites are anomalous and poorly representative of all original sites.

Ruins are Things in Themselves, Objects with Biographies

Ruin is not the end of the existence of an object; rather it is one more stage in the object's history and the ruins themselves continue to have a comprehensible history. The idea of object biography describes this ongoing progression. Kopytoff formulated the basic idea, which he called a "biography of things" (1986: 66; see also Gosden and Marshal 1999):

> In doing the biography of a thing, one would ask questions similar to those one asks about people: What, sociologically, are the biographical possibilities inherent in its "status" and in the period and culture, and how are those possibilities realized? Where does the thing come from and how is it made? What has been its career so far, and what do people consider to be the ideal career for such things? What are the recognized "ages" or periods in the thing's "life," and what are the

Figure 12.1.   The repurposing of abandoned structures protects them from ruin. The
                Theatre of Marcellus (a Late Republican structure in Rome) was overbuilt
                with apartments in Medieval times, which protected the ruins from the
                elements and from urban clearance. (Photo: Yair Haklai 2009, Creative
                Commons SA license. http://commons.wikimedia.org/wiki/File:Theater_of_
                Marcellus-Rome.jpg accessed 2/26/2011).

cultural markers for them? How does the thing's use change with its age, and what happens when it reaches the end of its usefulness?

Ruins reach us after a series of human choices about their fate. Particular cultural choices permit sites to escape (or at least delay) ruin. Woodward (2001) demonstrates this idea, which might be called "site biography," with his careful history of the Colosseum after abandonment. He is highly critical about the damage that happened to the site during the latest period in its history when it became an archaeological object and was stripped of human context, visual texture, and its ongoing ceremonial biography.

While the individual reuse of the components in a building destroys the structure, the reuse of an entire building will preserve it. Thus shrines or forts – or old barns and mills in the current Western landscape – that become homes are preserved against gradual decline, leaky roofs, or casual robbing (Figure 12.1). The repurposing of industrial structures – the knitting mill that becomes a condo or the brewery that becomes a shopping mall – is a favored way to preserve historic buildings.

Figure 12.2.
Refractory landscape elements – bells, corner stones, gates – outlast their original cultural functions, but maintain their nominal ceremonial importance within *ad hoc* shrines. The time-keeping function of church bells is lost in small town Pennsylvania, but the bells remain. A bell from a previous version of the First Baptist Church in Wellsboro is preserved as a purely symbolic object on a welded steel pedestal in sight of the tiny new steeple.

Sites, features, and artifacts with significant cultural value may be preserved in form but not in function. When churches, schoolhouses, or fire stations are razed in small-town US, the large bell that they had held often remains. The bell is a refractory object with obvious historic symbolic value, but it has become separated from its nineteenth-century time-keeping or public communication function; typically the bell gets built into a semi-formal shrine-like display at the site of the new structure (Figure 12.2). Millstones, cornerstones, cupolas, and gateways similarly remain stranded on the symbolic landscape long after their specific cultural functions are obscured.

A site that bears obvious symbolic weight is more likely to be preserved in some form. Temples and churches have long lives because of the cultural investment that has been made in them as sacred sites. The sacred valence of religious sites is often stable through major cultural changes, even a change of dominant religion. The cultural activities of a mosque will become located within the physical structure that was once a church (Hagia Sophia in Istanbul) or a mosque building will be situated onto the sacred space of an earlier Hindu temple (the Mosque of Babur in Ayodhya), or a cathedral will be built over an Aztec sacred precinct (Catedral Metropolitana de la Asunción de María in Mexico City) (Figure 12.3). Transferring the sacredness into a different tradition preserves the site and some basic structures, if not the details of its original meaning and features (Figure 12.4).

Figure 12.3. After Conquest, the Incan "Temple of the Sun" at Koricancha in Cusco, Peru, had its sacred space preempted by the Christian religious buildings. A Baroque Spanish convent building attached to the Church of Santo Domingo was built upon the massive basalt foundation of what had been the foremost temple in the Incan empire. Subsequent earthquakes damaged the rectilinear colonial building without affecting the sloping, rounded indigenous structure. (© 2002 Håkan Svensson, distributed under GNU Free Documentation License, accessed from http://commons.wikimedia.org/wiki/File:Cusco_Coricancha_Inti-Huasi_main_view.jpg, Feb. 25, 2011).

Figure 12.4. Christian symbols were erased from an interior balcony of Hagia Sophia cathedral in Istanbul after it was converted to a mosque in 1453 (authors' photo).

The Cultural Discourse about the Materiality of Ruin

Every human is an archaeologist at some level; everyone seeks to extract meaning about the past from whatever relicts they encounter. Culturally, we build a "popular archaeology" linking our present experiences to what came before. A significant part of that construction derives from our capacities to read ruins. The popular experience of antiquity is not much like the practice of formal archaeology, which seeks to look through the archaeological ruins to the earlier world that they represent. The popular experience is more often of the materiality of the ruins themselves. The look of the austere skeleton of the Acropolis in Athens is itself the monument; a reconstruction of the complete and painted earlier form would be less ancient and less impressive to the observer than the ruins. Object biography emphasizes the ways features continue to speak to humanity after they become ruins.

Ruins are rich in affective weight, a fact frequently remarked upon in scholarship. The ruin is situated in the mind of the observer as "a dialogue between an incomplete reality and the imagination of the spectator" (Woodward 2001: 139). Ruins provide a fogged mirror that permits the imagination to work at its best, in that it is "their fragmentary nature and lack of fixed meaning that render ruins deeply meaningful" (Edensor 2005). Ruins can evoke "the sense of loss, of harmony broken, and, at the same time, the hope of the future rebirth" (Mazzino 2009). A powerful dissonance develops between the previous value of a site and the now-seemingly-useless ruins. "[I]n its world-forming capacity, architecture transforms geological time into human time, which is another way of saying it turns matter into meaning. That is why the sight of ruins is such a reflexive and in some cases an unsettling experience. Ruins in an advanced state of ruination represent… the dissolution of meaning into matter" (Harrison 2003: 3).

Ruins draw their power from their materiality and their associations with site-specific cultural and historical facts. The ability of ruins to act as concrete links to legendary time encourages society to support archaeology as generously as it does. The cannonball in the castle wall links this specific place to that fabled war. The presence of ruins reifies our mental link to landscapes perceived as Eden-like within our cultural traditions – Rome, Athens, the Black Forest, the Celtic countryside. Ruins offer authenticity. A flag from a battle – the bombardment of Fort McHenry, say – carries its historicalness in the fact of it being physically deteriorated.

Ruins connect our minds to the ephemeral character of life and glory. Consider the cultural staying-power of the broken statue meme in Shelley's *Ozymandias*: "Nothing beside remains." Ruins evoke decay and disruption. "In Christianity the decay of the individual was a necessary prelude to

Figure 12.5. A Death's Head was a common symbol for the corruptibility of the flesh in English colonial North America, as seen in this early eighteenth-century stone on Burial Hill above Plymouth, Massachusetts (authors' photo).

resurrection. Ruins were a perfect metaphor for this process, for the skull beneath the skin; the more magnificent the edifice, the more effectively its skeleton demonstrated the futility of mortal pride. [The ruin of] Rome was a *memento mori* on a colossal scale" (Woodward 2001: 89). Cemetery monument symbolism is rich with ruins: the broken column, the fallen tree, or the cut stump all represent truncated life. The classic New England Death's-Head gravestone motif represents the ruin of the body out of which the soul must travel (Figure 12.5). Ruins are symbolic of decline, of the brevity of perfection: "Ruine hath taught me thus to ruminate / That Time will come and take my love away." (Shakespeare, Sonnet 64; see Vendler 1997: 301). Ruins offer an allegory of decline. A formal-garden monument constructed in the eighteenth century at Stowe was built as an already-ruined structure and titled "The Temple of Modern Virtues," thus alluding to the degenerate state of that erstwhile modernity (Wood 1979: 208).

To J.B. Jackson (1980: 102), ruins engender creation: "That is what I mean when I refer to the necessity for ruins: ruins provide the incentive for restoration, and for a return to origins. There has to be (in our new concept of history) an interim of death or rejection before there can be renewal and reform."

Ruins are preserved upon the landscape to indicate political superiority, or to remind viewers of a threat, or to display an animosity. Parts of the Berlin Wall are preserved as ruins, reminding viewers of the destruction of the Soviet system in Europe, in the same way that a Native American warrior might preserve a body part of his vanquished enemy. Medieval Christian artists used images of ruined classical Roman monuments to represent the triumph of Christianity over paganism (Worthen 2009).

Ruins are Constructed to Reflect Human Choices

In addition to constructing the meaning of ruins, people construct ruins in a literal sense. People have constructed pseudo-ruins for centuries. The freshly constructed ruin within an ornamental landscape, first popular in the mid-eighteenth century, provided the landowner with instant historicity for his estate. "If the vandalism of history doesn't conveniently provide a ruin, he has it built himself," as Evan says of the grandly Gothic Wimpole Folly built by Capability Brown in 1769 (2003) (Figure 12.6). More recent traditions have constructed ruins for ongoing use by living people. The various "rustic" architectural styles in the nineteenth-century US – Gothic-revival or Queen Anne domestic buildings, for example – conveyed a sense of wear and disorder to hearken to simpler times through the mimicking of primitive styles; the word '"authentic" was used at the time to describe the styles (Harris and Dostrovsky 2008). Re-creating ancient forms in venerable disrepair offers an explicit break from the pedestrian recent past to a finer earlier time.

Ruins are constructed in fiction as well – the famous broken Statue of Liberty in the 1968 pop-canonical post-apocalyptic movie *Planet of the Apes*, for example – and in cultural narrative. The military destruction of the battleship *Maine* was a political fact constructed by the Hearst newspapers out of entirely ambiguous historical raw material, in order to justify a war against the Spanish colonies. Civil War-era ruins of buildings in the American South were long preserved on the land and cherished in cultural memory as reminders of General Sherman's perfidy, an assemblage that included, to be sure, many ruins that were created by innocuous fire or by abandonment.

People guide or accelerate the process of ruination with the creation of proper ruins as their goal. Commercially offered antiques are often intentionally "distressed" with a length of chain or an ice pick, so they have a better mark of their antiquity. Newly woven carpets lie in the sun in "carpet farms" in Anatolia to fade to an appropriately aged shade, or are placed on

Figure 12.6. Wimpole Folly, built by Capability Brown in 1769, was meant to be a ruin
   from its conception; it lends a venerable Gothic aura to a rural English estate.
   (© 2006 Tysto, Nickarse2412, distributed under GNU Free Documentation
   License, accessed from http://en.wikipedia.org/wiki/File:Wimpole_folly.JPG,
   Feb. 25, 2011).

a road to be weathered by passing cars. Copper roofs get acid treatments
to produce the proper patina of age, and the steel in modern bridges is
engineered to rust in graceful ways. Through his "Theory of Ruin Value"
(*Die Ruinenwerttheorie*), Albert Speer urged that the Nazis design buildings
so that they would ruin magnificently – modern structures should eventually
fall apart into the finest ruins (Scobie 1990). Hitler planned for such ruins
to stand as a symbol of the greatness of the Third Reich far into the future,
as Greek and Roman ruins are now symbols of those civilizations.

Preservation is a cultural choice about ruins, too. The conspicuous
presentation of ruins is an important cultural landscape trope, and ancient
cities like Rome and Athens are gradually redesigned to show their ruins in
their best profiles. A ruin becomes a significant place by the formal fact of
someone preserving it. In recent times, explicit theories of cultural resource
management and historic preservation guide the self-conscious selection of
sites – but only certain sites – for protection. The processes of architectural
conservation alter a historic or archaeological site in significant ways, and
deny large parts its site biography. Citing J.B. Jackson's argument on the
necessity of ruins, Frisch (1989: 220) decries:

...the American tendency to require buildings or sites to go through phases of growth and decline before they seem eligible for saving, at which time historical significance is attached to a "Golden Age" whose restoration is then attempted. The result is not a reflection of the past, but a sanitized, present-day conception of one portion of that past. The very restoration can disrupt the 'sedimentation of culture' that has accumulated at the site; it demands that visitors suspend credulity by receiving the site not as a genuine remnant of history, but as a disjointed piece of the past that somehow has returned to pay us a visit in the present.

Archaeology and Ruins

Alternating rhythms of creation and destruction define much of cultural history, as the new grows out of the old. Now-abandoned landscapes that are the subject of archaeology were already partly ruins as they were occupied. The *höyük* or tell is a layered pile of ruins that was, even as it functioned to support the city, already the remnants of earlier cities. "So too are creation and destruction parts of a single process," as Michel (1988: 23) says of the Hindu idea of creative destruction, central to understanding temple architecture.

Much of the archaeological record describes sequences of growth and collapse. Timely ruin – luck – is a key to success in archaeological interpretation: if the pot hadn't broken, archaeologists wouldn't have the sherds. Archaeologists' ability to read the ancient landscape relies largely on individual snapshots given by specific events of ruin or collapse: the roof-fall in a cave, the military destruction a city, a burnt seed, or pyroclastic debris flowing out from Vesuvius. The stories of civilization are themselves punctuated most clearly by cataclysm – invasion, war, fire, plague, flood, death.

Archaeological excavation is itself a way that ruins are created. Archaeology transforms the ruins lying within a landscape into a different kind of ruin. Excavation strips the site is of its relationship to the contemporary world. An excavation slowly consumes its site, which becomes degraded in a stylized way – well-placed dumps, straight baulks, an orderly depot – but degraded nonetheless. An archaeologist who is working on a site that was excavated in earlier times, under earlier standards for documentation, becomes deeply aware of the loss created by the excavation: How does this old plan of a now-removed building in a higher layer align with the stones on the ground here? Were there carbon or iron stains on that long-removed floor? What might have been found if a flotation sample or a radiocarbon date had been taken from a now-removed pit? Even the parts that are revealed, rather than destroyed, are thus exposed to faster degradation after excavation. The driving force of the field of archaeological conservation is most immediately the vulnerability of artifacts and structures after they are removed from the ground where they may have lain safely for millennia.

Archaeology is an ephemeral enterprise based on a non-renewable resource, the set of archaeological sites. Cuyler Young hypothesized that only a century or so worth of high-grade "raw material" is left as sites are stressed from all sides (personal communication 1993). Archaeology itself is consuming many of the best sites, of course; robbers are ruining other valuable ones at an increasing rate as their tools and their information sources modernize; ordinary development and mechanized farming may obliterate most of the rest.

The act of archaeology forces the explicit definition of a ruin as valuable. One of the earliest instances archaeology was the veneration of a ruin, when Tuthmose IV excavated the Old Kingdom Sphinx at Giza, c. 1400 B.C., in response to a dream (Zivie-Coche and Lorton 2004; see Schnapp 1997 for parallel Mesopotamian practices). The administrative management of archaeology in many countries is housed in the same ministry as museums. Thus all sites, and all site activities, are presumed by the system (and, too often, by the workmen) to be involved in extracting museum-grade cultural value from the landscape. All archaeological materials – every sherd and bit of ash – are treated as though they were precious. Modern ecological archaeology is dramatically hindered as a consequence of this presumption that everything extracted is valuable. Even inert soil samples for geochemical analysis – 10 gm from a million tons of river bank – must be carefully documented and then formally exported through layers of bureaucracy in a museum.

Research and conservation also involve the reconstruction – de-ruining – of archaeological material. Research does it conceptually; it tells or shows what the site might have been like before ruin. Preservation or conservation physically returns an object to a similitude of its original form. Every reconstruction – even scraping the rust off a hinge – is predicated on a model of what the artifact or feature should look like. Site conservation results in a highly selective ruination, based on an explicit choice about the particular nature of the ruins at this excavation. During site conservation the archaeologist/conservator/architect makes a series of critical judgments about what the ruins should look like. A powerful aesthetic, which may not be at the level of consciousness to the planner, is applied to the site. For example, what level of disorder is acceptable? How ruined is okay? Should a site be stripped back to its stony skeleton, like Machu Picchu, or is it appropriate to leave some evidence of messy life around? Every subsequent viewer's experience of the site is conditioned by those choices, which then permit the viewer to forget the complexity of the site and to ignore its long history.

Reconstruction is fraught with cultural baggage. What period or stage is the "right" period? Evidence of later settlement is routinely stripped so that some favored period – and only that period – is most legible. Earlier excavators cleared sites quickly to the Pharaonic period on the Giza Plateau, or to the Classical period in Athens. The choice of "right" period for attention depends on the ideology of the preservers. Western excavations favor some art-rich urbanized "classical" period – which might be Iron Age in Anatolia, Bronze Age in the Troad, or Pharaonic in Egypt. In the Americas, the latest pre-European civilizations – Aztec, Maya, or Inca – may be "classical," so that earlier levels are under-explored. In the eastern Mediterranean, Roman and later levels were treated almost as overburden by the larger-than-life excavators of the early and mid-twentieth century, and were removed after a cursory examination. At Troy the entire Classical, Hellenistic, Roman, and later periods had been referred to as the PBA (Post-Bronze Age), implying a dismissal of the detail and significance of 2,000 years of culture history. Site biography may be truncated to some golden moment chosen by the project director or dictated by donors and funding sources.

Landscape and Ruin

Every landscape is a constellation of ruins. The landscape we see is the net product of a set of processes that built it up and a set of processes that reduced it. What we see everywhere are the most resistant elements of what came before; we see only those parts of geology, ecology, and human life that have stood up to assault of the time. The scientific study of the earth's form, geomorphology, acknowledges that all landscapes are degraded versions of earlier ones. In most places the mountains we see are ever-so-slightly lower versions of the mountains our grandparents saw. Physical landscapes are built by tectonic processes – volcanism, earthquakes, uplift – and the landscapes are reduced, or "leveled", by a suite of erosional and slope processes such as sheet wash, stream cutting, sedimentation, and slump or slide. Any geologic landscape, other than the freshest volcano or most active fault, reflects the differential leveling of an earlier framework. On the mature landscapes that constitute most of the world's surface, the hills are the places where geological chance brought resistant rock to the surface long ago, and the valleys are places that were underlain by weaker rock that has eroded away.

Archaeological landscapes have been leveled in much the same ways as natural ones but their construction was artificial, the result of the architectural and industrial projects that made the cities within them, as well as the walls, roads, field terraces, canals, and so forth with which the rural landscape was structured. Archaeological landscapes, like archaeological sites, have been affected by cultural processes that layer new meaning over old, that rob features of previous meaning, or that remove meaning entirely from the landscape.

Landscape Biography in Archaeology

Every site has reached the present day by being reshaped through long-term environmental influences: this is the taphonomy of the site. Those same changes are also reflected in the local landscape beyond the site, since the landscape is a repository of the environmental history. Environmental history includes natural processes of degradation, but also the human choices and values exercised on the landscape by subsequent users, and therefore it is an important part of the archaeological record. The term "landscape biography" emphasizes the comparison between the processes affecting archaeological landscape and the processes affecting the archaeological sites and artifacts contained in it. The landscape itself is subject to a large-scale kind of taphonomy; perhaps one could talk about the landscape biography subsuming some kind of "geotaphonomy". Cultural landscape histories are common in geography, developing in the US from the classic early twentieth-century works of Carl Sauer (1925) who traced the varieties of land use that had altered specific mid-western and western US environments from prehistoric to modern times.[2] Landscape focus in archaeology is growing in importance, both as a component of site-based research and as a self-contained field of study. Wilkinson (2003) explores the recent development of landscape archaeology and provides strong examples of its application to the environments of Near East.[3]

The most fundamental process of human impact on ancient environments has always been anthropogenic soil erosion, which is the work of raindrops on bare ground. Although it happens at the humble scale of a few square meters of bare ground, and occurs one rainstorm at a time, soil erosion is a process that can degrade civilizations (Montgomery 2008). In agronomic practice the key environmental factor affecting erosion rate is called cover. This parameter describes the vegetative coverage of the land and thus level of protection from erosion. Human change of vegetative cover is ultimately the biggest cause of environmental degradation in the Mediterranean and over most of the world. When the surface is protected from the raindrops by a well-developed tree canopy and an undisturbed vegetative under-story, soil erosion is close to zero. At the other extreme, with no vegetative cover at all soil frequently erodes at 300 to 1,000 times the natural background rate, much faster than natural processes create new soil.

Erosion denudes hillsides to bare rock, thins or removes the productive topsoil that enables plant growth, and washes the excess sediment into streams.

Those streams eventually silt up their channels, ruin lowland fields, and bury architectural features. Because humans so consistently accelerate the siltation of their environments, drainage structures are among the first features discovered in ancient cities – like the *Cloaca Maxima* in Rome – as early citizens made the land inhabitable by rectifying the environmental damage of their ancestors.

The loss of soil productivity decreases the population that can be sustained within an agricultural landscape. Indirectly, erosional processes starve water table recharge, dry out springs, and impoverish formerly perennial streams. Water features – such as Hittite spring shrines in central Anatolia – are particularly vulnerable to destruction because they are situated at the bottom of the landscape and thus they may be affected by burial, by stream scour, by desiccation, or by all three. Stream channel damage also ruins the opportunity for archaeologists to find the original stream-bank clay sources for ancient ceramics.

Most notable archaeological sites lie within specific resource regions that were exploited in antiquity to support the urban economy. That exploitation is likely to have initiated vegetation changes that disturbed the soil and subsequently buried or eroded sites. The timing of these landscape alterations is an important piece of the environmental history of a site. Earliest agricultural settlement of Mediterranean landscapes often coincides with rapid sedimentation of waterways after the degradation of the local landscape, and this sedimentary marker for timing changes in the subsistence system may be easier to observe than any artifacts to be found on the land (Marsh 2013). The very earliest occupation may have been so dispersed that the chances of finding an identifiable site are quite low, but the sediment yielded by heavy grazing or the earliest widespread farming would have accumulated in stream valleys at the bottom of the landscape and is well preserved and dateable under millennia of subsequent siltation.

Case Study: Gordion Landscape History

Landscape biography is a powerful tool to reveal the nature of ancient environmental changes and the responses of the rest of parts of the human ecology. A history of human use of the landscape at Gordion, the Iron Age Phrygian capital in central Anatolia, provides an example of the wide range of analyses that are possible. It can serve as a model for the integration of environmental and cultural chronologies at other sites.

The landscape evidence behind this example derives from our own field observations and research at Gordion (Marsh 1999; 2005), from the Gordion Regional Survey (Kealhofer 2005; Marsh and Kealhofer 2014), from the work of other Gordion researchers (e.g., Sams 2005), as well as from comparative

Figure 12.7. Fragments of Iron-Age Gordion are buried 4 m below the modern floodplain. Wall tumble, collapsed buildings, and a 2,500-year-old stump (in the foreground) emerge from the banks of the Sakarya River. The exhumed surface that the city occupied had been buried by river overbank sedimentation at about 20 cm per century. This exposure was created during a 1967 flood-control project (authors' photo).

studies in nearby human landscapes (Boyer et al. 2007; Matthews and Glatz 2009; Marsh 2011). We have allowed our history to be somewhat conjectural about the nature of evolving human landscape use in this place, rather than being definitive of the actual chronology at Gordion, which is still being unraveled.

The distinctive fact about the archaeological landscape at Gordion is the magnitude of human environmental impact that is visible there. The city lies on the floodplain of the Sakarya River, but the river has undergone huge changes since the Bronze Age (Figure 12.7). By modern times, the river had silted in at least 4 m, had buried substantial parts of the lower town, had obliterated other parts of the urban area as it meandered laterally over walls and other structures, and had finally jumped from its original bed and resituated itself amongst the dense wall systems on the west side of the citadel mound (Figure 12.8).

The underlying physical cause of this sequence of events is obvious. Massive post-settlement environmental degradation is a hallmark of archaeological landscapes in eastern Mediterranean. This has been recognized since Vita-Finzi's classic study on the geomorphology of Mediterranean valleys (1969), and the Gordion area shows this impact clearly. Early and ongoing cultural pressure on vegetation – timbering, fuel gathering, grazing, and farming – exposed soils to vastly accelerated erosion rates, which yielded sediment to the Sakarya River in excess of the stream's capacity to transport it; subsequently the valley floor filled in. The geomorphic evidence in the upland near Gordion readily supports this model for the changes in the Sakarya River. Much of the steeper land is cut by sharp gullies, and small streams are as heavily alluviated as the river. Human landuse practices are responsible for the denudation of this landscape.

What is hidden in such a report is the question of when – and why – that happened. A naive view of such a landscape might suggest that it was in one state when it was first occupied, now it is in another state, with the change happening during a limited, undifferentiated transitional period. But in fact the transformation of this landscape from some pre-settlement form happened over an extended period, and that biography is knowable and significant.

What follows is a broad, and occasionally hypothetical, biography of the landscape at Gordion, offered as a series of stages that human land use passed through.

Paleolithic Landscape Choices

The first thing to note about the landscape biography at Gordion is that there was no meaningful initial state. The earliest effective settlement in the Holocene was on a landscape that had already been occupied by humans. Human occupation of the landscape began in the Pleistocene, prior to an extended period of accelerated landscape processes during the late Pleistocene glacial maximum climate that would mask most previous human impact. The oldest cultural material in the Gordion region shows up as scatters of Middle Paleolithic lithics, mostly chipping debris and coarse tools, on hill-crests overlooking the wide lowlands. The evidence suggests that these lithics were produced by Neanderthal hunters from hundreds of thousands of years ago who had no cultural continuity to later occupations (Matthews and Glatz 2009: 76). The consistent upland location of these scatters – typical of such sites elsewhere in northern and central Anatolia – reflects the landscape needs of the hunters who left them. Those people occupied the land in a way that enabled them to see great distances across an unforested countryside, an optimal situation for tracking big game.

Landscape Effects of the Last Glacial Stage

Prior to 12,000 B.P., late Pleistocene glacial and periglacial climates accelerated surface processes throughout Anatolia, even on an unglaciated landscape like Gordion. Slopes became gentler, as wet hillsides relaxed from the weight of the water or under the influence of intensified freeze-thaw cycles. Hills became more rounded as rocks weathered to coarse soil. This climate produced the thick soil mantles onto which the first agriculturalists moved, soil that subsequently eroded so rapidly.

Stream valleys were widened by melt-water and pluvial-climate rainfall. The Bronze Age Sakarya River occupied the middle of a kilometer-wide, long-wavelength meander belt adjusted to huge floods from pluvially enlarged freshwater sources to the south. That well-drained, sandy-bottomed, relict valley was the site of the ancient city and most of its early suburbs.

The Neolithic Skips Gordion

The next major landscape stage is distinctive for what did not happen in the Gordion region. Although the earliest domestication of wheat involved the nearby Taurus Mountains ecosystems, and although world-famous Neolithic sites like Çatalhöyük are just 240 km to the south, there is scant evidence of Neolithic settlement at Gordion, nor further north in Anatolia (Matthews and Glatz 2009: 77). This landuse pattern – an absence of early farming – suggests an important fact about how the would-be settlers read the landscape. The wooded northern Anatolian land was apparently unconquerable with Neolithic tree-felling technology. Instead early farmers migrated northwestward, finally into Europe, where better adaptations for woodland farming were developed and then brought back to Anatolia.

Earliest Farmers and Stream Sedimentation

The magnitude of earliest human impact at Gordion is remarkable, for the first agricultural users of the land may have been the most destructive of all. The best evidence of the time of their arrival is within the earliest observable human impact on the streams around Gordion during the middle Chalcolithic, about 4000 B.C. The artifactual signature of settlement at that period is subtle – a few lithics and sherds on upland fields – but the sedimentary evidence is very clear in the bottom layers of silt in the smaller stream valleys. Although non-agricultural settlers may have been present at some density below the threshold for landscape visibility to present researchers, all concrete evidence indicates an abrupt and widespread influx at the Chalcolithic by farmers with sufficient technology – copper axes, in particular? – finally to control that environment. The impact was immediate and dramatic. Sedimentation in the small streams – reflecting rapid destruction of surface soil profiles – progressed at the highest rate in the local human record, before or since (Marsh and Kealhofer 2014).

Perhaps such dramatic early soil alteration is to be expected, since early human alteration of any sort would upset the precarious ecological balances that protected the most vulnerable soil deposits, and those fragile deposits would therefore not be available for later farmers to abuse or protect. Any cultural soil conservation practices whatsoever – relating to grazing intensity, soil-turning technology, or cropping cycles – are important parts of farming that could only develop over time, as farmers had the chance to study their own impacts over many generations.

Earliest Holocene Settlement Induces Earliest Land Degradation

The evidence of post-Chalcolithic environmental alteration is visible not only in the sedimentary deposits in the stream valleys, but on the overall landscape as well. The earliest Chalcolithic settlements were on lands that were subsequently degraded beyond usability through human action. One Chalcolithic site in the Gordion area was a small lithic scatter at the edge of an ancient spring. But the spring is now completely dry, identifiable only from relict humic-rich soils around a shallow basin. The spring was destroyed by the same soil depletion that filled the lowland valleys. Thinned soils permanently accelerated the runoff of winter rains so the groundwater reservoirs that once fed the springs are no longer recharged. Unlike at most spring sites in the area, no Bronze Age settlement was located there, suggesting that the spring may have been degraded very early on.

A Weak Bronze-Age Landscape Signature

Early Bronze Age environmental impact on the upland landscape near Gordion is not easily distinguishable from prior periods. Sedimentation rates did decline during the Late Bronze Age, apparently for the first time since earliest agriculture. This could be related to population declines associated with the Hittite collapse to the east. Streams near the Hittite capital at Hattuša show a similar pattern of early sedimentation (from Chalcolithic vegetation destruction?), followed by later stream incision as the sediment supply decreased (Marsh 2011). The shift at Gordion could also be part of a long-term trend of sediment decrease as degraded agricultural landscapes were abandoned. This would be similar to the (much briefer) post-European-settlement evolution of stream valleys in the eastern US, which show a peak of anthropogenic sedimentation in the nineteenth and early twentieth century, just before a sedimentation decrease resulted from the abandonment of eroded farms.

Site and Situation of the City at Gordion

The citadel mound at Gordion must have been very challenging as an occupation *site* for an Iron Age city. It is bounded by many kilometers of poorly watered upland to the west, the entire region is almost devoid of good building materials, and it was been swampy or flooded for most of its history. It is, however, a very good *situation* for a city. ("Site" refers to the local conditions, in economic geography; "situation" is the larger geographic relationships to other places.) The situation of the city was optimal for control of a river-crossing on a crucial east-west route, and the city lay near the important junction of the Sakarya with the Porsuk River which linked the Phrygian uplands with the rich lands and diverse cultures to the east.

Earliest River Impact is Late and Modest

The larger Sakarya River watershed behaved quite differently from the smaller local watersheds. The river floodplain showed its earliest evidence of anthropogenic sedimentation 2,500 years after the impact became visible in the smaller streams. In fact, the sedimentation increase in the river plain was during the same period that sedimentation started to decline significantly in the smaller local watersheds. A thin layer of silt was laid onto the Sakarya floodplain over a period of at least several hundred years in the Late Bronze Age, growing slowly enough that the sediment developed into a soil as it was laid down – very differently than rapid the aggradation by eroded soil in the local stream valleys.

Iron Age Initiation of Major Regional Sedimentary Impact

Destructive landuse affected the larger Sakarya basin in the Iron Age. The Sakarya River became engulfed in a wave of sedimentation like the little streams had, but the wave in the river rose steeply 600 years after river floodplain sedimentation began, and 2,000 years later than the rapid increase had happened in the local watersheds. The sedimentation rate on the river climbed sharply during the Iron Age, and remained at a high level until recent times (Figure 12.7). The landscape event responsible for the increase was presumably the expansion of intense human use over a significant portion of the large watershed of the Sakarya River, producing enough sediment to shift the river's flow characteristics to a meandering and aggrading regime. The Iron Age city would have had a very large ecological footprint because of consumption of tree cover driven by the rapid expansion of pyrotechnical industries for the sophisticated population – abundant ceramics, specialized glass production (Jones 2005), metallurgy, baking, etc. – as well as the need for food production from plowed fields.

The expanding city of Iron Age Gordion drew on ecological resources from across the river's large watershed, which accelerated soil erosion enough that the river silted in over the lower parts of the city to several meters deep

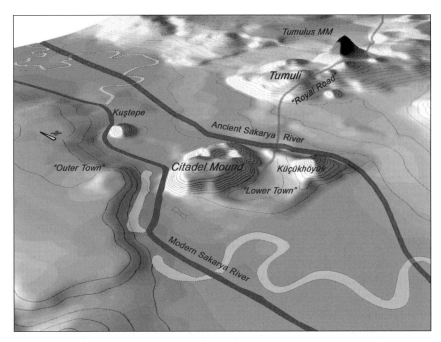

Figure 12.8. The map of the river plain at Gordion shows the physical impact of the
heavily alluviated river on the city and the location of the river after its
translation to the west side of the mound. Discontinuous fragments of eroded
wall now extend in both directions from the destroyed defensive tower at
Küçükhöyük. Before stream attack and burial, those walls linked to Kuştepe,
a kilometer to the north (left), and to the uplands west of the modern river
(image by authors).

in a millennium (Figure 12.8). The city drowned itself in sediment by over-
exploiting its extended hinterland.

Environmental Response to River Changes in Ancient Gordion

The city at Gordion had to respond to rapid river sedimentation in the Iron
Age and later. Site evidence shows that they did so in several in several ways.
This ancient urban response to an ancient environmental shift is a distinctive
characteristic of Gordion archaeology. Occupation shifted gradually away
from the lower southern parts of the city toward higher parts of the site,
moving onto the adjacent uplands by Roman times as the floodplain parts
got muddier and more mosquito-ridden. Floodwalls were apparently built to
hold the river in its own channel through the narrow river section adjacent to
Küçükhöyük, the upstream defensive tower. Large volumes of river sediment

were removed to relieve the channel, and were used in various massive construction projects such as Gordion's renowned Clay Layer, used to bury the Phrygian Destruction Level, as well as building a large pad of fill, 4 m deep, that raised the occupation sites just east of the ancient river above the rising groundwater. Roads across the floodplain had to be rebuilt repeatedly as the accreting floodplain buried the previous levels in sediment.

Political Stability and Settlement Clustering

Landuse patterns in the local watershed shifted as political stability changed. The Roman political hegemony permitted dispersed settlements, including some in areas that had not been used intensively before then. In less secure earlier times, settlements were probably more clustered. The several occupation mounds in the eastern foothills all show a concentration of Bronze Age artifacts at their highest levels, suggesting that later residents built more widely across the landscape when they no longer needed the security that mound living provided. In Paphlagonia, several hundred kilometers to the northeast, Bronze Age settlements similarly favored especially defensible and enclosed hill-top locations (Matthews and Glatz 2009). This clustering of an insecure population for military reasons would limit intensive agriculture to smaller areas around the mounds, while secure times could permit widespread farming (and thus widespread environmental damage).

Arraying the Urban Landscape onto the Site

The city of Gordion used the physical landscape of the river valley in different ways at different times. The riverbank and some nearby escarpments provided especially defensible locations for Phrygian-era city walls. Later settlement shifted west of the river valley, beyond the Iron Age defensive perimeters on the uplands above the floodplain. Iron Age tumuli had been carefully situated on hilltops visible from the city or along major transportation corridors. Hellenistic tumuli were appended onto the early geometry, but clustered more in the western uplands.

Utilization of the Altered River

By Medieval or Ottoman times, the Sakarya had become an important resource for water energy because of the physical obstruction of the river by the degraded city mound. The mound blocked the normal migration of the river across the floodplain, creating a sharp hydraulic drop at an area to the west and northwest of the mound that was shielded from the north-flowing stream. Mill-races, fed from low weirs across the river, would have been extended across the western part of the site to exploit that topography, to supply waterpower for grain mills.

Human Action Initiated the Shift of the River across the Mound

Human action inadvertently altered the course of the Sakarya River. The long-term sedimentation of the river valley made the river's position inherently unstable as its bed was raised, and thus prone to catastrophic shift. But the immediate cause of the shift was probably the dams and mill-races. It is likely that the river broke out of its ancient bed in the eighteenth or nineteenth century, shifting to the west side of the mound where it flows now by occupying and enlarging one of those mill-races. Over time, the new course became stabilized as the stream cut downward into the new path. The new course was even more well-suited to mill construction, and a complex system of dams and races – built with robbed Roman sculpture in some cases – was maintained at the western base of the mound into the twentieth century.

The Mound as a Quarry

The citadel mound became a quarry as it lost its major symbolic importance. Stone construction in villages throughout the area relied on the squared basalt blocks that the mound yielded – which had originally been hauled many kilometers from the eastern mountains in Phrygian times. The still-active railroad overpass 400 m southwest of the mound was built by German engineers in the early twentieth century out of handsome Middle Phrygian ashlars (Figure 12.9). It was the attention of those engineers to the "quarry" from which the rocks came that brought the mound at Gordion to modern archaeological notice.

The Site Formally Becomes "Archaeology"

Human use of the landscape around Gordion today is heavily affected by the modern awareness that the site is ancient Gordion. The archaeological fact has created a clear value in the landscape that had been absent before the site was recognized. Towns around Gordion, especially the closest village of Yassıhöyük, owe their well-being in good part to the economic benefits of the site, including tourist-based employment in the museum area and intermittent employment at the excavation. Much regional landuse is affected by the governmental goal of preserving the site. The awareness of the region as an archaeological landscape has also encouraged the robbing of nearby tumuli and other presumed sites.

Figure 12.9.
The Gordion Citadel Mound served as a quarry for the early twentieth-century German railroad construction teams. Middle-Phrygian ashlars, brought from many kilometers away during the Iron Age, were robbed to build this railroad underpass immediately across the modern river from the site (photo: Gareth Darbyshire).

Solving the Problem of River Sedimentation through Technology

Into the mid-twentieth century, the foremost environmental challenge from the Sakarya River was the wide, swampy floodplain created over three millennia by the deposition of eroded soil. In the 1960s the Turkish government solved that problem by a massive excavation project to cut a 4m-deep channel into the floodplain for the stream to follow. The floodplain was drained by this action, and the river has stopped depositing material on that surface, although upland erosion continues at a reduced rate. That excavation was a boon to archaeological research at the site, cutting sharp sections into the edge of the mound, and casting up sculpture and building stone in the dredgings.

Modern Farming and the River

Farming has been evolving rapidly in the local area over recent decades.[4] Labor-intensive, traditional methods have been displaced by high-technology farming, with significant effects on the landscape. River water is pumped out for irrigation until the river is nearly dry in some years, perhaps with as low a flow as it ever experienced under natural conditions. The river is also badly polluted by fertilizer, pesticides, and raw sewage, causing large algal blooms and impoverished fish life. The river is no longer a safe food source, nor a pleasant recreation site, or source of good quality water, while the inefficient spray irrigation aerosolizes the toxins and pathogens from the river into the local atmosphere. The process of laying irrigation pipes revealed some significant archaeological evidence, but damaged much more. Low Bronze Age mounds in the watershed are being graded to the level of the fields to facilitate mechanized farming.

Modern Farming and the Rural Landscape

The loss of farm jobs under expanding mechanization has led to the gradual depopulation of the rural landscape. Fewer young people remain in villages, accelerating the demographic collapse, which will be followed by physical collapse over the next decades. The lack of young rural workers has decreased sheep-herd densities enormously, with a beneficial effect on the ecology: trees are returning year by year to the upland landscape, and soil loss rates should continue to decrease. This improvement will happen in spite of the expansion of centrally irrigated fields to 7–8 km from the river and the resultant shift of regional agriculture from low-impact wheat cropping to water- and chemical-intensive onions and sugar beets.

This case study is intended to show that the landscape biography of the Gordion region contains cycles of construction and destruction, of human environmental impact and subsequent response to environmental change, and of valuation and devaluation of the landscape; these cycles began in the Chalcolithic, acted at nearly every stage, and continue to today.

Impediments to Reading Landscape Degradation in Archaeology

Understanding the sequence of events through which archaeological landscapes have been ruined is important, because the hinterland contains the resource base that once supported the city under excavation, and the history of the adjacent landscape resembles and reveals the history of the site itself. Yet few major excavations attend to the biography of their landscapes and surroundings with a fraction of the enthusiasm that they apply to the architecture and the artifacts on the site. A small number of excavation projects in Anatolia have integrated their regional surveys well with their excavations: Sagalassos, Çatalhöyük, and Gordion come to mind. At these sites, the influence of extra-site landscape processes on the occupation at the site has only gradually become apparent, over the course of decades. For 40 years of its excavation history, it was not known to archaeologists at Gordion that the lower city was buried in four meters of sediment, for example, and the associated changes in local soils and hydrology over historical time are only now becoming clear.

But essentially every ancient site has undergone parallel changes. Why does the specific local environmental history remain unexplored at most excavations? What impediment discourages many archaeologists from examining the archaeology of their local landscapes, and from seeing the nearby environment as part of the site? Many archaeological projects are indifferent to questions of landscape history, and some seem almost hostile.

There are comprehensible reasons why traditional archaeological projects tend to diminish the landscape as an object of study. Landscapes are more or less legible to different observers, depending on their perspectives and experiences. Archaeologists often show a constrained facility for observation and interpretation at a landscape level. Geography and archaeology may be kindred and complementary fields, but they are fundamentally different disciplines with contrasting epistemologies (Marsh 2001), which is precisely why they can be such strong partners. The strength of archaeology is in the interpretation of cultural changes over time, which may have displaced a focus on changes over space – in short, archaeologists read up the section rather than across the landscape; spatial patterns in the environment are less salient to many standard archaeological questions than patterns over time. Similarly, the basic unit of research in archaeology has been the site – a bounded, human-dominated piece of the landscape defined by the presence of artifacts. An entire landscape, without inherent limits and often not marked by artifacts, is not a natural unit of investigation within traditional realms of archaeology.[5]

We all live with an illusion of landscape stasis that our psychology demands in order to create a stable world for our minds to trust. It is easy to overlook the amount of change that a site undergoes. An impediment to human understanding of environmental change is the slow rate at which alteration occurs. We live in a changed and changing world, but it is a challenge to recognize the magnitude of these changes within our own limited time horizons. Floodplain deposition at one millimeter per year is very fast to a geomorphologist, but imperceptibly slow to a human on the ground – ankle deep over a lifetime. If we cannot directly see change happening at its slow rate, it is hard to believe that the world is, in fact, persistently unstable. (Societal inability to respond adaptively to long-term environmental problems like global warming is a product of this same innate human resistance to recognizing slow change.)

We are better at recognizing change in retrospect, but only to a certain extent. It is easy for the inexperienced observer to underestimate both components of landscape leveling around a site – upland erosion as well as lowland deposition. The removal half is usually obvious on a site – walls are reduced, buildings collapse, and mounds slump and flatten. But removal from an entire landscape can be subtle: a few gullies among square kilometers of thinned soil profiles can be all that shows of a major degradation event. And the deposition part is often even harder to read, since observers are typically standing on top of a seemingly natural floodplain surface.

The natural processes that are affecting the landscape around a site were peripheral to the education of many archaeologists. As a result, conventional archaeological explanations of site degradation tend to draw on a narrow suite of more newsworthy landscape processes: earthquake, conflagration, military attack, etc. The mundane tools that nature has used to shape most of the world since the Cambrian – rain, soil erosion, slope failure, and stream migration – do not show up as often in the literature as they do on the land. Most researchers should expect to find significant influence – more influence than they might be prepared for from reading traditional archaeological reports – from the natural post-occupation processes that degrade, bury, and alter a site. Certain markers are important clues that a site-related landform or deposit is the product of geomorphic wasting. Young floodplains, slumps, and debris flows all have clear signatures, and always tell of changed environmental conditions. The discovery of cultural material – sherds, usually – within a stream bank or slope deposit is the most common convincing evidence about rapid, late landscape change, which is the most critical physical transformation within the typical landscape biography at a site.

Landscape study will expand in archaeology as its utility becomes clearer, but the long-term integration of the landscape paradigm – the assertion that local space and environment are crucial dimensions of all archaeological studies – depends on changes in the training of graduate students. Coursework in human ecology, geomorphology, and cultural landscape will enable the next generation of archaeologists to see their sites better within their larger environmental contexts.

The Future of Ruin

Historically, archaeology has broadened its analytic gaze from an early focus on precious artifacts and religious relics, to a nineteenth-century infatuation with classical architecture, and recently to efforts to understand entire urban sites as dynamic units. Now, enlarging environmental sophistication has permitted the focus to shift again, from the site to the regional landscape, which permits the integration of the city into the area that supported it. Simultaneously, the ultimate objects of archaeological analysis have become

more democratic, shifting from the elites who commissioned the golden
bowls, to all the inhabitants of a city, and now to include rural workers and
even the non-human world.

Understanding landscapes as ruins with ongoing histories is a way to
facilitate this step, but this is just a step. In the near future, archaeology
will need to look not only at changes in the regional landscape, but to start
talking about environmental change at a global level. This shift would change
the highest level of archaeological landscape analysis one more step, from
humans' cultural landscape to the entire ecosphere.

Future ruins are a common trope in fiction: *The Time Machine*, *The
Postman*, or *Ridley Walker*. But the world as we know it might itself become
ruins as the effects of global environmental change send repercussions
through the various life-giving systems, and degrade entire landscapes
upon which human life depends. The millennia-long trends of increasing
levels of environmental alteration documented in the Near East are sure to
continue, with more intensification of extraction, more mechanization, more
urbanization, and more heedless construction in more places. Global climate
change will force sea-level rise, desertification, ecological shifts, and major
changes in hydrological systems, which can obliterate landscapes that have
been stable for millennia.

Perhaps the best preparation for humans to understand those widespread
changes is to understand better the changes that humans have already induced
in large ecosystems, by looking at the ruins of archaeological landscapes. By
knowing how to read the history of landscape degradation from the past and
by valuing that information, we can better understand our human prospect,
and thus to know how to value our present.

History and Environment in the Cultural Landscape

The idea of landscape is powerful because it is so broad. It can erase the
division between site and environment (e.g., a city and its resources are a
single landscape). The idea of cultural landscape further weakens another
culturally constructed divide, the one that splits human agency from
natural process, by acknowledging the landscape to be inextricably affected
by both actions simultaneously. Agriculture, for example, is neither natural
nor artificial alone, but is combined of the two. Landscape biography takes
the generalization of the study of the landscape one step further, by de-
emphasizing some privileged stages of landscape alteration, and thus denying
the primacy of the "archaeological" past over all the other pasts that humans
have lived on this land. The meanings of archaeological features and their
artifact assemblages have been constructed and reconstructed repeatedly

through time. Neither ours nor the Phrygians' construction is inherently superior. The history of any landscape – any feature, really – reaches us only through some intermediate states of consciousness, just as the materiality of landscape itself reaches us having passed through those intermediate times. We would not know the feature in the same way if its intermediate history had not told us how to see it (Lowenthal 1985: 192).

Every impact acting on a landscape shifts both the materiality of the landscape and also the history. A job of archaeology – this hybrid of craft, science, and art – is turning materiality into history, processing objects into stories. Archaeology is an especially powerful object-biographical agent. It is seemingly the end-point of the biography of the site, because the site simultaneously gets consumed and explicated. Perhaps it is because the materiality is consumed – and alternate histories are foreclosed – that excavation archaeology is so definitive.

But let's step back. The lesson of landscape biography is that there are neither beginnings nor ends to the history of a place. The past is not one archaeological moment; it is the sweep of time in which the site and landscape have existed, a sweep that embraces today and tomorrow as well. The pairing of the ideas of ruin and of environment within the concept of landscape biography provides an effective way to understand the continuity – in time, space, and agency – of the processes that construct cultural landscapes, including archaeology itself. Landscape biography pulls us away from the particularities of one place, one time, one agency, one reader, one story, to a broader view of landscape as a set of places, processes, perceptions that interact in complex ways over extended time.

Notes

1. For discussion of the concept of ruin in architecture see Harbison 1991; Piper 1947; in landscape architecture, Jackson 1980; in history, Woodward 2001; in cultural geography, Lowenthal 1985; and in philosophy, Ginsberg 2004; Trigg 2006.

2. Hoskins' *The Making of the English Landscape* (1955) is a seminal work in English landscape studies broadly comparable to Sauer. See also Rackham 1995; Yamin and Metheny 1996.

3. See Alcock et al. 2003; Bottema et al. 1990; Grove and Rackham 2003; Shipley and Salmon 1996.

4. Recent research at Gordion offers an unusual opportunity to compare the ancient story of regional use of plant resources at one site (Marston 2011; Miller 2010) with the modern evolution of farming (Gürsan-Salzmann 2005).

5. But this is changing rapidly. The broader study of prehistory has always been hungry for systemic accounts of how sites fit into the larger world. Landscape archaeology is evolving quickly. At the same time that site-based archaeology is becoming more interested in

integrating landscape-scale knowledge into its explanations, more regional landscape surveys are being planned and executed with weak or no connection to central sites – e.g., Matthews and Glatz in Paphlagonia (2009), Luke and Roosevelt in Lydia (2009), or Nixon et al. on Crete (2009).

References

Alcock, Susan E., Jennifer E. Gates, and Jane E. Rempel
 2003 Reading the Landscape: Survey Archaeology in the Hellenistic *Oikoumene*. In *A Companion to the Hellenistic World*, edited by Andrew Erskine, pp. 354–372. Wiley-Blackwell, Oxford.

Bottema, Sytze, Gertie Entjes-Nieborg, and Willem van Zeist (editors)
 1990 *Man's Role in the Shaping of the Eastern Mediterranean Landscape*. A.A. Balkema, Rotterdam.

Boyer, Peter, Neil Roberts, and Douglas Baird
 2006 Holocene Environment and Settlement on the Çarşamba Alluvial Fan, South-central Turkey: Integrating Geoarchaeology and Archaeological Field Survey. *Geoarchaeology* 21(7): 675–698.

Edensor, Tim
 2005 *Industrial Ruins: Spaces, Aesthetics and Materiality*. Berg, Oxford.

Evans, Peter
 2001 Wimpole Hall. http://hoary.org/snaps/engl/wimp.html (Accessed December 12, 2013).

Frisch, Michael
 1989 *A Shared Authority: Essays on the Craft and Meaning of Oral and Public History*. SUNY Press, Buffalo.

Ginsberg, Robert
 2004 *The Aesthetics of Ruins*. Rodopi Press, Amsterdam.

Gosden, Chris, and Yvonne Marshall
 1999 The Cultural Biography of Objects. *World Archaeology* 31(2): 169–178.

Grove, Alfred T., and Oliver Rackham
 2003 *The Nature of Mediterranean Europe: an Ecological History*. Yale University Press, New Haven.

Gürsan-Salzmann, Ayşe
 2005 Ethnographic Lessons for Past Agro-Pastoral Systems in the Sakarya-Porsuk Valleys. In *The Archaeology of Midas and the Phrygians: Recent Work at Gordion*, edited by Lisa Kealhofer, pp. 172–189. University of Pennsylvania Museum Press, Philadelphia.

Harbison, Robert
 1991 *The Built, the Unbuilt, and the Unbuildable: In Pursuit of Architectural Meaning*. MIT Press, Cambridge, MA.

Harris, Richard, and Nadine Dostrovsky
 2008 The Suburban Culture of Building and the Reassuring Revival of Historicist Architecture since 1970. *Home Cultures* 5(2): 167–196.

Harrison, Robert P.

2003 *The Dominion of the Dead*. University of Chicago Press, Chicago.

Hoskins, William G.

1955 *The Making of the English Landscape*. Leicester University Press, Leicester.

Jackson, John Brinckerhoff

1980 *The Necessity for Ruins, and Other Topics*. University of Massachusetts Press, Amherst.

Jones, Janet

2005 Glass Vessels from Gordion: Trade and Influence along the Royal Road. In *The Archaeology of Midas and the Phrygians: Recent Work at Gordion*, edited by Lisa Kealhofer, pp. 101–116. University of Pennsylvania Museum Press, Philadelphia.

Kealhofer, Lisa

2005 The Gordion Regional Survey: Settlement and Landuse. In *The Archaeology of Midas and the Phrygians: Recent Work at Gordion*, edited by Lisa Kealhofer, pp. 137–148. University of Pennsylvania Museum Press, Philadelphia.

Kopytoff, Igor

1986 The Cultural Biography of Things: Commoditization as Process. In *The Social Life of Things: Commodities in Cultural Perspective*, edited by Arjun Appadurai, pp. 64–91. Cambridge University Press, Cambridge.

Lowenthal, David

1985 *The Past is a Foreign Country*. Cambridge University Press, Cambridge.

Luke, Christina, and Christopher H. Roosevelt

2009 The Central Lydia Archaeological Survey: Documenting the Prehistoric through Iron Age Periods. In *Tree-rings, Kings, and Old World Archaeology and Environment: Papers Presented in Honor of Peter Ian Kuniholm*, edited by Sturt W. Manning and Mary Jane Bruce, pp 199–218. Oxbow Books, Oxford.

Marsh, Ben

1999 Sakarya River History and the Alluvial Burial of Gordion. *Journal of Field Archaeology* 26(2): 163–173.

2001 Kindred Scholars: In the Field with Archaeologists. *Geographic Review* 91(1–2): 231–238.

2005 Physical Geography, Human Adaptation, and Human Impact at Gordion. In *The Archaeology of Midas and the Phrygians: Recent Work at Gordion*, edited by Lisa Kealhofer, pp. 162–171. University of Pennsylvania Museum Press, Philadelphia.

2010 Globalization and the Cultural Landscape. In *A Dictionary of Cultural and Critical Theory*, edited by Michael Payne and Jessica Rae Barbera, pp. 159–161. Wiley-Blackwell, Chichester.

2011 Geoarchaeology of the Human Landscape at Boğazköy-Hattuša. *Archäologischer Anzeiger* 2010: 201–207.

2013 Reading Gordion Settlement History from Stream Sedimentation. In *The Archaeology of Phrygian Gordion, Royal City of Midas: Gordion Special Studies 7*, edited by C. Brian Rose, pp. 39–46. University of Pennsylvania Museum of Archaeology and Anthropology, Philadelphia.

Marsh, Ben, and Lissa Kealhofer

   2014   Scales of Impact: Settlement History and Landscape Change in the Gordion Region, Central Anatolia. *The Holocene* 24(6): 687–699.

Marston, John

   2011   Archaeological Markers of Agricultural Risk Management. *Journal of Anthropological Archaeology* 30(2): 190–205.

Matthews, Roger, and Claudia Glatz (editors)

   2009   *At Empire's Edge: Project Paphlagonia. Regional Survey in North-Central Turkey.* British Institute of Archaeology at Ankara, London.

Mazzino, Francesca

   2009   Landscape and Ruins – Planning and Design for the Regeneration of Derelict Places. http://www.eclas.org/eclas-conference-details.php?konferenz_id=29 (Accessed December 12, 2013)

Miller, Naomi F.

   2010   *Botanical Aspects of Environment and Economy at Gordion, Turkey.* University of Pennsylvania Press, Philadelphia.

Michell, George

   1977   *The Hindu Temple: An Introduction to its Meaning and Forms.* University of Chicago Press, Chicago.

Mitchell, Donald

   2000   *Cultural Geography: A Critical Introduction.* Blackwell Publishers, Malden, MA.

Montgomery, David R.

   2008   *Dirt: The Erosion of Civilizations.* University of California Press, Los Angeles.

Nixon, Lucia, Simon Price, Oliver Rackham, and Jennifer Moody

   2009   Settlement Patterns in Mediaeval and Post-Mediaeval Sphakia: Issues from the Environmental, Archaeological, and Historical Evidence. In *Medieval and Post-Medieval Greece: The Corfu Papers,* edited by John Bintliff and Hanna Stöger, pp. 43–54. BAR International Series 2023. Archaeopress, Oxford.

Piper, John

   1947   Pleasing Decay. *Architectural Review* 102(609): 85–94.

Rackham, Oliver

   1995   *The History of the Countryside.* Weidenfeld and Nicolson, London.

Sams, G. Kenneth

   2005   Gordion: Exploration Over a Century. In *The Archaeology of Midas and the Phrygians: Recent Work at Gordion,* edited by Lisa Kealhofer, pp. 10–21. University of Pennsylvania Museum Press, Philadelphia.

Sauer, Carl Ortwin

   1925   The Morphology of Landscape. *University of California Publications in Geography* 2(2): 19–54.

Schnapp, Alain

   1997   *The Discovery of the Past.* Harry N. Abrams, New York.

Scobie, Alexander
    1990 *Hitler's State Architecture: The Impact of Classical Antiquity.* Penn State Press, University Park.

Shipley, Graham, and J.B. Salmon (eds.)
    1996 *Human Landscapes in Classical Antiquity: Environment and Culture.* Routledge, London.

Trigg, Dylan
    2006 *The Aesthetics of Decay: Nothingness, Nostalgia, and the Absence of Reason.* Peter Lang, New York.

Vendler, Helen H.
    1997 *The Art of Shakespeare's Sonnets.* Harvard University Press, Cambridge, MA.

Vita-Finzi, Claudio
    1969 *The Mediterranean Valleys: Geological Changes in Historical Times.* Cambridge University Press, Cambridge.

Waters, Michael R., and David D. Kuehn
    1996 The Geoarcheology of Place: The Effect of Geological Processes on the Preservation and Interpretation of the Archaeological Record. *American Antiquity.* 61(3): 483–497.

Wilkinson, Tony J.
    2003 *Archaeological Landscapes of the Near East.* University of Arizona Press, Tucson.

Wood, Eric S.
    1979 *Collins Field Guide to Archaeology in Britain.* Collins, Hammersmith.

Woodward, Christopher
    2001 *In Ruins.* Pantheon Books, New York.

Worthen, Amy N.
    2009 *Art in Ruins.* Des Moines Art Center, Des Moines.

Yamin, Rebecca, and Karen B. Metheny
    1996 *Landscape Archeology: Reading and Interpreting the American Historical Landscape.* University of Tennessee Press, Knoxville.

Zivie-Coche, Christiane, and David Lorton
    2004 *Sphinx: History of a Monument.* Cornell University Press, Ithaca.

Archaeological Landscapes, Pushed Towards Ruination

JOHN F. CHERRY

> But upon these stones
> the wind of wrath will blow,
> the dust of cholera and death
> will make the gardens wither.
> The statues will be blackened,
> the domes will crack open.
> the cisterns will turn brackish,
> the porticos will fall.
> Moss will cover the capitals;
> Slowly, the sea will begin to invade.
> These mountains will be islands.[1]

It is strange that archaeology – which is, after all, the study of actual ruins – has so far (with rather few exceptions: e.g., Dawdy 2010; Shanks 2012) done a rather poor job of theorizing the concept of *ruin*, at least as compared to work in architecture, landscape architecture, history, cultural geography, and philosophy. Archaeologists have not (yet) written books with titles such as *The Aesthetics of Decay*, *In Ruins*, or *The Necessity for Ruins*, nor have they contributed much to the welter of blogs and websites that have sprung up recently around the topic of "ruin porn."[2] Is this precisely because archaeologists are *always* working with ruins, and over-familiarity has obscured the fact that the concept might repay closer interrogation? And will the development of more nuanced notions of *ruin* and *ruination* emerge from cross-disciplinary encounters which give standard archaeological ways of thinking a jolt, as well as from more capacious views of ruins that go well beyond fallen-down buildings and abandoned sites to embrace entire landscapes, that are always in the process of becoming? On the evidence of the previous chapter, which offers an unusual mash-up of disciplinary perspectives, both of these conjectures may have some truth.

The argument would go as follows. During the Holocene, many – perhaps almost all – of the landscape changes we can detect are anthropogenic in origin, and thus landscapes themselves are artifacts of human action; this, in fact, is one basis for suggesting that the newly-coined "Anthropocene" era began by the onset of the Holocene, if not earlier (Smith and Zeder 2013). So if landscapes and the ruins within them are human creations and things in themselves, then we can extend to them similar outlooks and approaches as have been applied, productively, in anthropological and archaeological discussions of the "cultural biography" of things (e.g., Kopytoff 1986; Gosden and Marshall 1999; Gosden 2005; Hodder 2012). Thus Marsh and Jones (Ch. 12), from a starting-point in cultural geography and environmental science, provide a sketch of the long-term landscape history of Gordion and its region that falls broadly within the standard realms of geoarchaeology or archaeological geomorphology. And yet, significantly, the term they themselves employ in characterizing their work is *landscape biography*, "a way to conceptualize the continuous and ongoing story that a cultural landscape presents to the observer, throughout its entire history" (p. 170).

Ruminating on ruins inevitably makes for depressing, if also very interesting, reading. The bottom line is that the world is disintegrating, always moving towards ruin, subject to utterly inevitable entropic processes. All the products of human effort and imagination are ultimately doomed to erasure: by ineluctable natural processes, obviously, but equally by cultural processes that degrade sites, and by memory work that elides or rewrites the material record of the past. Some fascinating *aperçus* emerge from this perspective, the sorts of observations that make one want to kick oneself for not having grasped them before. So, for example, the reason why pyramids, ziggurats, and burial mounds are among the most resistant and long-lived of structures is because they "mimic the stable and low-energy shape of a pile of dirt" (p. 173) and cannot fall down – having already done so, in geomorphic terms. Similarly, the ways humans preserve food co-opt the same conditions (dry, frozen, waterlogged, salty, etc.) that result in excellent archaeological preservation; and yet, precisely because the absence of such degrading situations is so unusual, sites with the very best preservation often turn out to be atypical and far from representative of the general run of all sites. That is a fascinating paradox, one that has yet to be unpacked. It feeds back into one of the messages of this book as a whole, which is that archaeologists tend to be attracted (for understandable reasons) to sites where preservation is spectacular, yet this comes at the cost of failing to attend to "ordinary" places. The vast growth of intensive survey in recent decades, as well as greater interest in ethnoarchaeology, have helped enormously in redressing this imbalance.

Recognizing that the much-changed, degraded landscapes we see today are not those of the past does not always require rocket science. In some cases, spotting these changes was easy even long ago – especially in those areas most susceptible to rapid geomorphological change, namely, along major river systems and adjacent to oceans (which, conveniently perhaps, have always been preferred loci of human settlement and activity). For example, when early travelers in Crete noticed that Hellenistic harbor towns, such as Phalasarna, on the west coast of the island were now perched high and dry 6 to 9 m above sea-level (Frost and Hadjidaki 1990), and, conversely, that Roman-period, rock-cut fish-tanks in the central and eastern parts of the island were now submerged in shallow water (Davaras 1974; Mourtzas 2012), they knew something was up, that the land itself had changed – although it was a long time before the basic causative mechanism (plate tectonics) came to be understood. Similarly, it was quite apparent to early archaeologists and travelers alike that a number of the Greco-Roman harbor cities at the mouths of the major rivers in Aegean Turkey (such as the Maeander) were in fact no longer harbors at all, but drowned in silt and now located several miles from the sea, as a result of fluvial deposition and shoreline progradation (which were the causes of their final demise in late antiquity). This, of course, was why one of the Seven Wonders of the Ancient World, the Temple of Artemis at Ephesus, went missing, and it is an interesting question why no-one before the 1860s, when John Turtle Wood spent seven years grubbing around in the alluvial mud, thought to dig through the silt to try to locate such a famous lost religious monument (Romer 2000: 130–142). Oddly enough, another of the Seven Wonders fell victim to the same processes – the site of the temple and statue of Zeus at Olympia in Greece, where progressively more severe flooding by the Kladeos and Alpheios rivers in late antiquity eventually left the entire sanctuary covered by several meters of silt and entirely lost to view, until its largely serendipitous rediscovery by Richard Chandler in 1766.

Finding a lost site is one thing. But in other instances, conceptually "undoing" the alterations to a site and its contemporary setting – "walking back the landscape," as it were – have proven more difficult. The debate concerning the geography of Homeric Troy is a good case in point, one that has perplexed scholars for more than 2,000 years. As far back as the 1800s, it was realized that, in "Homeric" times, the coast at the mouth of the Scamander and Simois rivers was well inland of its present position. But it took geological science to sort things out: the floodplain of the two rivers adjacent to Troy provided an excellent opportunity for geoarchaeologists to use environmental core-drilling to reconstruct the movement of the ancient shoreline of the earlier marine embayment, as sediment infill forced marine regression. This, in turn, has necessitated a reassessment of our view of the

Trojan coastal topography in the late second millennium B.C., and the epic events that supposedly took place there (Rapp and Gifford 1982). Another comparable example would be the palaeogeographic reconstruction of the Plain of Thermopylae in Greece, again with the help of coring, which finally set to rest conflicts among historians concerning inconsistencies between historical accounts of the great battle of 480 B.C. and the modern topography (Kraft et al. 1987).

Work in this vein is, in general, relatively recent. The late development of geoarchaeology as a discipline is interesting. For example, the Archaeological Geology division of the Geological Society of America was formed only in 1977, while the leading journal in the field, *Geoarchaeology*, was not founded until 1986. In the Mediterranean context, the timing is not coincidental, I believe. It was the huge surge in diachronic, intensive surveys from the late 1970s (for quantification see, e.g., Cherry 2003: figs. 9.1–9.3) that created the urgent need for trained geomorphologists to work as members of regionally-focused archaeological fieldwork teams (they still remain, unfortunately, in very short supply). If sites are being discovered in one part of a region but not another, or if artifacts predating a certain horizon seem generally absent, the first thing to be established – with the assistance of those trained to read environmental history from landscape traces – is whether this is mainly a function of geomorphic processes, rather than of cultural choice. Recognizing areas of soil deflation, hillslope erosion, or valley-bottom alluviation is usually the easier part; dating those episodes is much harder; and establishing causation, and especially whether human activity is implicated, hardest of all. The seeming verities of an earlier generation of research, best epitomized by Claudio Vita-Finzi's influential book *The Mediterranean Valleys: Geological Changes in Historical Times* (1969), have collapsed in the face of a great deal of subsequent research (most often in the context of diachronic, regional archaeological survey projects) that has pointed towards much more local sequences of landscape change, driven in large part by the consequences of human-environment interactions (see, most recently, Walsh 2013). Not all such changes, incidentally, are deleterious. For example, systems of stone-built terraces for farming on hill-slopes trap sediments, promote soil formation, and arrest downslope erosion, even in the absence of pristine vegetation cover; this is, in general, a good thing. And yet it is merely a delay of the inevitable: when the terraces are abandoned and revert to natural vegetation grazed by goats, lack of regular maintenance results in the dislodgement of stones by livestock, eventual breaching of the terrace-walls, and, in short order, the catastrophic release of soil down onto valley floors below (Van Andel et al. 1986).

Marsh and Jones draw a contrast between archaeologists as concerned with time, and geographers with space. They also suggest that an entire landscape "is not a natural unit of investigation" (p. 196) for archaeology as traditionally practiced. On these points I must register some disagreement. Archaeology's involvement with regional-scale analysis and with the history of cultural landscapes has a long history, for example in the German *Landeskunde* tradition that predates the Second World War; and the massive growth of survey projects all around the Mediterranean since the 1970s has resulted in considerably more parity between archaeologists who dig stratigraphically ("time") and those who survey regionally ("space"). The authors' outlook arises, perhaps, from long-term association with research at an Anatolian mega-site (Gordion) dominated by excavation. For various reasons (some purely bureaucratic, some disciplinary), landscape archaeology and regional survey in Turkey have developed rather differently than in a number of other Mediterranean countries. Compared to Greece, Italy, France, Spain, Israel, and even Tunisia, rather fewer such projects have yet taken place there. Moreover, as Doonan's (2012) useful summary makes clear, surveys in Anatolia have followed different, admirably flexible paths – some have been rescue projects, others in the historical topographic tradition, and yet others pulled either towards the methods of Near Eastern tell surveys, or of high-intensity surveys elsewhere in the Mediterranean. Significantly, some of the archaeologists associated with several major, long-term excavation projects in Turkey have – eventually, and not always with great enthusiasm – come around to realizing that the city cannot be properly understood without also investigating its surrounding landscapes and sustaining hinterland (see, most recently, Ratté and De Staebler 2012 on Aphrodisias, where systematic excavations began in 1961, but survey beyond its walls only in 2005). It is a truism that cities and their territories in the Greco-Roman world formed an inseparable unit; but of course numerous case-studies have by now also revealed how quickly meeting a city's ongoing requirements for food, water, fuel, and other resources results in massive damage to the regional environment, primarily by exposing soils to greatly accelerated erosion rates. The history of the city as a place is also the history of the landscapes outside it; sites are parts of larger ecological wholes, and both are pushed to ruination.

Ruin, ruination, damage, deterioration, degradation: Marsh and Jones's chapter is replete with such gloomy notions. This last term "degradation", it is true, is generally used in the technical sense of "a wearing down by erosion", and they are right to remind us that all geomorphological processes ultimately act to level the landscape, even if their rates are accelerated and their unfortunate outcomes exacerbated by incautious human actions; but the word also has connotations of degeneration, debasement, even disgrace. Similarly negative overtones also surround the use of the term "damage" to describe these processes. Yet perhaps we should pause for reflection here.

Several years ago I co-organized a symposium at the annual meeting of the Archaeological Institute of America on "The Archaeology of Damaged Landscapes." It was prompted directly by the experience of trying to do survey archaeology in a part of southern Armenia badly impacted by Khrushchev-era Soviet agricultural practices – widespread bulldozing to level new fields, deep plowing, the installation of extensive networks of buried irrigation pipes and concrete water-canals to feed them, the trenching of hill-slopes to plant vast stands of coniferous trees as an agro-industrial monocrop – all in the service of the official policy of (so-called) "land amelioration" (Alcock et al. 2008). Initially, we lamented the level of damage and degradation we could see all too clearly in this environment, since it seemed probable that it would greatly curb our ability to study all earlier, pre-Soviet landscapes. (In the event, several seasons of fieldwork by the Vorotan Project [Zardarian et al. 2007] showed this to be a less severe problem than at first envisioned; but that is a separate discussion for another place.) Nonetheless, as we studied the situation more carefully, we came to realize that this supposed Soviet "damage" was itself in fact the creation of yet another landscape – albeit very intrusive, environmentally unsound, and now defunct – one equally worthy of our attention as grand-scale ruins of the near-contemporary past. Furthermore, as the archaeology itself showed us, there had been repeated previous episodes of human exploitation and intervention, stretching back into prehistory, that had likewise generated landscape change. Should these too be regarded as "damage"? The danger in conceptualizing archaeological landscapes as constantly undergoing a material process of ruination and degradation is the temptation to turn that into a moralizing story of steady decline from some imagined, originary, pristine, "undamaged" state, much as in Hesiod's presentation of human history in his *Works and Days*.

But now we come back to Marsh and Jones's framing concepts. Landscapes were being degraded long before there were humans in them. Archaeological landscapes are ruins whose biographies can be narrated through human interactions with, and interventions in, the environment – an environment that is simultaneously both natural and cultural. That is why human experiences of place, and the place-making activities that occur there, are (in the words of Harmanşah's Introduction [p. 8]) "mediated through an animated world that is always already at a state of ruination, teeming with memories, deep histories, stories, monuments, and traces of past human activities."

The time-frame of these processes is critical, and it is hard not to think about them in terms of Braudelian *annaliste* notions of differing kinds of time. One might imagine, for instance, a Hittite sacred spring drying up virtually overnight as the result of (say) a local earthquake, and its startling, even terrifying impact on those who were engaged with such a place. Yet were the inhabitants of those Roman port cities in Aegean Turkey aware of the centuries-long process of siltation that was ultimately to wreck their homes and livelihoods – let alone what was causing it? The long-term effects were plain to see ("We can no longer sail into the harbor our forefathers built"); steps, futile in the long run, could be taken to stem the damage (divert or canalize the river, move to higher ground, establish a new settlement). But if the accretion of sediment on a floodplain at 1 mm each year is lightning-fast in geomorphological terms, it is change far too slow to be obvious to people on the ground, making it next to impossible to grasp that this ruination is the environmental damage of their own ancestors. Humans have a hard time dealing with slow change that cannot be seen directly, which is one reason why the lessons of archaeology are so important. Those politicians who are deniers of sea-level rise, global warming, even evolution itself, are trapped in the dissonance between incrementally slow change and the brevity of the next electoral cycle, and of their own lifetimes; their failure to support adaptive solutions to environmental crises may yet lead to catastrophic ruination – this time, potentially, of humankind itself.

Notes

1. Translation by Felipe Rojas of stanza 2 of the first of the Cuban poet Severo Sarduy's *Poemas bizantinos* (*Obras I: Poesía*, Fondo de Cultura Económica, México, 1999); I thank him for drawing my attention to this poem, which is so germane to the present topic.

2. A notable exception is the *Ruin Memories* project (ruinmemories.org/). Stemming from the recent growth of interest in the archaeology of the contemporary past (e.g., Harrison and Schofield 2010), it focuses mainly on the material ruins of modernity (closed-down shopping malls, abandoned prisons and military establishments, industrial wastelands, derelict mining towns, empty apartment houses, etc.), "a ghostly world of decaying modern debris mostly left out of academic concerns and conventional histories – and also considered too recent, too grim and repulsive to be embraced as heritage" (http://traumwerk. stanford.edu/archaeolog/2013/05/ruin_memories_a_portfolio.html). This laudable development is, however, far less expansive than the notion of ruin as embraced by Marsh and Jones.

References

Alcock, Susan E., John F. Cherry, and Jennifer E. Gates-Foster

2008 Archaeological Impacts of Soviet-era Land Amelioration Programs in the Southern Caucasus. Paper presented at the 109th Annual Meeting of the Archaeological Institute of America.

Cherry, John F.

2003   Archeology Beyond the Site: Regional Survey and its Future. In *Theory and Practice in Mediterranean Archaeology: Old World and New World Perspectives*, edited by John K. Papadopoulos and Richard M. Leventhal, pp. 137–159. Cotsen Advanced Seminars 1. Cotsen Institute of Archaeology, University of California, Los Angeles.

Davaras, Costas

1974   Rock-cut Fish-tanks in Eastern Crete. *Annual of the British School at Athens* 69: 87–93.

Dawdy, Shannon

2010   Clockpunk Anthropology and the Ruins of Modernity. *Current Anthropology* 51: 761–793.

Doonan, Owen

2012   Surveying Landscapes: Some Thoughts on the State of Survey Archaeology in Anatolia. *Backdirt* 2012: 118–123.

Edensor, Tim

2005   *Industrial Ruins: Spaces, Aesthetics, and Materiality.* Berg, New York.

Frost, Frank J., and Elpida Hadjidaki

1990   Excavations at the Harbor at Phalasarna in Crete: The 1988 Season. *Hesperia* 59: 513–527.

Gosden, Chris

2005   What Do Objects Want? *Journal of Archaeological Method and Theory* 12.3: 193–211.

Godsen, Chris, and Yvonne Marshall

1999   The Cultural Biography of Objects. *World Archaeology* 31.2: 169–178.

Harrison, Rodney, and John Schofield

2010   *After Modernity: Archaeological Approaches to the Contemporary Past.* Oxford University Press, Oxford.

Hodder, Ian

2012   *Entangled: An Archaeology of the Relationships between Humans and Things.* Wiley-Blackwell, Malden, MA.

Kopytoff, Igor

1986   The Cultural Biography of Things: Commoditization as a Process. In *The Social Life of Things: Commodities in Cultural Perspective*, edited by Arjun Appadurai, pp. 64–91. Cambridge University Press, Cambridge.

Kraft, John C., George Rapp Jr., George J. Szemler, Christos Tziavos, and Edward W. Kase

1987   The Pass at Thermopylae, Greece. *Journal of Field Archaeology* 14: 181–198.

Mourtzas, Nikos D.

2012   Archaeological Indicators for Sea Level Change and Coastal Neotectonic Deformation: The Submerged Roman Fish Tanks of the Gulf of Matala, Crete, Greece. *Journal of Archeological Science* 39: 884–895.

Rapp, George Jr., and John A. Gifford

1982   *Troy, The Archaeological Geology.* Princeton University Press, Princeton, NJ.

Ratté, Christopher, and Peter D. De Staebler (eds.)

    2012   *The Aphrodisias Regional Survey. Aphrodisias* V. Phillipp von Zabern, Darmstadt/ Mainz.

Romer, John

    2000   *The Seven Wonders of the World: A History of the Modern Imagination.* Seven Dials, London.

Shanks, Michael

    2012   *The Archaeological Imagination.* Left Coast Press, Walnut Creek, CA.

Smith, Bruce D., and Melinda A. Zeder

    2013   The Onset of the Anthropocene. *Anthropocene.* http://dx.doi.org/10.1016/ j.ancene.2013.05.001.

Van Andel, Tjeerd H., Curtis N. Runnels, and Kevin O. Pope

    1986   Five Thousand Years of Land Use and Abuse in the Southern Argolid. *Hesperia* 55: 103–128.

Walsh, Kevin

    2013   *The Archaeology of Mediterranean Landscapes: Human-Environment Interaction from the Neolithic to the Roman Period.* Cambridge University Press, Cambridge.

Zardaryan, Mkrtich H., Armen V. Tonikyan, Susan E. Alcock, and John F. Cherry

    2007   Les investigations du project "Vorotan" dans le région de Syunik. *Les Dossiers d'archéologie [Arménie des origines à la Christianisation]* 321: 60–63.

(Dis)Continuous Domains: A Case of "Multi-Sited Archaeology" from the Peloponnesus, Greece

CHRISTOPHER L. WITMORE

Introduction

The task of the following article is threefold. First, in looking to another "historical archaeology" (Morris 2000; Snodgrass 1987; 2006), it lays out a case for what a "multi-sited archaeology" might resemble. The article discusses an example of boundary and group maintenance related to an arbitration dispute between two Greek *poleis*, Hermion and Epidauros, in the 2nd century B.C. This exemplification moves through a series of vignettes which detail the diverse locales, materials, and relations implicated in the act of arbitration. Along the way, I take the opportunity to present some considerations of the dynamic and repetitive practices necessary for *polis* maintenance.

Second, the article addresses the empirical project of working with bits and pieces – how do archaeologists and ancient historians connect sites up? This question will bring us to the complex and convoluted ways in which archaeology has accounted for, or rather tracked, the heterogeneous elements caught up in this act of *polis* maintenance over the last two centuries.[1] This activity is closely related to the question of how the *polis* is viewed – not from above as a regional entity at a particular scale, but as a moving assemblage of connected and, every so often, contested, *topoi*.[2] Arriving at the interrelation between these *topoi* rests upon the circulation of various media at a distance; such labor also draws upon much longer chains of reference involving stone stelae, Milesian judges, goats, ridgelines, Pausanias, military geographers, Classical topography, excavation, epigraphy, and intensive surface survey.

With a handle on how Classical archaeology builds this story of distributed relation, the third and final task will be to determine whether the term "multi-sited" has stood up to the rigorous road conditions connected with an archaeological and metaphysical trial of strength. On the one hand, it is fair to say that "multi-sited archaeology" is very much a practice in the making (cf. Ryzewski 2012); on the other hand, it is equally fair to say that the multi-sited goes to the heart of what archaeologists have been *doing* from the beginnings of the profession. By keeping both "hands" in view, so to speak, this article, it is hoped, will make a contribution to the collective process of understanding and enhancing the empirical practices of archaeology. However, before we get underway in these tasks, one is obliged to address the question: what is "multi-sited archaeology"?

Locating Multi-sited Archaeology

By now the scenario is a familiar one. All the so-called radical shifts behind those unwieldy forces of globalization – i.e., transnational economic and political integration, cross-cultural flows and diasporas, world networks of digital cultures, and so on – have necessitated the retooling of various disciplinary methodologies across the sciences and the humanities (see, e.g., Gupta and Ferguson 1997; Hodder 1999; Morris 2003).[3] In anthropology this retooling has precipitated the development of a "multi-sited ethnography" (Marcus and Fischer 1986; Marcus 1995; Falzon 2009). The adjective "multi-sited" designates topographically discontinuous yet topologically continuous settings, all of which become legitimate sites of ethnographic engagement. Mobility, displacement, connectivity, interaction: such features of our 21st-century cultures seem to have complicated the notion of "the local" to the degree that the *mise-en-scène* of single-site research may *no longer* provide a sufficient basis for tracing the associations and connections implicated in a given situation. De facto, these features of global humanity often oblige researchers to abandon the creature comforts of the immediate, local setting (Appadurai 1996). From here to there, relations overflow the research "site" and spill out across numerous locales.

A fresh swell is forming in the wake of this multi-sited ethnography, and faithful to its inspiration, it has been dubbed "multi-sited archaeology" (Hodder 1999; Lucas 2001; Hicks 2003; Beaudry 2005). Like its anthropological counterpart, a multi-sited archaeology aims to track dislocated sets of relations wherever they may lead. Such an approach presents numerous challenges. Foremost among these is the fact that the multi-sited lays emphasis upon the relational character of matters of archaeological concern and this is regarded by some as a significant alternative to conventional area/period specialization in archaeology (Hodder 1999; Lucas 2001). Discussions under the rubric of "multi-sited archaeology" are largely centered upon historical archaeology, and yet there are actually few developed examples (Hicks 2003; Beaudry 2005;

Ryzewski 2008; 2012; although see Hamilakis and Anagnostopoulos 2009). This is because most work has arisen through comparative juxtaposition rather than by actively tracing the various strands of particular networks to the variegated locales which may lie along these paths (Hall 2000; Lucas 2006). Consider how the collective network of 18th-century tobacco was never staged at a few choice sites; rather, this industry rested upon myriad linkages which take us from a South Carolina plantation, to a Charleston dockyard, to the Thames, to a snuff shop at the upper end of the Haymarket, London. The distributed character of such networks suggests an altogether different topography for archaeological fieldwork (also see Smith 2005); that is, archaeological fieldwork deployed to address the sorts of questions that oblige a researcher to follow these linkages.

Another strain of multi-sited archaeology lays emphasis on the assorted groups – merchants in the tourist trade and archaeological site workers, government or heritage industry officials, and laboratory specialists – through which disparate forms of information are produced in relation to a given archaeological site (Bartu 2000: 101–109; Lucas 2001: 143–144).[4] This distribution takes archaeologists to other places: town squares during local festivals, ballrooms during conferences, websites, tourist shops, laboratories, libraries, wherever relevant materials are presented, manifested, or rearticulated (Hodder 2000).[5] These locales all come to perform, no matter how minuscule or massive the part, in the constitution, the co-production, of particular material pasts (Witmore 2004).[6]

The "multi-sited" is not to be confused with interregional systems. Mediterranean archaeologists, for example, are quite familiar with how connectivity and interaction take one far beyond local circumstances in certain scenarios (Horden and Purcell 2000; Morris 2003). If you want to find out where the bread, wine, and oil consumed on an early spring afternoon in 5th-century B.C. Athens came from, then holding fast to those interactions associated with agricultural production in Attica (including that of crop yields, rotation, soil fertility, and the carrying capacity of land) only takes you so far. To be sure, this question leads one much farther afield: to the breadbaskets of the Black Sea, Magna Graecia, Western Sicily, and Egypt; to the islands of Knidos, Thasos, and Rhodes; to the 5th-century oil amphorae stored in the apotheke of the Agora Excavations in Athens (Grace 1979; Garnsey 1998). The web of linkages associated with the trials and tribulations behind this simple meal stamps out any notion of regional coherence. While its ingredients are not sanctioned by any hard and fast boundaries delimited in the flatlands of Euclidean space, such an account clearly implicates many different settings, many diverse objects, and many diverse relations.

Unlike interregional systems, the coherence of a multi-sited account rests upon the meticulous detailing of all the heterogeneous locales and linkages involved. Unlike interregional systems, the "Mediterranean panorama" is not a starting point for the investigation because, to the contrary, the "big picture" is the outcome of practices that require one to move from locale to locale in an effort to build an image of how particular networks constituted themselves. To underline the distinction between interregional systems and the "multi-sited", the differences come down to where one begins, how one moves, and how one frames. If anything, because a multi-sited archaeology requires one to put in a great deal of labor into tracking associations to various places, it *should* ask us to hold arguments of scale until all the hard work of rebuilding paths, tracing associations, and connecting diverse locales has been accomplished (though the question of scale remains and we will postpone that discussion until later in the chapter). As we will see in the following case study, this prohibition can last quite some time.

While archaeology has long thrived on those roots which draw upon anthropological practice, it is in sticking too closely to a path forged by anthropology that archaeology has neglected its unique contribution: underneath all these over-dramatized processes, the notion of location was never straightforward.[7] And this is not limited to the post-1500 A.D. worlds of "nautical globalization" and "global provincialism" (Sloterdijk 2005a). When considered in terms of *what we actually do*, as I mentioned in the introduction, archaeologists have pieced together all the ingredients necessary for "multi-sited" work before. A 7th-century perfume jar may take us from a display case in the Rhode Island School of Design museum, to a tomb in Etruria, to a workshop in Korinth (Shanks 1999). X-ray fluorescence may suggest (re)connecting a quarry at Gkiafa in the southern Argolid of Greece with cut stone on the *Bisti* of Ermioni, formerly ancient Hermion, or with a series of houses in the old town of Idhra – houses likely constructed out of stone taken from remains on the *Bisti* in the 18th century.[8] A multi-sited account is not only about such sites; a multi-sited account also addresses the relations between them.

Whether we speak of food, pots, or coins, myriad relations distant in both time and space are folded into things (Webmoor and Witmore 2008). Whether A.D. 1500 or 1500 B.C., global networks exist, but it requires work to connect the components of these networks and maintain those connections (compare Whitehead 1978 [1929] to Harman 2002, 2009; also Serres 1995, on the notion of "world object"). However, to repeat, the extent, composition, and weight of these networks cannot be settled in advance. To clarify, the point here is that groups are connected through heterogeneous, multifarious elements. Certainly, it would be more than foolish to claim that Egyptians had an impact on Mesoamerican pyramid construction. One could

Figure 14.1. Hermionian version of the arbitration inscription in 2007 (author's photo).

make a case, however, for a global network associated with the carving knife in your kitchen drawer; that is, provided one travels far enough and puts in the requisite genealogical work. A world object, the blade, has been part of the composition of humanity over the very long term (Hodder 2013: 132).

This discussion, no doubt, begs a few key questions, to which we will return later in the chapter. How do I retrace connections that have in most cases long since perished? How do I connect sites in a text with sites on the ground? Even if I can trace these former associations, how far do I go?[9] And how do the chains of labor spawned through addressing these questions factor into the accounts archaeologists generate? Let us now turn to the example of arbitration between two 2nd-century B.C. *poleis*.

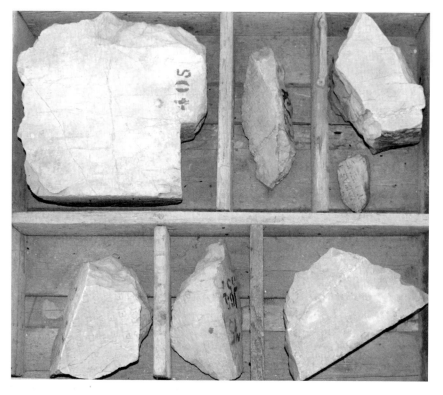

Figure 14.2. Epidaurian version of the arbitration inscription in 2008 (author's photo).

Boleoi Lithoi

The term *boleoi lithoi* is inscribed on two stone stelae (Figures 14.1–14.2). Translated as "heaped" or "thrown stones", *boleoi lithoi* serves as a reference for a series of border cairns tracing a section of the territorial boundary between Hermion and Epidauros at some point in the early 2nd century B.C. (Dixon 2001). Only after two centuries of topographical speculation and survey work have we come to establish with a degree of cautious certainty that this reference was *possibly* attached to a series roughly circular concentrations of unhewn rubble along a ridgeline between the Dhidhima basin and the Fournoi valley in the southern Argolid. If these 7- to 10-m diameter stone clusters are indeed the *boleoi lithoi* (an attribution that will be characterized always by indeterminacy), then they are the erstwhile materializations of a border dispute between Hermion and Epidauros. In this context, the thrown heaps of stone also inscribe the settlement of an arbitration.

Boleoi lithoi are both textual references on stelae and large gatherings of rough limestone cobbles on a juniper-covered ridgeline in the countryside. In aspiring to immutability, the arbitration of this land dispute was materialized as two stone stelae.

Things and Politics

According to the narrative as inscribed on the stelae, the dispute arose out of disparate claims over cropping and pasturage (for the full text, see Peek 1934: 47–52; cf. Ager 1996: 170–173). Arbitration by Milesian judges led to the delineation of a boundary defined by prominent geographical features. It was along the most contentious section that the stone cairns, the *boleoi lithoi*, were piled out in a line along the spine of a ridge.

The identity of the arbiters, according to Sheila Ager (1996: 9), was one of the most important things to be specified in the negotiation of a border dispute among Greeks. The Hermion version of the arbitration, from which much of the fragmented Epidaurian version has been restored, lists the judges and witnesses in the dispute:

> Zenippos son of Gongylos, Phanokles son of Polystides, Demetrios son of Maiandrios, Demetrios son of Histiaios, Hegelochos son of Themistokles, Anthiades son of Simos. These judges were conducted from Kleitor in Arkadia by two Hermionians, Philon son of Kallistratos and Menekrates son of Menkrates, and two Epidaurians, Damokles son of Kallimenes and Timainetos son of Kallikon [Jameson et al. 1994: 596].

The issues of concern that brought these judges and witnesses together at the place of contention had to do with rights of pasturage and cropping in and around the area of the Sellas (a stream) and the wild harbors up to Strouthous or Sparrow Point (Jameson et al. 1994: 596–597). This gathering of people together delegated a task to gatherings of stone and these cairn piles then come to modify subsequent affairs. In this transaction the relevant parties are not only judges and witnesses from the different *poleis*. Prominent topographical features and a series of cairns, the *boleoi lithoi*, are also designated:

> This is to be common territory for the Hermionians and the Epidaurians. It is in the Didymia and is defined by the following boundaries: the *boleoi lithoi* established on the border of Philanoreia, as it is called, and along the dock-tailed heights straight down to the sea – the south side of the watershed (for the full translation, see Jameson et al. 1994: 596–597).[10]

Along with six judges and four witnesses, *things* are also specified on both stelae and, in this, I will take certain liberties in arguing that the *boleoi lithoi* should also be considered as both arbiters and witnesses.

Returning to the stelae, one (*SEG* 11.377) was located in a public space somewhere in Hermion. The other (*IG* IV².1.75) was placed in the Asklepieion of Epidauros.

The Asklepieion of Epidauros

All discussions pertaining to the Epidauros version of the inscription provide no more than the obligatory contextual reference – "found in the Asklepieion of Epidauros." No-one has attempted to follow this link farther in terms of the situated display of the stelae in the sanctuary. Instead, scholars keep to the paths offered by the epigraphic details of the inscribed text or trudge on to the potential topographic associations given over by the toponyms (e.g., Peek 1934; Wilhelm 1948; Jameson 1953). However, it is the site-specificity of the inscription in a public space that stabilizes the shared commitment it inscribes. Of course, establishing the location with any degree of detail is by no means an easy task. When it comes to inscriptions excavated in the 19th century, site reports are often sparing on contextual particulars. Still, given the importance of location, this issue warrants further consideration.

From 1891 to 1928 the Archaeological Society of Athens under Panayotis Kavvadias carried out excavations of the sanctuary; a sanctuary to a hero-healer turned god-healer. By the 2nd century B.C. the sanctuary was a complex polychronic aggregate of buildings, monuments, and infrastructures centered upon the Temple and Altar of Asklepios, the tholos, or Thymele, the Abaton, a building simply labeled E argued to be a cult complex and the temple of Artemis. This central area was the focus of the late 19th-century excavations of Kavvadias (1891).

Unlike the most venerable of sacred objects, which are only seen by a privileged few deep in the interiors of buildings, the arbitration text was by necessity something to be observed in the open. The key official inscriptions, many related to the *polis* of Epidauros (situated 10 km to the east on the coast), were not only located within the sacred precinct, they were also assembled around and, especially, in front of the temple of Asklepios (Figure 14.3). Amidst building accounts, records of miraculous cures, and other monuments, the inscription was set up within visual, corporeal proximity to the religious heart of the sanctuary. Stone stubborn, the inscription persisted within earshot of the gold and ivory Asklepios upon his throne, scepter in hand, dog at feet. Priests and pilgrims, physicians and healers, athletes and the infirm, animals bound for sacrifice and the sacred dogs of Asklepios whose powerful tongues cured disease: all amassed, intermingled, and circulated in the open areas formed amidst the buildings near the temple. Such spaces of coexistence are of particular significance for it is precisely the

Figure 14.3. Temple of Asklepios and the adjacent areas as seen in 2007 (author's photo).

repetitive interactions of such groups as observers with the installation of stelae near the temple that stabilize and strengthen a shared commitment inscribed in stone.

Still, ambiguous piles of rubble cannot hold the line alone and neither can a single stele in only one of the *poleis* involved. It takes two. The settlement must be mutually respected by Epidauros and Hermion.

Hermion

With regard to the Hermion inscription, we know little of the context of display in the second century B.C. In 1953 Michael Jameson speculated that the inscription was found somewhere on the *Bisti* by Alexandros Philadelpheus during his excavations in 1908–09 (Jameson 1953: 160; Philadelpheus 1909, 174).

The *Bisti* (Albanian for "tail") is the peninsula of ancient Hermion, later Kastri, and today Ermioni (Figure 14.4). Roughly divided in two, the western half is occupied by the contemporary town, which continues to rise up the *Pron* ("the foreland"). The eastern half, which begins at the Medieval crosswall, was planted with pines in the early 20th century and is now an archaeological park. Because the village is constructed on top of the ancient town, there have been few excavations apart from those carried out on the *Bisti* and in the course of rescue work by the Archaeological Service in the town. All discussions of Hermion are heavily reliant upon Pausanias.

Stone inscriptions may become lintels, thresholds, wall fabric, garden decorations, or objects on a storeroom floor. Many of the Hermion inscriptions met with such fates in the various transformations of the *sites*. We know as much because in 1729 the notorious Abbé Fourmont located perhaps as many as three

Figure 14.4. A segment of the peninsula of Ermioni (ancient Hermion) from the north in 2012. The wooded portion of the Bisti on the left ends at the medieval crosswall; the Pron begins with the slope outside of the photograph to the right (author's photo).

dozen such inscriptions in the Medieval crosswall of the *Bisti* (Omont 1902). Almost two centuries later, Philadelpheus focused his efforts upon dismantling what was left of this crosswall (see figs. E.1 and E.7 in Jameson et al. 1994). In so doing, his team displaced numerous inscriptions, old statue bases, and reused bits of architectural fabric. Many of these inscriptions were located in the second tower along the medieval wall and in the Chapel of Ayios Nikolaos when Jameson documented them in the winter and spring of 1950. At the time, the Hermion copy of the inscription was set up in a garden just outside Ermioni (Jameson 1953: 154–155). The garden belonged to the Papabasileios family. After 2000 the inscription was moved to the Porto Kheli apotheke (the crack seen in Figure 14.1 resulted from this relocation); now, however, it is in the Archaeological Museum in Nafplion.

Speculation as to Pausanias' reading of the inscription suggests that it was perhaps still situated in a public space four centuries after the dispute had taken place. As with the sanctuary of Epidauros, the location of these inscriptions entered them into a complex exchange with communal space. There are several points that we may raise here for consideration. First, a literate audience is important insofar as its members insure an active, iterative, and mutual observation – mutual, that is, on the part of both Epidauros and Hermion. Memory must be practiced and, for this to occur, observers must be strengthened in order to undertake these practices. Second, observation does not require all to be literate.

William Harris estimated the level of literacy in Attica to have ranged from

5% to 10% at most for both the Classical and Hellenistic periods (1989: 114, 146). Literacy, no doubt, fluctuated among various groups and *poleis*, but, for the sake of comparison, if we take the degree of literacy in second-century B.C. Hermion to be analogous to Harris's estimate, then inscriptions such as the Hermion stele would enter into quite different relationships with the majority of the population, relationships that were mediated by an unread stone. Stelae neither move in the same way as papyrus or goatskin, nor the paperwork or pixelwork before us. As we witnessed with the example of the Epidaurian version of the arbitration, understanding stone inscriptions has a great deal to do with their material presence in a situated context.

James Whitley, in his study of law inscriptions from Crete, argued that, in the absence of widespread literacy, such texts in stone were "as much symbolic as practical." As such, the nature of an attentive person's engagement with a stelae-in-a-public-space rests upon their personal life history, training, and skill. As Whitley emphasizes, inscriptions such as the Gortyn Law Code transform the regulations and practices of a small city-state into "eternal and immutable" form, but in this role they are "just as effectively incoherent as coherent, read as unread" (1997: 660–661). While Whitley assumes "coherence" of legible texts,[11] it is certainly the case that the meanings, associations, and understandings connected with stone inscriptions are modified by the architectures, things, and relations facilitated within a particular locale – whether *polis* center, wall fabric, garden, storehouse, or museum. In the 2nd century B.C. such relations also involved repetitive practices in these public spaces of coexistence. And yet there are important differences in how the inscribed events of these stelae are brought to life through such variable interactions.

With both inscriptions the spoken word is given spatial presence, and the difference between literate participants and casual beholders will be in how the specificities of these events linger a little longer. Without this means (and end) of rendering the arbitration public, one cannot, as Peter Sloterdijk puts it, "stabilize fleeting events and cannot give voice to them in the political domain" (2005b: 949). Materialized in stone, the availability of these events to be called upon at will is key to the longevity of these *poleis*; while this casts literate citizens in a very different role with respect to the on-going maintenance of the *polis*, no one would get very far without the stelae that pool the event of arbitration and lure the attentive observer.

Pausanias (2.36.3)

Pausanias also mentions the *boleoi*. Having passed along the straight road to Mases from Hermion, Pausanias points out the road on the right from Mases to Strouthous ("Sparrow Peak" or "Promontory"). Beyond the latter, at a distance of 250 stades according to Pausanias, lies the area of Philanorium and the *boleoi*. The latter he describes as piles of rough stones. At the equivalent of 50 km, Pausanias' measurement of 250 stades for this distance is, to borrow the words of William Martin Leake, "quite extravagant." Most argue for a more circumscribed distance of 55 stades or 11 km. If Strouthous is indeed Cape Iria, then this distance is apposite.

Almost two centuries of topographical research, speculation, and reconnaissance by Classical topographers was given over to the search for these long-lost and forgotten arbiters of, and witnesses to, a territorial dispute. Their location was posited to be as far south as the area of Fournoi and as far north as the heights above the Bedheni valley adjacent to the Dhidhima basin. Michael Jameson located the most likely candidates for the *boleoi lithoi* in the early 1990s on a ridge called Vigla.

A Ridgeline

Maintaining the integrity of the *polis*, which fundamentally includes its common territory, requires constant work. Unlike the stelae which were deployed in order to be beheld by crowds, the *boleoi* hold the line of the Philanoreia in the area of Didymoi (Figure 14.5). This was not the only demarcated section because the boundary was specified as continuing "along the dock-tailed heights straight down to the sea – the south side of the watershed." Following Pausanias, "dock-tailed heights" can be taken as "along the summits of the mountains" (Jameson et al. 1994). No cairns have been found upon Malavria or the Voskaria. The area of the Sellas and the Agrioi Limenes up to the Strouthous was to be held as common territory. Here, the karst topography and craggy texture of the mountain heights play a role in the line.

Nine candidates for the *boleoi*, along with potentially two others obscured by now ruined windmills, lie upon a rocky spur of a juniper-covered ridgeline, the summit of which is today known as Vigla. There is more to be said regarding this attribution, not only in terms of forging a connection between archaeological materials and historical referents (cf. Snodgrass 1987: 36–66, 2006: 45–62; also Morris 2005: 93–102), but also in terms of the presumed associations between several piles of unhewn rubble – we will return to these issues below. For now, aerial photographs dating to the mid-20th century show rocky limestone heights speckled with the ruins of two windmills and stone animal enclosures. This rocky exposure gives over to slopes covered in contour terracing high on the Dhidhima side of the rise (the modern village of Dhidhima retains its ancient place name, *Didymoi*).

The *boleoi lithoi* are potentially visible from both the upper plateau of Dhidhima and the lower valley of Philanoreia (the Fournoi valley); I say

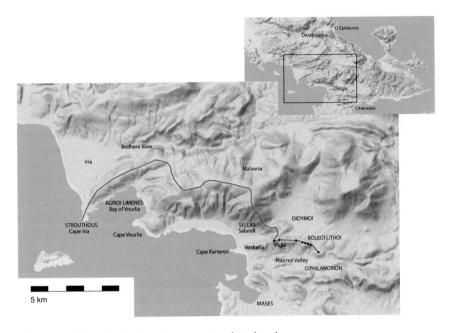

Figure 14.5. Map showing locations mentioned in this chapter.

"potentially", as the question of visibility will not only depend on the height of the pile, but also the surrounding vegetation. Indeed, the densest concentration of *boleoi lithoi*, tightly grouped, four of nine (and possibly two more) are located near the main road between the two districts. Travelers in their comings-and-goings between Didymoi and the Hermionid, shepherds conducting their herds of goats, farmers of "dusty feet" working at their tasks in fields below, or people collecting herbs or snails on the hillside: all these activities were mediated by the cairns. The presence of the *boleoi lithoi* on the ground not only provides a material basis for demarcating the boundary for those living in close proximity, but, given their visibility, the *boleoi lithoi* also sanction the actions of people, droves, and plants from a distance.

Relations between Spaces of Coexistence

Inscribed texts at the "center" of the community space in the city and sacred space at the heart of a sanctuary *temenos* maintain an inscribed border at the fringes of their mutual territory. In this, divine associations were not specific to the Epidauros inscription. According to Pausanias (2.34.12), Hermion manifested this exchange between center and boundary in the duplicate shrines of Demeter Thermesia – one rested somewhere within the city walls of Hermion and the other on the border with Eileoi, perhaps in the area of what the Argolid Exploration Project (AEP) denoted as "G1."[12]

The enrollment of these hard, immutable *immobiles*, nevertheless, hardens borders and extends the community. Delegated the task of articulating and holding on to something of the event of arbitration, the Hermion and Epidauros inscriptions also continue to mediate relationships between two city-states concerning borders through the years. As such, these modes of inscription are fundamental entities within the heterogeneous collective that constitutes the *polis* of 2nd century B.C. Hermion. Lures for observation, reservoirs for memory, maintainers of border integrity: such roles, in every sense, make these stelae viable members of the community themselves, with their own histories, their own stories, and their own place in the public space.

That is not all. In this field of relations, the *boleoi lithoi* were tracers of community, judicial and divinely sanctioned bonds. *De iure*, they held the border and in this way fulfilled a contract; a role that was further guaranteed by their common reference upon stone stelae. As *quasi-objects*, a term I borrow from Michel Serres (2007), the cairns and stelae were part of the composition of these Greek societies. They were ingredients necessary to on-going *polis* formation and maintenance. The constituents of these "social" aggregates are adjacent to the temple of Asklepios, in a visible setting on the *bisti* of Hermion, and thrown up into piles along the spine of a rocky ridgeline. The *boleoi lithoi* perform the work of maintaining common borders. The *boleoi* contribute to community cohesion among those who dwell behind shared walls. This living together is also tied up with grazing droves, shepherds and farmers, crops and herbs, third-party arbitration and tax collection.

Connecting Things Up

Relationality, by which I mean the connections among various *topoi*, is not given over so easily when dealing with old things around which former networks of relations have atrophied to the point of non-association. We simply lack many of the elements which were situated in past networks. They have broken down, perished, and/or transformed; they have been forgotten, usurped, or rendered void in new sets of relation. Once the links have been severed (and reformed elsewhere), how do we follow connections among these heterogeneous elements? How do we establish relationships between entities on the move, as in the case of the *boleoi lithoi*? One answer would be that we first have to build associations between the materialized remnants of past relationships, and these usually involve long chains of scholarly production, circulation, debate, reassessment, and further production.

Save the possibility that some new "monumental evidence" might surface, the 19th-century polymath William Martin Leake left the matter of *boleoi* to future topographers (1846: 290). Leake's problem was one of a reference without its referents. But he had already covered a great deal of ground with the *Periegesis* of Pausanias as his guide (he probably carried either the 1794 Thomas Taylor translation or one of the two 1516 Aldine texts of Pausanias: Wagstaff 2001: 192–193). The *Periegesis* provided Classical topographers with a mode of engagement, a basis for reference, orientation, and negotiation on the ground, not only in the Greek countryside (Wagstaff 2001), but also in the study, the map room, or the library. Whether in Greece, London, Paris, or Providence, it provided answers to questions of "what to observe" and it continues to do so today (Witmore and Buttrey 2008).

Writing as he moved on the ground – by autopsy – Pausanias, it is commonly held, hoped his book would become a guide for subsequent travelers (Habicht 1985: 20). The 2nd-century Baedeker (metaphorical reference after Carroll 1907) focused on gathering together the things that were most memorable along his routes by sea and countryside (Pausanias 3.2.1). *Logoi*, both spoken and written words, and *theoremata*, what is to be seen on the ground, are the two core features of his witnessing. A well-blended mixture of observation, discussions of inscriptions read, and storytelling on the basis of local oral accounts characterizes Pausanias' route through the Hermionid. The order of these routes, along with distances to other locales, provided topographers with something of a sequential word map.

Of his path from Hermion Pausanias states:

> 2.36.3 From Mases there is a road on the right to a point called Strouthous. From this point along the tops of the mountains it is a distance of 250 stades to the place called Philanorion and the *Boleoi*. The *Boleoi* are piles of rough stones. There is another place, which they call Didymoi, 20 stades from there [translation by Jameson et al. 1994: 575].

Pausanias tied the *boleoi* to the site of *Philanoreia*, which he places 250 stades along the tops of the mountains from Mases. Speculation, however, as to the location of Philanoreia was hindered by the excessive distance given by Pausanias (2.36.3). Puillion de Boblaye (1836: 61–62), on the basis of observations made during survey reconnaissance by M. de Vaudrimey as part of the *Expédition Scientifique de Morée*, and perhaps in connection with a similar assertion by Gell (1810: 132), conflated Mases with Halieis, which he took to be "les ruines d'une ville considérable, dont une grande partie se prolonge sous les eaux" at Porto Kheli or Bezáti, as the bay was also known.[13] Having done so, he relates Philanoreia with remains, probably those associated with the areas denoted as "C11" and "C17" by the AEP at Koiladha

Bay (Puillion de Boblaye 1836, 62; also see Jameson et al. 1994: 466–467, 469). Leake corrected Puillion de Boblaye's mistake by placing Halieis at Porto Kheli and Mases at Koiladha. Subsequent work would verify Leake's associations. Having settled one dispute, there was still the unresolved matter of Philanoreia, a locale to which the *boleoi* were closely attached. Here new controversies would arise.

In 1953 Michael Jameson speculated that Philanoreia lay in the vicinity of Lambayana, at the western end of the Fournoi valley near the shore (Jameson 1953: 166). In so doing, he championed the area around the Lambayana tower as a possible candidate for the ancient place-name. However, nearly 25 years later John Bintliff suggested that Philanoreia be associated with a cluster of sites in and around the contemporary village of Fournoi some 4 km farther up the valley from the Lambayana shore area (1977: 204, 234).[14]

Soon after Bintliff's study, a small fountain was constructed in the center of the village; it incorporated 2 marble lion-head spouts dated by the Argolid Exploration Project to the 4th century B.C. These features and materials come together to provide the material evidence on the ground for the association of ancient Philanoreia with Fournoi village by Jameson et al. (1994: 519). All that remained was the matter of the *boleoi*.

Earlier attempts to determine the location of the *boleoi* focused on the area north of the Dhidhima basin. Both Werner Peek (1934) and Adolph Wilhelm (1948) had associated the Sellas with the Bedheni River which drained into the Iria Plain to the north (see Figure 14.5). Parting ways with Peek and Wilhelm, Jameson (1953: 161–167) associated the Sellas with the valley of Salandi (the genitive of Sellas is *Sellantos*). Thus, place-names still in existence, such as Salandi and Dhidhima, also play a role. Of course, we know to look for piles of rough stone. We know that they are plural in number. It is fairly safe to say that there are more than two, given their former roles in delineating a border, but how many? And how can one be sure that such cairns remain?

I will spare the reader more details related to the controversies that arose over the exact course of the border, but, as I indicated earlier, there is more to be said regarding the association of several piles of stone with historical referents. Clusters of unhewn stone are very high on the scale of ambiguity. It is, moreover, an audacious and risky enterprise to connect things on the ground to things in a text. Given the radical differences between archaeological and historical data, the repetitive roster of cautions and criticisms levied at such work is lengthy.

Anthony Snodgrass, for example, has taken issue with a tendency among Classical archaeologists to grasp for any possible historical event that might provide grounding for the archaeological evidence under consideration

(Snodgrass 1987: 36–66; 2006: 45–62). Snodgrass targets a series of underlying assumptions associated with the interpretation of excavated settlement-sites. Why, for example, should one jump from isolated evidence of destruction by fire to a historically documented event, if a site is not fully excavated? Could there be other episodes of burning that might have escaped the historical record? Could the historical accounts of such events be problematic? There is admittedly too much noise ever to expect a clear signal. Unlike many of Snodgrass's examples, with the case of the *boleoi* we are dealing with a scenario of connecting textual *topoi* with potential locations on the ground. Still, even beyond the issue of attribution, one cannot even be certain whether isolated clusters of stone on Vigla are constituted as part of a common episode.

In his discussion of the rupestral *horoi* of Attica, Josiah Ober lays caution against the possibility of linking together such markers in a series (1995). He emphasizes the difficulty involved not only in ascertaining the simultaneity of multiple rupestral *horoi*, but also in even proving a marker to have been established between two demes in a particular period (1995: 119–120). Beyond the uncertainties of serial connection, piles of stone do not even give one the benefit of the inscribed term *horos*.

As an archaeologist, I do not "discover" the past, as it is often held. Rather, I work with what is coextensive with me and such work requires great care and creativity. In the end, archaeologists never find the past as it was; they, as a matter of fact, are caught up in the articulation of something entirely novel. Rife with indeterminacy, this work does not fail by proposing a *possible* connection between historical references and archaeological materials, or even between discrete concentrations of stone; it fails by insisting on a *necessary* one. Plausibility increases in one's favor when weighed in light of the chain of labor and the network of other relations that lie behind the tentative attribution of Vigla as the site of the *boleoi lithoi*.[15]

Indeed, with the case of the *boleoi lithoi*, epigraphy, Classical topography, excavation, the *Periegesis*, two stone stelae, intensive survey, toponyms, reiterative practices, and multiple return trips staggered over 200 years, all come together in the process of reconnecting referents as locations on the ground. In this, one link depends on others. Halieis and Mases, Philanoreia and the *boleoi*, Salandi and Dhidhima, the shape of a coast or a peak, materials indicative of an ancient site, piles of stone: it is never an issue of a single reference associated with a single site, but rather each and every one relies on a whole web of other connections and long cascades of achievement. So, in returning to the question of linking things up, how do we get from one site to another? We just stubbornly follow the traces of associations no matter where they may take us.[16] Dead ends are frequent. Attributions are always tentative. And the field of relations manifest in the 2nd-century B.C.

arbitration is the outcome of a chain of scholarly labor spread out over two centuries.

It is in following such paths that we encounter a false detour with regard to the issue of scale. With some recent work embracing the rubric of multi-sited archaeology, it is all too common to find the local and global treated as two different scales, micro and macro, between which we may freely travel back and forth (Hicks 2003: 324; Beaudry 2005: 309–310).[17] From a pile of rocks on the ground is there any path, direct or otherwise, to the nature of "interstate relations", "economic models", or the "ancient state"?[18] One should rightly hesitate over the answer. Consider how goats in pursuit of vegetation stray across a boundary that brings shepherds into contention with vested parties in the area of Didymoi and Philanoreia. From here fees are imposed. Tax collectors seek payment for pasturage. Concerned citizens from Epidauros and Hermion become involved, leading to a commission for Milesian judges who pass a decision on the matter. Though our picture is admittedly fragmentary and opaque, the materialized rendering of the circuitous path that begins with ravenous goats and ends with interstate arbitration suggests an altogether different topography of interaction, one that is characterized by connectivity between many sites, and not by zoning limits set up in advance.

As long as we cradle the *polis* in two dimensions alone, we will continue to turn around this problem – the *polis* is never at rest, it is never static. Yet our mode of rendering the past mobile flattens this dynamism into Euclidean space.[19] For shepherds, literate citizens, judges, or tax collectors, a border was never experienced as a scaled line from above, but as movements between a series of connected, coexistent *topoi*. No boundary as viewed from the cartographer's table can proclaim the proper delimitation for such relations, because these were never framed by Euclidean space (Witmore 2013); they were caught up within ever-fluctuating relations between, for example, vegetation, goats, piles of stone, and citizens ablaze with discontent on the ground. We may further clarify these points through a brief discussion of a critique leveled at Mediterranean intensive surface survey by Richard Blanton (2001) in his review of the POPULUS Project (Bintliff and Sbonias 1999; Leveau et al. 1999; Gillings, Mattingly and van Dalen 2000; Pasquinucci and Trément 2000; Francovich, Patterson and Barker 2000) in the journal *Antiquity*.

Intensive surface surveys in the Mediterranean generally rest upon methodologies which are oriented toward areas of 100 km² or less (what Blanton calls "microregions"). For Blanton, the "myopic" scales at which these projects are conducted are too small to represent the past regional systems of which these areas were once a part. Such a critique, however, puts the cart before the horse in such a way that neither the horse nor the driver can make out the road in front of them. Clearly, not all groups operated at the same "scale" in the past: *poleis* do not have the same borders as goats, vegetation, and shepherds, or sea currents, red mullet, and fishermen. As such, we might regard scale as an outcome of certain relations rather than a predetermined envelope for all such interactions. Scale, in short, is assembled through backbreaking, labor-intensive, empirical work, and not, as Blanton would have it, defined *a priori* (cf. Alcock and Cherry 2004). Consequently, the best place to begin is *in medias res* with specific connections underneath the over-dramatized processes of interstate dynamics. As archaeologists we are always dealing with many spaces – stelae in a sacred precinct or in an area of community display, cairn piles along a ridgeline – which are more or less connected (Marcus 1995:99; Latour 2005). The problem of scale should be replaced with the challenge of connection.

Let us now move on to our third and final task related to whether the notion of "multi-sited" holds up to the needs of archaeology.

A Multi-sited Archaeology?

Grazing droves and boundary lines between *poleis*; the arbitration of a land dispute in the 2nd century B.C., and piles of unhewn rubble along a ridgeline in the southern Argolid; a reference to the *boleoi* mentioned in Pausanias' *Periegesis* and two stone stelae, one in Epidauros and one in Hermion: all these heterogeneous elements are linked up within a complex and perpetually fluctuating network of relations. Archaeologists, along with ancient texts, stone stelae and rubble, and chains of previous labor, must build these associations, and such referentiality, such relationality, explodes any notion of a vacuous unity of place-in-itself. For a "multi-sited archaeology," a seemingly unassuming pile of rubble is not simply lying upon a ridgeline in the midst of low juniper bushes, but it is of many different places (and times) simultaneously. Something of these stone cairns is caught up in relations on the ground in Epidauros, Hermion, or even Jameson's topographical surveys from the 1950s on. Whether dealing with stone stelae or stone cairns, all are simultaneously located and dislocated, defined and distributed, singular and collective. They circulate in a variety of forms and extend their webs of relation, which are constantly fluctuating. Given this, we are now well positioned to ask: what does the term "multi-sited" actually designate?

As the concept arose to address multi-cultural, long-distance sets of relation, some readers may take issue with how far this essay has cast its net under the rubric of "multi-sited". As with the Travelers Club of 19th-century London, the length of your journey should not be a requisite criterion for membership in such studies. We might even say that space and time do not define particular relations, but, to the contrary, they are defined out of them (Latour 2005; Harman 2007: 43; Witmore 2007a).[20] Still, we could with a great deal of hard work continue with, for example, Michael Jameson's notebooks, photographs, and squeezes[21] – these media circulate both the inscriptions and the locales at an even greater distance, thus linking up more locales.[22] However, this would miss the point. So long as we trace out the salient heterogeneous elements we need cross neither longitudes nor latitudes as an obligatory condition for a multi-sited study. Sometimes, we need not stray very far from the same spot. Under your feet there are potentially many sites but, more often than not, you have to go elsewhere to get to them (Sloterdijk 2009).

Archaeology, though it is never specified in this way, consistently reveals how a place is never the *same* "site" (or even a "site") over the long term (consider, for example, David Pettegrew's [2001] discussion of "Classical farmsteads"). This, at first, may seem to be captured by the common-sense proposition: locales change, but this too holds for entities, which are often painted as consistent, irrespective of the changing climate around them. The cairn piles are potentially many distinct entities depending on what set of relations they have entered. Arbiters of a dispute (the *boleoi lithoi*), markers for a boundary, obstacles for passing goats, wind screens for a campfire, quarries for a windmill, topics of academic interest and debate: the cairn piles are many different things, many different sites, performing many different roles, offering up many different properties, and yet they are singular events on a ridgeline simultaneously! The same locale may be *places* or *sites* in the plural, depending on the rapports into which it enters. But, I hasten to add, these sites are neither reducible to, nor exhausted by, their relations. They hold something in reserve; they have an integrity that exceeds the vast majority of their interactions (Harman 2002: 233; Olsen 2010).

If the relational nature of things is such that they are, as I have specified, simultaneously located and dislocated both spatially and temporally, what are we to make of the notion of "multi-sited"? There is much more at stake here than issues of semantics. The term "multi-sited" breaks down with respect to how it prioritizes particular metaphysical ingredients. This happens in two ways: it either designates the located character of all interactions or it refers to the situated circumstances of all entities whether they are on the ground, on a page, in cyberspace, etc. Either way the "multi-sited" prioritizes the spatial grounds for various relations. And this would be perfectly fine if it were not for other components of reality which are potentially over*looked*.

Certainly, if we trace the associations, we will arrive at other sites, possibly at many; but we will also come across other times, other materials, and other agencies (Latour 2005: 166).[23] As I have argued, there is more to any site than relations among materials on the ground, because they are linked up with varieties of articulations whether as paperwork or pixelwork. We can say for certain there are many sites – a ridgeline, museum containing an inscription, the desk in my office, or the line on my computer screen; there are many agencies – Pausanias, a map in a book, cairns on a ridge, judges, topographers, goats and shepherds; there are many times – the 1950s, 1890s, 2nd century B.C., 2nd century A.D. – and all are *now* simultaneously at play.[24]

Conclusions

We have covered many grounds in the course of this chapter and we are now in a position to conclude with the question of "so what?" Let us return to the three tasks I set for myself in the introduction by placing emphasis on three arguments. First, boundary maintenance is a distributed affair with interactions counting for as much in sanctuaries and town "centers" as on the "periphery". Understanding these dynamics compels one to carefully trace the connections between many different places, temporal *topoi*, materials, and agencies. There is also a lesson here of specificity and scale. One cannot presuppose the relevant paths in advance with some macro framework. All together the network of things, locales and times one traces out will come to count for more than any predetermined, overarching big picture.

Second, a multi-sited archaeology is full of many detours, but it should seek to recognize the heterogeneous nature of societies in the past and the ways in which contemporary archaeologists are themselves all mixed up with their fields of study. I have engaged in a form of archaeological practice, which puts the act of tracing relations right up front (cf. Shanks 1999: 32). This does not occur at the expense of previous work. On one level, this is what good archaeology has been about for some time now – we build upon the achievements of actors whose work has often been regarded as outmoded.

Third, there are bolder possibilities concerning the referential character of things and the nature of people/thing, animal/thing and thing/thing relations which could be pushed even farther (Whitehead 1978 [1929]). There are more ingredients to the heterogeneous network than *place*. Again, there are also *other times*, *other materials*, and *other agencies* that come into play (Latour 2005: 166).

The decisive problem with the term "multi-sited" is metaphysical – it simply does not cover the quadruple folding of agencies, materials, times, *and* spaces. So if multi-sited archaeology does not sufficiently address the range of issues I have specified, with what then do we replace it? Symmetrical Archaeology? Actor-Network Archaeology? I hope that by revealing the features of the connectedness, the depth of the chains of reference, the multiplicity of the various times, I have made the case that we would recognize we are dealing with good practice under a single, sufficiently encompassing rubric: "archaeology."

Acknowledgements

Behind this article runs a cascade of numerous versions. It largely developed out of a paper given in a workshop, "Drawing on Rocks, Gathering by the Water," sponsored by the Joukowsky Institute for Archaeology and the Ancient World at Brown University in March of 2008. I would like to thank Susan Alcock, John Cherry, Elliot Colla, Ömür Harmansah, Krysta Ryzewski, and Bradley Sekedat for their insights into that paper. Portions of the section covering the *boleoi lithoi* draw upon an earlier case-study from my 2005 dissertation, and here I am indebted to Ian Hodder, Michael Jameson, Ian Morris, Michael Shanks, and Fred Turner. This paper has also benefited from feedback by Jason Banta, Alfredo González-Ruibal, Ömür Harmansah, David Larmour, Timothy Webmoor, and Joseph Zehner. In the course of the background fieldwork to this article, I received much help and support from Georgia Ivou, Michael Jameson, Evangelia Pappi, Lena Zgouleta, and Zoi Zgouleta.

Notes

1. In so doing, I do not relegate previous work to the realm of the outmoded. Instead, I recognize previous endeavors, whether antiquarian or topographical, as achievements to be built upon (on the rhetorical strategy of the so-called gesture of "Copernican Revolution" in archaeology, see Witmore 2007a, 2007b).

2. The term *topos* is recognized in its full ancient Greek sense of referring to a place, a position, or a passage in a text.

3. To be sure, the picture is infinitely more complex – in short, because these processes are the over-dramatized images of macro-processes. In this essay, we will walk underneath these grand canvases to engage micro-relations below.

4. It would also be fair to label such work as multi-sited anthropology focused on fields of archaeological production.

5. Elsewhere, in lieu of a notion of multi-sited archaeology, I have deployed the notion of multiple fields (Witmore 2004, 2007b). Multiple fields cover the various links and nodes caught up in webs of knowledge co-production in archaeology. My rationale for this is further articulated below.

6. There has been a fair amount of debate in Mediterranean archaeology over the notion of "site" with regard to delimiting the extent of materials on the ground (Cherry 2003). Here, the notion of a site refers to those loci which have acquired sufficient definition to a allow movement from one to the next.

7. While it is so much easier to hold on to a former and simpler image of a world bifurcated into separate hemispheres of the global and local, it is much more difficult to argue that it was never as simple as many would have us believe. Arguments for multi-sited archaeology often play upon such rhetoric for former dichotomies which are subsequently either taken on their own to account for both sides, or unified into a composite (Hodder 1999).

8. The question of whether or not particular 18th-century structures in Idhra are constructed out of stone quarried from the ruins of Hermion remains an open one in need of further work. This supposition partially rests upon comments by 18th- and 19th-century travelers and topographers. William Martin Leake, in his discussion of the site for example, comments: "its situation near the sea, and not far from some islands of recent populousness, has been very unfavorable to the preservation of its remains of antiquity" (1830 II: 461). Leake, however, never visited Ermioni in the course of his travels and relied upon either local informants or other traveler accounts.

9. Ian Morris has criticized recent work on connectivity in the Mediterranean for its ill-defined nature (2003). Arguing that the reliance on networks by scholars such as Horden and Purcell (2000) has to do with the work of contemporary notions of global capitalist economies, Morris suggests that there is a need for more precise analytical categories, and an explicit recognition of the impact of globalization on these frameworks. The notion of connectedness discussed here owes more to the work of STS, which in some strains draws from the philosophy of Leibniz and Diderot (cf. Latour 2009). The thrust of this body of work is to put to one side over-dramatized processes like globalization as starting points, because it seeks to understand how they come about by moving empirically from site to site.

10. Jameson translates the participial clause *boleoi lithoi keimnoi* as the "*boleoi lithoi* set up" (Jameson et al. 1994: 597). However, *keimai* also carries more connotations, especially in legal terms, related to 'laying down', 'establishing', or 'ordaining law' (see, e.g., Thucydides 2.37; Lysias 1.48).

11. Alfred North Whitehead warned against the presupposition that language enunciates "well-defined propositions… Language is thoroughly indeterminate, by reason of the fact that every occurrence presupposes some systematic type of environment" (1978 [1929]: 12).

12. Pausanias (2.35.3) also tells us of the temple of Apollo Horios (Apollo "of the borders") that is also located in Hermion.

13. Puillon de Boblaye attributed Halieis to "les ruines d'une forteresse hellénique à 5,000 mètres sud de Castri, sur les bords de la mer; une petite île formait son port" (1836: 61). Leake suggested that this site, probably Petrothalassa (denoted as "E6" by the AEP), which is located near a small island by the same name 5.5 km northeast of Porto Kheli, was "some dependency of Hermion, of which the name is not recorded in ancient history" (1846: 287). Faraklas (1973) published a plan of the circuit wall at Petrothalassa.

14. Bintliff's "Fournoi Focus" was comprised of numerous sites with surface remains (labeled "F6," "F13," "F15," "F17," and "F32" by the AEP); all culminated in a low, exposed hill with a limestone summit known today as Profitis Ilias (dubbed "F5").

15. Even the suggestion that stone concentrations are cairns requires a combination of trust in this interpretation by Jameson and further acts of retroactive verification. I revisited the ridgeline on August 19, 2007 with Bradley Sekedat, who was at that time a PhD student at Brown University. We walked for several hundred meters through the thick

cover of juniper along the top of Vigla until circumstances prevented us from pushing farther. We were able to locate 4 of the 9 cairns mentioned by Jameson along with the ruined windmills, which may, as Jameson suggested, sit atop other stone piles. All, save the easternmost cairn, were dispersed out into low clusters of stone ranging from 10 to 15 m across; the easternmost was more densely packed into an area roughly 7 m across, as described by Jameson et al. (1994: 599).

16.   We should say "to explain is," as Bruno Latour puts it, "not a mysterious cognitive feat, but a very practical world-building enterprise that consists in connecting entities with other entities, that is, in tracing a network" (2005: 103).

17.   Connecting the foreground and the background has never been archaeology's strong suit (Pearson and Shanks 2001).

18.   Here I am paraphrasing Bruno Latour (2005: 167): "from the floor of a sweatshop is there any canal that goes to a 'capitalist mode of production' or to an 'empire'?"

19.   Stability, thus, requires constant labor on the part of concerned citizens. At the same time, no ideology, no political power, no set of values, no economic models, no agreements among citizens alone could sustain the *polis* without minions of much more humble and mundane things. From this angle, the labor of maintenance and repair is far more important to the longevity of the *polis* than has been previously acknowledged.

20.   It is necessary to remember that calendars are standardized blocks on a page; clocks are composed of cogs and gears which translate into consistent movements of hands on a dial.

21.   A squeeze is filter paper that is wetted and brushed onto the surface of an inscription. With this compression, the paper takes on the three-dimensional qualities of the inscription in reverse.

22.   Scholarly media, too, are coexistent. Their referentiality in relation to the *boleoi* adds to the network of relation. They perform in the on-going definition of these locales. Each new account takes part in the performance of not only other accounts, but also the things, materials, matter dealt with. Each, if they are solid accounts, adds to the complexity of the *boleoi* (they may also subtract from it, and often do).

23.   All along my road map has been Actor-Network-Theory (Callon and Law 1997; Latour 2005; Law 2008). Actor-network-theory teaches us to be open to all possible mediators and to follow all possible paths of association. The act of arbitration folds together heterogeneous spaces, times and agencies which are not necessarily contemporary with the dispute resolution. Arbitration, the form of a ridgeline, the gods, and many diverse elements play a role. And we cannot presuppose what is relevant in a given situation.

24.   This is why I prefer notions such as topology, as the Greek term "topos" can refer to a place in general or "a room in a house, a part of the body, a position in the zodiac, a place of burial, a passage in a text, or even a topic or theme within rhetoric" (Witmore 2007a).

References

Ager, Sheila L.
    1996   *Interstate Arbitrations in the Greek World, 337–90 B.C.* University of California Press, Berkeley.

Alcock, Susan E., and John F. Cherry (editors)
    2004   *Side-by-Side Survey: Comparative Regional Studies in the Mediterranean World.* Oxbow, Oxford.

Appadurai, Arjun

1996 *Modernity at Large: Cultural Dimensions of Globalization*. University of Minnesota Press, Minneapolis.

Bartu, Ayfer

2000 Where is Çatalhöyük? Multiple Sites in the Construction of an Archaeological Site. In *Towards a Reflexive Method in Archaeology: The Example at Çatalhöyük*, edited by Ian Hodder, pp. 101–109. The McDonald Institute for Archaeological Research, Cambridge.

Beaudry, Mary C.

2005 Concluding Comments. In *Industrial Archaeology: Future Directions*, edited by Eleanor Conlin Casella and James Symonds, pp. 301–314. Springer, New York.

Bintliff, John L.

1977 *Natural Environment and Human Settlement in Prehistoric Greece*, 2 Vols. British Archaeological Reports 28. Archaeopress, Oxford.

Bintliff, John L., and Kostas Sbonias (eds.)

1999 *Reconstructing Past Population Trends in Mediterranean Europe (3000 B.C.–A.D. 1800)*. Oxbow, Oxford.

Blanton, Richard

2001 Mediterranean Myopia. *Antiquity* 75: 627–629.

Callon, Michel, and John Law

1997 After the Individual in Society: Lessons on Collectivity from Science, Technology and Society. *Canadian Journal of Sociology* 22(2): 165–182.

Carroll, Mitchell

1907 Pausanias: A Second Century Baedeker. *The George Washington University Bulletin* 5: 61–67.

Cherry, John F.

2003 Archaeology Beyond the Site: Regional Survey and Its Future. In *Theory and Practice in Mediterranean Archaeology: Old World and New World Perspectives*, edited by John K. Papadopoulos and Richard M. Leventhal, pp. 137–159. Cotsen Institute of Archaeology, Los Angeles.

Dixon, Michael

2001 *IG* IV2.1.75 and the Date of the Arbitration between Epidauros and Hermion. *Zeitschrift für Papyrologie und Epigraphik* 137: 169–173.

Falzon, Mark-Anthony (editor)

2009 *Multi-Sited Ethnography: Theory, Praxis and Locality in Contemporary Research*. Ashgate, Burlington.

Faraklas, Nikolaos

1973 *Ermionis–Alias*. Ancient Greek City Reports 12. Athens Center of Ekistics, Athens.

Francovich, Riccardo, Helen L. Patterson, and Graeme Barker (eds.)

2000 *Extracting Meaning from Ploughsoil Assemblages*. Oxbow, Oxford.

Frazer, James George

1898 *Pausanias's "Description of Greece"*. 6 Vols. Macmillan, London.

Garnsey, Peter
 1998   *Cities, Peasants and Food in Classical Antiquity: Essays in Social and Economy History.*
        Cambridge University Press, Cambridge.

Gell, William
 1810   *The Itinerary of Greece, With a Commentary on Pausanias and Strabo, and an Account
        of the Monuments of Antiquity at Present Existing in that Country, Compiled in the
        Years 1801, 2, 5, 6 etc.* T. Payne, London.

Gillings, Mark, D.J. Mattingly, and Jan van Dalen (eds.)
 2000   *Geographical Information Systems and Landscape Archaeology.* Oxbow, Oxford.

Grace, Virginia
 1979   *Amphoras and the Ancient Wine Trade.* American School of Classical Studies at
        Athens, Athens.

Gupta, Akhil, and James Ferguson (eds.)
 1997   *Anthropological Locations: Boundaries and Grounds of a Field Science.* University of
        California Press, Berkeley.

Habicht, Christian
 1985   *Pausanias's Guide to Ancient Greece.* University of California Press, Berkeley.

Hall, Martin
 2000   *Archaeology and the Modern World: Colonial Transcripts in South Africa and the
        Chesapeake.* Routledge, London.

Hamilakis, Yiannis, and Aris Anagnostopoulos
 2009   What is Archaeological Ethnography? *Public Archaeology: Archaeological Ethnographies*
        18(2–3): 65–87.

Harman, Graham
 2002   *Tool-Being: Heidegger and the Metaphysics of Objects.* Open Court, Chicago.
 2007   The Importance of Bruno Latour for Philosophy. *Cultural Studies Review* 31(1):
        31–49.
 2009   *Prince of Networks: Bruno Latour and Metaphysics.* Re.Press, Melbourne.

Harris, William V.
 1989   *Ancient Literacy.* Harvard University Press, Cambridge, MA.

Hicks, Dan
 2003   Archaeology Unfolding: Diversity and the Loss of Isolation. *Oxford Journal of
        Archaeology* 22(3): 315–29.

Hodder, Ian
 1999   *The Archaeological Process.* Blackwell, Oxford.

Hodder, Ian (ed.)
 2000   *Towards Reflexive Method in Archaeology: The Example of Çatalhöyük.* The McDonald
        Institute for Archaeological Research, Cambridge.

Hodder, Ian, with William Rathje, Michael Shanks and Christopher Witmore
 2013   Ian Hodder. In *Archaeology in the Making: Conversations through a Discipline,*
        edited by William Rathje, Michael Shanks and Christopher Witmore, pp. 122–138,
        Routledge, London.

Hordon, Peregrine, and Nicholas Purcell

    2000 *The Corrupting Sea: A Study of Mediterranean History.* Wiley-Blackwell, Oxford.

Jameson, Michael H.

    1953 Inscriptions of the Peloponessos. *Hesperia* 22(3): 148–171.

Jameson, Michael H., Curtis N. Runnels, and Tjeerd H. van Andel

    1994 *A Greek Countryside: The Southern Argolid from Prehistory to the Present Day.* Stanford University Press, Stanford.

Kavvadias, Panagiotis

    1891 *Fouilles d'Épidaure.* S.C. Vlastos, Athens.

Latour, Bruno

    2005 *Reassembling the Social: An Introduction to Actor-Network-Theory.* Oxford University Press, Oxford.

    2009 Spheres and Networks. Two Ways to Reinterpret Globalization. *Harvard Design Magazine* 30 (Spring/Summer 2009): 138–44.

Law, John

    2008 Actor-Network Theory and Material Semiotics. In *The New Blackwell Companion to Social Theory*, edited by Bryan S. Turner, pp. 141–158. Wiley-Blackwell, Oxford.

Leake, William Martin

    1830 *Travels in the Morea.* Vol. II. J. Murray, London.

    1846 *Peloponnesiaca: A Supplement to Travels in the Morea.* J. Rodwell, London.

Leveau, Philippe, Frédéric Trément, Kevin Walsh and Graeme Barker (eds.)

    1999 *Environmental Reconstruction in Mediterranean Landscape Archaeology.* Oxbow, Oxford.

Lucas, Gavin

    2001 *Critical Approaches to Fieldwork: Contemporary and Historical Archaeological Practice.* Routledge, London.

    2006 *An Archaeology of Colonial Identity: Power and Material Culture in the Dwars Valley, South Africa.* Springer, New York.

Marcus, George E.

    1995 Ethnography in/of the World System. The Emergence of Multi-Sited Ethnography. *Annual Review of Anthropology* 24: 95–117.

    2005 Multi-sited Ethnography: Five or Six Things I Know About It Now. In *Problems and Possibilities in Multi-sited Ethnography Workshop*, 27–28 June 2005, University of Sussex. (Unpublished)

Marcus, George E., and Michael J. Fischer

    1986 *Anthropology as Cultural Critique: An Experimental Moment in the Human Sciences.* University of Chicago Press, Chicago.

Miliarakis, Antonios

    1886 *Geographia tou Nomou Argolidos kai Korinthas.* Bibliopoleion Estias, Athens.

Morris, Ian

    2000 *Archaeology as Cultural History.* Blackwell, Oxford.

    2003 Mediterraneanization. *Mediterranean Historical Review* 18(2): 30–55.

    2005 Archaeology, Standards of Living, and Greek Economic History. In *The Ancient*

Economy: Evidence and Models, edited by Joseph G. Manning and Ian Morris, pp. 91–126, Stanford University Press, Stanford.

Ober, Josiah

1995 Greek Horoi: Artifactual Texts and the Contingency of Meaning. In *Methods in the Mediterranean: Historical and Archaeological Views on Texts and Archaeology*, edited by David B. Stone, pp. 91–123. Brill, Leiden.

Olsen, Bjørnar

2010 *In Defense of Things: Archaeology and the Ontology of Objects*. AltaMira Press, Lanham, MD.

Omont, Henri Auguste

1902 *Missions archéologiques françaises en Orient aux XVIIe et XVIIIe siècles*. Vol. 1. Imprimerie Nationale: Paris.

Pasquinucci, Marinella, and Frédéric Trément (eds.)

2000 *Non-Destructive Techniques Applied to Landscape Archaeology*. Oxbow, Oxford.

Pearson, Mike, and Michael Shanks

2001 *Theatre/Archaeology*. Routledge, London.

Peek, Werner

1934 Griechische Inschriften. *Mitteilungen des Deutschen Archäologischen Instituts, Athenische Abteilung* 59: 35–80.

Pettegrew, David K.

2001 Chasing the Classical Farmstead: Assessing the Formation and Signature of Rural Settlement in Greek Landscape Archaeology. *Journal of Mediterranean Archaeology* 14(2): 189–209.

Philadelpheus, Alexandros

1909 Ai en Hermionidi Anaskaphai. *Praktika*, 172–184.

Puillon de Boblaye, Emile

1836 *Expédition scientifique de Morée. Recherches géographiques sur les ruines de la Morée*. F.G. Levrault: Paris

Ryzewski, Krysta

2008 Archaeology of a Colonial Industry: Domestic Ironworking and Industrial Evolution in Rhode Island, 1642–1800. Unpublished Ph.D. Dissertation, Brown University.

2012 Multiply Situated Strategies? Multi-Sited Ethnography and Archaeology. *Journal of Archaeological Method and Theory* 19(2): 241–268.

Serres, Michel

1995 *The Natural Contract*. University of Michigan Press, Ann Arbor.

2007 *The Parasite*. University of Minnesota Press, Minneapolis.

Shanks, Michael

1999 *Art and the Early Greek State*. Cambridge University Press, Cambridge.

Sloterdijk, Peter

2005a *Im Weltinnenraum des Kapitals: Für eine philosophische Theorie der Globalisierung*. Suhrkamp, Frankfurt am Main.

2005b Atmospheric Politics. In *Making Things Public: Atmospheres of Democracy*, edited by Bruno Latour and Peter Weibel, pp. 944–951. MIT Press, Cambridge, MA.

2009 Spheres Theory: Talking to Myself About the Poetics of Space. *Harvard Design Magazine* 30 (Spring/Summer 2009): 126–137.

Smith, Monica L.
2005 Networks, Territories, and the Cartography of Ancient States. *Annals of the Association of American Geographers* 95(4): 832–849.

Snodgrass, Anthony M.
1987 *An Archaeology of Greece: The Present State and Future Scope of a Discipline.* University of California Press, Berkeley.
2006 *Archaeology and the Emergence of Greece.* Cornell University Press, Ithaca.

Wagstaff, J. Malcolm
2001 Pausanias and the Topographers: The Case of Colonel Leake. In *Pausanias: Travel and Memory in Roman Greece*, edited by Susan E. Alcock, John F. Cherry, and Jaś Elsner, pp. 190–206. Oxford University Press, Oxford.

Webmoor, Timothy, and Christopher L. Witmore
2008 Things are Us! A Commentary on Human/Things Relations under the Banner of a "Social" Archaeology. *Norwegian Archaeology Review* 41(1): 53–70.

Whitehead, Alfred North
1978 [1929] *Process and Reality: An Essay in Cosmology.* Free Press, New York.

Whitley, James
1997 Cretan Laws and Cretan Literacy. *American Journal of Archaeology* 101(4): 635–661.

Wilhelm, Adolph
1948 Ein Gebietstreit in der Argolis. *Anzeiger der Wiener Akademie der Wissenschaften, Philosophisch-Historischen Klasse*, 57–80.

Witmore, Christopher L.
2004 On Multiple Fields. Between the Material World and Media: Two Cases from the Peloponnesus, Greece. *Archaeological Dialogues* 11(2): 133–164.
2007a Landscape, Time, Topology: An Archaeological Account of the Southern Argolid Greece. In *Envisioning Landscape*, edited by Dan Hicks, Graham Fairclough, and Laura McAtackney, pp. 194–225. Left Coast Press, Walnut Creek, CA.
2007b Symmetrical Archaeology: Excerpts from a Manifesto. *World Archaeology* 39(4): 546–562.
2013 The World on a Flat Surface: Maps from the Archaeology of Greece and Beyond. In *Representing the Past: Archaeology through Text and Image*, edited by S. Bonde and S. Houston, pp. 125–149. Joukowsky Institute Publication 2. Oxbow, Oxford.

Witmore, Christopher L., and T.V. Buttrey
2008 William Martin Leake: A Contemporary of P.O. Brøndsted in Greece and in London. In *P.O. Brøndsted (1780–1842) – A Danish Classicist in his European Context*, edited by Bodil Bundgaard Rasmussen, Jørgen Steen Jensen, John Lund, and Michael Märcher, pp. 15–34. Historisk-filosofiske Skrifter 31. Det Kongelige Danske Videnskabernes Selskab, Copenhagen.

— 15 —

Moving On:
A Conversation with Chris Witmore

GAVIN LUCAS

In reading Chris Witmore's paper, I was impressed by his engaging and clever progression from multi-sited archaeology to relational ontology. To the dispersal and de-centering of place/space into a network or chain of connections, Witmore adds a complementary dispersal of time and agency, creating a trinity – a triple folding – for which the term "multi-sited archaeology" does not do full justice. Inspired by Witmore's train of thought, I want to retrace his footsteps, but follow the journey back from the relational to the multi-sited, taking in some rather different issues along the way.

Everything is connected to everything else – or so it is often claimed. One of the problems with relational ontologies is that pushed to their full logical conclusion, the very heterogeneity that is their strength is in danger of melting into an homogeneous oneness. As Graham Harman has argued, if objects have no essence, if they are pure relations, what stops these relations from dissolving into one big soup: why are there *beings* instead of just Being? Harman's reversal of Heidegger's ontic-ontological division in terms of its philosophical relevance is a powerful critique of relational ontologies and in Harman's view (2002; 2005), objects are not pure relations, but always hold something back. Indeed, everything is *not* connected to everything else – a rock is immune to a gust of wind, while a feather floats away. Causal relations between objects vary not only in intensity, but in actuality – some objects just do not connect at all. Such a recognition preserves the heterogeneity that Witmore discusses, but also takes us one step backward, away from relational ontologies to a multi-sited archaeology.

Let me take a slightly different tack and draw on a more archaeological example here. I have always been struck by Colin Renfrew's critique of the culture group concept, where the archaeological record is portrayed as a uniform continuum in terms of spatial variability, but due to the randomness of where one starts, boundaries emerge and culture groups are defined. Renfrew explains this better:

> For it is easy to show how spatial distributions, equivalent to the traditional cultural entities, can be generated by the archaeologist out of a continuum of change. If uniformities and similarities in artefact assemblages are viewed as the result of interactions between individuals, and if such interactions decrease in intensity uniformly with distance, each point will be most like its close neighbors. Consider the point *P* lying in a uniform plain, with its neighbors fairly regularly spaced around it. ... If the excavator first digs at *P* and recovers its assemblage, he will subsequently learn that adjacent points have a broadly similar assemblage, which he will call "the P culture". Gradually its boundaries will be set up by further research, with the criterion that only those assemblages which attain a given threshold level of similarity with the finds from *P* qualify for inclusion. So a "culture" is born, centering on *P*, the type site, whose bounds are entirely arbitrary, depending solely on the threshold level of similarity and the initial, fortuitous choice of *P* as the point of reference [Renfrew 1977: 94–95].

There is an interesting parallel here with Witmore's suggestion of immersing oneself *in medias res*. On the one hand, Witmore's and Renfrew's strategies are quite opposite: in Renfrew's approach, the arbitrariness of the starting point *does matter*, because it is linked to identifying bounded places (i.e., culture areas), while for Witmore it is irrelevant, since it is about looking for connections between places, not circumscribing such places. One is about boundedness and fixity, the other about connectivity and fluidity. On the other hand, however, they both share a certain presumption of spatial homogeneity, which neither of them actually might really believe. The very arbitrariness of the starting point which makes culture groups a purely archaeological construct in Renfrew's case, or that makes ontologies relational in Witmore's, also acts to underline the specter of homogeneity that Harman raises.

I fully agree with Witmore's threefold of space, time and agency, but what needs exploring – and explaining – is not purely relationality tripled, but how this trinity creates and maintains heterogeneity. That is, if each object is defined by its connection to other objects, what prevents all objects from collapsing into one; what is it that preserves difference? There are connections between things, but not everything is connected to everything else. A South Carolina plantation may well be connected to a Charleston dockyard and a snuff shop in London, but not necessarily to a small farm in the northwest of Iceland. What enables or prohibits these connections? What restricts a multi-sited archaeology from becoming a pan-sited archaeology (which is where a relational ontology is in danger of taking us)?

As Witmore suggests, it is all about tracing the connections but, more than that, about thinking of these connections, in turn, as materialized; in short, the connection between a South Carolina plantation and a Charleston dockyard is not one of action-at-a-distance, but the materialized transfer or exchange of mobile objects or bodies between the two sites and the materialized routes and paths along which these objects travel. It seems to me that in working back towards a multi-sited archaeology, a rather different – but complementary – set of concerns is raised to those offered by Witmore. I agree completely with his suggestions that scale is irrelevant, and that time and agency cannot be ignored or space/place privileged – as a conventional multi-sited archaeology might seem to indicate. But it is not enough to posit the heterogeneous nature of networks; what maintains this heterogeneity? I want to suggest that a multi-sited archaeology leads us to questions of mobility, to *an archaeology of mobility* which engages with how and why things move, and how other things may facilitate or prohibit such movement.

Mobility has become a topic of great interest recently, spawning its own journal *Mobilities* – and some have even argued for a 'mobility turn' in the social sciences and humanities (Sheller and Urry 2006). Of course, mobilization has also been an important element in Bruno Latour's view of science, through his 'immutable mobiles' and circulating references (e.g., Latour 1987). In archaeology, mobility has always been a subject of investigation, whether in terms of people (from long-distance diffusion/ migration to localized nomadism) or objects (distribution and exchange networks) (for recent literature on mobility in archaeology, see Beaudry and Parno 2013; Leary 2014). Practically, this usually involves studies such as provenancing (both objects and people through elemental and isotopic analysis) or the investigation of material culture associated with transport (roads, boats, etc.). As Oscar Aldred has pointed out, however, such studies tend to reduce mobility to the connection between points A and B (Aldred 2014). Thus, *Spondylus* shells found in central Europe during the Neolithic must have moved from the Mediterranean, their native habitat, indicating exchange networks between the two areas – however indirect.

Such connections are of course only the *beginning* of a multi-sited archaeology, which, as Witmore rightly points out, is about much more than exchange networks. But what such traditional archaeological studies of movement also lack is a proper attention to movement *in itself*. While there are various models about the process of migration or diffusion or about how exchange systems work, they all remain fairly abstract and movement remains reduced to a line between points. In such models, it is almost the points that matter most: the lines merely connect up the dots. What Aldred is suggesting is that we pay greater attention to movement as a *constitutive* factor in creating places – and the network which links places together, rather than just an assumed factor needed to get from A to B (Aldred 2014; also see Aldred and Sekedat 2010).

This is a notion in its infancy and it will be interesting to see how it develops. But by paying greater attention to the materialization of mobile practices – or mobilities – archaeologists ought to gain a much sounder understanding of the networks which constitute a multi-sited archaeology. More importantly, it may also help us to understand the intensity or actuality of connections between places, people, and objects. Of course, Witmore is quite right in questioning the validity of the term multi-sited archaeology and my discussion of mobility is in some ways simply an addition to his expansion of the multi-sited; from the threefold, we now have the quadruple of space, time, agency and mobility. While it may not immediately solve the problem of why some things are connected and others not, it does provide the basis for exploring this issue in concrete ways. Thus, having traced Witmore's path in reverse, I do not think we are in the same place he started, namely a multi-sited archaeology – but neither are we where he ended. But then that is perhaps the sign of a good conversation.

References

Aldred, Oscar
   2014   Past Movements, Tomorrow's Anchors: On the Relational Entanglements between Archaeological Mobilities. In *Past Mobilities: Archaeological Approaches to Movement and Mobility,* edited by Jim Leary. Ashgate Publishing, Farnham.

Aldred, Oscar, and Bradley Sekedat
   2010   Moving on to Mobility: Archaeological Ambulations on the Mobile World. *Archaeolog* (accessed January 2011): http://traumwerk.stanford.edu/archaeolog/2010/12/moving_on_to_mobility_archaeol.html

Beaudry, Mary C., and Travis G. Parno (eds.)
   2013   *Archaeologies of Mobility and Movement*. Springer, London.

Harman, Graham
   2002   *Tool-Being: Heidegger and the Metaphysics of Objects*. Open Court, Chicago.
   2005   *Guerilla Metaphysics: Phenomenology and the Carpentry of Things*. Open Court, Chicago.

Leary, J. (ed.)
   2014   *Archaeological Approaches to Movement and Mobility*. Ashgate, London.

Renfrew, Colin
   1977   Space, Time and Polity. In *The Evolution of Social Systems*, edited by Jonathan Friedman and Michael J. Rowlands, 89–112. Duckworth, London.

Sheller, Mimi, and John Urry
   2006   The New Mobilities Paradigm. *Environment and Planning A* 38: 207–226.

Index